To Tina and Bill Baker,

Respected colleagues and

great friends

Love John

Southern Struggles

NEW PERSPECTIVES ON THE HISTORY OF THE SOUTH

Florida A&M University, Tallahassee
Florida Atlantic University, Boca Raton
Florida Gulf Coast University, Ft. Myers
Florida International University, Miami
Florida State University, Tallahassee
University of Central Florida, Orlando
University of Florida, Gainesville
University of North Florida, Jacksonville
University of South Florida, Tampa
University of West Florida, Pensacola

Southern Struggles

The Southern Labor Movement and the Civil Rights Struggle

John A. Salmond

Foreword by John David Smith, Series Editor

University Press of Florida

Gainesville | Tallahassee | Tampa | Boca Raton

Pensacola | Orlando | Miami | Jacksonville | Ft. Myers

09 08 07 06 05 04   6 5 4 3 2 1

Library of Congress Cataloging-in-Publication Data
Salmond, John A.
Southern struggles: the southern labor movement and the civil rights struggle /
John A. Salmond; foreword by John David Smith.
p. cm.—(New perspectives on the history of the South)
Includes bibliographical references (p.) and index.
ISBN 0-8130-2703-9 (alk. paper)
1. Textile workers—Labor unions—Southern States—History—20th century.
2. African Americans—Civil rights—Southern States—History—20th century.
3. Labor movement—Southern States—History—20th century.
4. Civil rights movements—Southern States—History—20th century.
I. Title. II. Series.
HD6515.T4S25 2004
323.1196'073075'09046—DC22   003066577

The University Press of Florida is the scholarly publishing agency
for the State University System of Florida, comprising Florida A&M University,
Florida Atlantic University, Florida Gulf Coast University, Florida International
University, Florida State University, University of Central Florida, University
of Florida, University of North Florida, University of South Florida,
and University of West Florida.

University Press of Florida
15 Northwest 15th Street
Gainesville, FL 32611-2079
http://www.upf.com

This book is for my children, Kerry, Nikki, Paul and Mark;
their partners, John, Leigh, Helen, and Lee;
and their children, Bill, Hilary, Jim, and Tom Washington,
Lucy and Bob Henningham, Alexander and Rachel Salmond,
and Saitong, Somrudee, and Sasipapa Tapat.

Contents

Figures

Figures follow page 83

Foreword

Whether they view southern history through the lens of continuity or discontinuity, scholars generally agree that conflict lies at the core of the region's past. Over the course of his long and distinguished career at Australia's La Trobe University, labor historian John A. Salmond has reflected analytically, sensitively, and thoughtfully on the complexities of racial and class conflict over the sweep of southern history. In many books and articles, Salmond has sketched the contours of the idealism and passion of southern laborers, chronicling their quest for equal opportunity and social justice.

In his engagingly written *Southern Struggles: The Southern Labor Movement and the Civil Rights Struggle,* Salmond underscores the commonalities between the struggles for economic and social justice for white textile workers in the 1930s and those of black southerners in the 1960s. Drawing on the vast scholarship in labor and civil rights history, Salmond probes the "shared traditions" of repression and struggle that working-class white and black southerners experienced in the last century. He identifies similar leadership styles, similar inspirations, similar strategies of protest, and similar opposition—"the ferocious determination of the upwardly mobile white middle class to resist challenges from below, whether white or black."

To illustrate his points, Salmond paints sparkling word portraits of the men and women who championed the labor and civil rights struggles. He analyzes the role of religion in their crusades and assesses the contributions of the struggles' "outside" and "inside" agitators. Salmond compares and contrasts the methods and tactics strikebreakers used to stymie unionists and white supremacists employed to resist racial change. He charts the role of the federal government in ushering in labor and civil rights legislation. "Throughout the twentieth century," Salmond writes, "those white and black southerners determined to bring change to their region, faced common and equally determined resistance. . . . They were spied upon, they were denied the space to expand their lives, to enlarge their horizon, not those of their children. And yet they endured, till finally the federal government acted on at least some of the injustices that had long been part of the very fabric of their lives."

Salmond selects three violent incidents as symbols of the twentieth-century South's working-class struggles. The first occurred in Marion, North Carolina, in 1929. The second took place in Honea Path, South Carolina, in 1934. And the third happened in Orangeburg, South Carolina, in 1968. According to Salmond, these case studies illumine "the dark underside of southern history"—the horrendous murders of innocent men and women and the tragic failure of class to override race in uniting working-class southerners.

Historians remember Marion as the most violent of the labor strikes that occurred in the southern textile industry in 1929. In October, when striking unionists at the East Marion Mill refused to disperse, county deputies fired tear gas into the crowd and then shot workers as they fled—hitting most in the back—killing six and seriously wounding many others. Assessing the tragedy at Marion, Salmond notes that "the combination of intransigent management, state and local power, the weakness of the UTW [United Textile Workers of America], and a hostile social environment would defeat those workers struggling against workplace conditions deplorable even by the South's lax standards."

The 1934 strike at Honea Path ended similarly. In September, the owner of the Chiquola Mill, who also served as the town's mayor and police chief, approached a group of striking textile mill workers with a small army of special deputies. Fistfights ensued as striker breakers attempted to cross the workers' lines. Suddenly, as in Marion, deputies opened fire on the strikers, many of whom were wounded. Seven died, most having been shot in the back. The shooting at Honea Path, according to Salmond, "was a body blow to the strike effort because of the sanction it gave state governors for widespread use of the national guard to maintain public order—and, incidentally, to keep the mills open if management so desired."

The 1968 Orangeburg killings, in Salmond's words, "bore eerie resemblance to the massacres of Marion and Honea Path all those years before." They occurred not in the crucible of labor strikes, but within the context of voter registration drives and challenges to Jim Crow discrimination during the civil rights era. State police fired upon a crowd of unarmed African American student protesters, killing four and injuring scores of others. At Marion, Honea Path, and Orangeburg, Salmond explains, "police had fired on angry demonstrators, people had died as a consequence, yet no one was held accountable."

Salmond's powerful essays establish what he terms the "grim continuity between the drive of white textile workers for economic justice and that of black southerners for racial equality." In various locales throughout the South and over the course of the twentieth century, "those who challenged the social order did so at the daily risk of their lives; they could be shot down by those sworn to uphold the law." White textile mill workers and black civil rights activists exhibited similar characteristics—"dignity, bravery, commitment to the struggle, even the strength to die for it. They held to their humanity, to their sense of self-worth, even as their opponents tried to strip them of it."

Ironically, Salmond notes, while working-class southerners, white and black, shared similar enemies, until the second half of the century "they were also enemies to each other," a circumstance he considers "the greatest tragedy of all." This is just one of many telling insights that readers will welcome in Salmond's compelling book.

John David Smith
Series Editor

Preface

I first experienced the American South in September 1961, as a young man from Dunedin, New Zealand—the uttermost end of the earth it seemed then. I had come to Durham, North Carolina, to enter Duke University's graduate history program. Unknowingly, I had arrived just as the civil rights revolution was gathering speed, and it became impossible not to become caught up in its idealism and passion. This spirit is with me still, more than forty years later, as it has been throughout my life. This book, coming as it does at the culmination of a career spent engaged with many of the issues raised so unflinchingly by Martin Luther King and his fellow fighters, is my acknowledgment of their continuing importance.

Dunedin, where I grew up, was a staunchly Presbyterian town, and was then, equally staunchly, devoted to the principles of equal opportunity and social justice embodied in the political philosophy of the New Zealand Labour Party. My father, a Presbyterian clergyman, described himself as a Christian socialist and was deeply steeped in the philosophy of the social gospel. As such, he was a firm believer in the right of working men and women to organize and bargain collectively, a conviction he transmitted to me early and which has remained with me. This book, drawing heavily as it does on my previous research on union struggles in the South's textile mills, in part has its roots in my childhood.

As always, there are many people to thank. Writing American history so far from its sources is no easy task, and certainly my work could not have been done without the generous and continuing assistance of the Australian Research Council and the La Trobe Faculty of Humanities and Social Sciences. My vice chancellor, Michael Osborne, my dean, Roger Wales, and my colleague and friend Alan Frost have been unstinting in their institutional support, and I thank them sincerely for it. Librarians and archivists at La Trobe University and at scores of depositories in the United States have tirelessly followed up my frequent and not always clear requests for books, documents, and photographs, and my research has been made much easier as a consequence. To them all, my gratitude.

My colleagues and friends Bruce Clayton of Allegheny College in Meadville, Pennsylvania, and Bill Breen at La Trobe, have both read sections of the manuscript to its certain benefit. Tim Minchin of the University of St. Andrews in Scotland has generously shared ideas with me on many occasions. David Kennedy of Stanford University, Jim Patterson at Brown University, and Bill Chafe at Duke University have all helped clarify my notions during brief visits to Melbourne. Felicity Turner and Kerrie Newell were willing and efficient research assistants, while once more Heather Wilkie has, miraculously, turned my barely legible scribblings into camera-ready script. I thank, too, Meredith Morris-Babb and the editorial staff at the University Press of Florida for their encouragement and efficiency. My greatest debt, as always, is to the steadily growing group named in the dedication, my children and grandchildren.

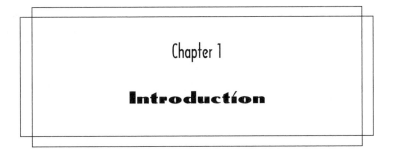

Chapter 1

Introduction

Let me first talk of two small towns in the twentieth-century South, less than 200 miles apart, and certain events which happened in them within a five-year span. The towns shall go unnamed for a time.

Both these towns were rigidly segregated. There was a white middle class, well-fed, reasonably prosperous, contented, even self-satisfied, living in modern, well-appointed houses. And there was another group, mostly unskilled laborers who were kept apart, confined to one section of these towns in unsanitary, crowded housing fronting unsealed roads, lacking plumbing, exploited at the workplace, working long hours at minimal rates of pay, much of their paltry wages already committed to paying off debt at the employer-owned stores they were forced to patronize. Their children soon learned to wear the badge of inferiority. Confined to their own inadequate schools, kept away from the children of the middle class, refused entry to most of the places of entertainment, denied in one town even the prospect of post-elementary education, they knew their lives would be like those of their parents, exploited, controlled, kept in their place, in the last resort, by the local law-enforcement officers, creatures of the white middle class.

But, as often happens, there were in these two confined communities a few brave men and women unwilling to suffer these conditions any longer, determined to seize the rights to full citizenship the Constitution promised them—their civil rights—determined to take control of their own lives. Inexperienced in the politics of resistance, they looked outside their communities, indeed, outside the South, for people to help them. Soon, dedicated young volunteers answered their call and helped them challenge the local forces that oppressed them. In both towns they waged their campaign peacefully; indeed, nonviolence was always a central concern. They paraded, often under the banner of the Stars and Stripes, they held mass meetings to reinforce their resolve, they sang songs of resistance, they prayed—how they prayed—and they withdrew their labor. They fought valiantly for their freedom, but they did not break the law.

The forces arrayed against them, however, had no such compunction against illegality, and in the end they proved too strong. The town councils, the mayors, the local law enforcement officers, the police chiefs, the county sheriffs and their men, were determined to keep these people in their place. They were, of course, aided by friendly state power, in the menacing shape of the national guard, by the courts, and most dangerously, by well-armed vigilante groups, their membership comprising the towns' most upright citizens. Some of them even wore white sheets, and called themselves by the most peculiar titles.

Soon the peaceful parades were ordered to cease by court injunction, but the protesters were far too committed, far too convinced that the right was on their side to obey. And so they ignored this legal blockade. They kept on marching and singing. Then the violence began, the savage beatings, the jailings on trumped up charges, the night attacks, the bombings and the burnings, as the conflict escalated and the politics of confrontation took over.

Then came, in these two towns, the inevitable, the ferocious act of violence. In both communities the sheriff and his men used their guns on unarmed demonstrators, and when the shooting ceased, men and women lay dead—six in one case, seven in the other—and scores were wounded, mostly shot in the back as they fled, terrified, from the carnage. Some died later from their wounds. The guns had served their purpose. The protests were over.

In both cases those who had fired the shots were well known, some even boasted about it. Because of outside pressure, there had to be some attempt to bring the murderers, for that is what they were, to justice. Men were indicted in both towns for these crimes and put on trial by prosecutors outwardly determined to do their duty. But the victims were not fooled for a moment. They knew what the verdicts would be. This was the South, after all, and those who died had challenged the social order. And, of course, they were right. All those tried were quickly acquitted, and the townspeople tried to get on with their lives.

Most will find the lineaments of this story disturbingly familiar. Such illegalities have always been part of the dark underside of southern history, and no more so than during the 1960s, on the bloody battlefields of the Mississippi Delta, of Alabama, of Georgia, where the civil rights struggle was fought. We know those who died, John Dittmer's "local people," the brave African Americans and those, white and black, who came to help them fight the forces of oppression. And we know the profile of the oppressors, the local Bull Connors and Jim Clarks, the sheet-covered Robert Sheltons, the Al Lingos. Such incidents as those briefly described are now part of the fabric of the civil rights story.[1]

The towns in the story, however, are not part of that particular tale. They are not civil rights battlegrounds of the Deep South but Marion in the North Carolina mountains and Honea Path in the South Carolina Piedmont. The time is wrong, too, because the incidents described took place not in the 1960s but thirty years earlier, in Marion in 1929, Honea Path in 1934. Those brave local men and women who lost their lives were not African Americans but largely of Scottish-Irish extraction, not agricultural workers or unskilled laborers, but textile operatives, and those who came to help them were not idealistic student volunteers but organizers for the United Textile Workers Union (UTW), an AFL affiliate. The reaction, however, remained the same, the official violence by those who ostensibly upheld the law, the compliant courts and juries, the unpunished murderers, the ferocious breaking up of the local movements, the reluctance of government to prevent this. Indeed, during the whole of the civil rights struggle no single act of violence approached in its scale of death the shootings at Marion or Honea Path.[2]

Southern police would not shoot into an unarmed crowd, obviously intending to kill, for another thirty-four years. This time the context was the waning years of the civil rights movement, exacerbated by the bitter division of the Vietnam War, and those who died were not white textile workers but black students protesting the continuation of segregation in their community, despite all the tumultuous changes of the 1960s. This is not to say that the civil rights movement had not produced a casualty list. Of course it had, and a good number of those who died had done so at the hands of local sheriffs and their deputies, particularly in the struggle's prime battleground, the lawless state of Mississippi. But they had mainly been killed in their ones, their twos, and even their threes, like Medgar Evers, like Florida's Harry Moore, like Michael Schwerner, James Chaney, and Andrew Goodman, like Viola Liuzzo, and usually under the cover of darkness and white sheets. Though lines of police often did battle with angry demonstrators in those years, they used teargas, clubs, and water cannon rather than lead. However, in May 1968, a confrontation took place in Orangeburg, South Carolina, which bore eerie resemblance to the massacres of Marion and Honea Path all those years before.

Orangeburg, less than an hour's drive due south of Columbia, and a typically segregated southern town in the 1960s, was also the site of two black colleges, South Carolina State and the private Clafin College. For this reason, the Student Non-violent Coordinating Committee (SNCC) decided to establish a voter registration project there, far from its main center of activity, Mississippi. Accordingly, SNCC field worker Reggie Robinson went there in early 1963 to start things up. His initial reports were not encouraging, but more because of the lack of cooperation he received from the local NAACP branch, which had given him the "run around," than the opposition of the town's whites. Yet he persisted, and by April he was able to report that "the project is really moving forward." SNCC maintained a presence in Orangeburg for the next five years, as the legal walls of segregation were finally breached.[3]

Still, there were many whites who simply refused to acknowledge their world had changed. In Orangeburg, one such was the owner of the All Star Bowling Alley, who despite the Civil Rights Act of 1964, stubbornly refused to admit black patrons. In February 1968, local students decided to force his hand, marching to the establishment on February 5 and demanding entry. Rather than comply, the owner locked the doors, prompting three days of sporadic violence, during which local whites drove through the South Carolina State campus, shooting into dormitories and classrooms, and, reportedly, at individual students. In an endeavor to restore order, the beleaguered local police were reinforced by 127 state patrolmen and 450 members of the national guard.[4]

This tense situation became tragic on the night of February 8. Around 10:00 p.m., 66 patrolmen and 45 guardsmen confronted an angry crowd of about 200 students, some armed with rocks and bricks but most only with insults as they moved to where the patrolmen were grouped, shotguns at ready. Without warning, the police opened fire. When the volley was over, three students were dead and twenty-seven lay injured, many seriously—one died of his wounds within a few hours. Also wounded was former SNCC program secretary Cleveland Sellers, who was shot in the arm. Sellers, a veteran of many a struggle, was later arrested as he lay on a hospital trolley and charged with inciting to riot, arson, and assault with intent to kill. Nine state policemen, too, were eventually charged with various offenses.[5]

The evidence at the various inquests, FBI inquiries, and trials which followed was both voluminous and confusing, yet several clear points emerged, most of which were undisputed. First, despite the contention of the nine patrolmen, there was no credible evidence that the students had fired first. No firearms were confiscated from those students arrested following the shootings, no witness saw any of them with a gun, though there was evidence that some were hurling missiles. The leading students were still at least seventy-five feet away from the patrolmen when they were caught in a crossfire of shotguns, loaded with lethal double-aught buckshot and pistols. Many were in fact shot while lying on the ground, attempting to evade the volley, others while trying to crawl away. A few, indeed, were hit from a distance of 100 yards. There was no evidence that any of the national guardsmen present had discharged their weapons; all the shots had come from the police. Moreover, all of the nine patrolmen charged admitted firing on the students, claiming self-defense.[6]

No one was found guilty of any crime arising from the shooting, nor was Sellers brought to trial. The tragedy, indeed, was quickly forgotten, a small part of the general national agony of 1968. For his part, Jack Nelson concluded that the police acted as much out of panic as from racist malevolence. "The state forces had every reason to be prepared to cope with student violence that night," he later wrote. They had been in Orangeburg for two days. They had smelled "the tension of the situation," but they were ill prepared to deal with it. Whatever the explanation, as in Marion and Honea Path, all those years before, police had fired on angry demonstrators, people had died as a consequence, yet no one was held accountable.[7]

These three sites of death, Marion, Honea Path, and Orangeburg, show, at one level, a grim continuity between the drive of southern white textile workers for economic justice and that of black southerners for racial equality. Those who challenged the social order did so at the daily risk of their lives; they could be shot by those sworn to uphold the law. Of course, white textile workers were not the only southerners to try to bring social change through union action and, sometimes, to die in the attempt. White coal miners did so in Matewan, West Virginia, and Wilder, Tennessee, for example, as did paper workers throughout the region. Black southerners, too, used those few unions they controlled to fight for economic justice and their civil rights. They did so in Birmingham, Alabama, and on the Memphis docks. And on rare occasions, black and white workers joined together in their struggles, forming fragile coalitions based on class, the racial divide at least temporarily bridged, providing poignant glimpses of what might have been an alternative South.[8]

From 1943 to 1950, for example, in Local 22 of the Food, Tobacco, Agricultural and Allied Workers of America, black and white tobacco workers in Winston-Salem's gigantic R. J. Reynolds plant, then the largest in the world, not only forced the company to accept a union contract but also took their coalition into the wider community. In 1947, whites and blacks in Local 22 were the impetus behind the election of a black minister to Winston-Salem's Board of Alderman, the first African American to defeat a white candidate in any election in the twentieth century South. The success of Local 22, while not unique, was unusual, resulting from the fortunate conjunction of several forces: the entry of blacks and women into the industrial labor force during World War II, New Deal labor legislation, the labor-friendly policies of the early National Labor Relations Board, the brief radicalism of the CIO, and the latter's connection with the New Deal's social democratic temper. Moreover, such interracial unionism had a fragility that could not survive the postwar ferocity of the employers' fight back, aided as it was by national political reaction. Nevertheless, Local 22, and a very few like it, provide poignant glimpses of what was possible when class interests overrode race and black and white southerners joined together.[9]

There were no such glimpses in the South's flagship industry, textiles. Blacks were never allowed inside the mills. They remained lily-white until the equal employment provisions of the 1964 Civil Rights Act at last forced change. And yet the focus of this book is on those mills, despite there seemingly being few points of comparison between the struggle for economic and social justice for white textile workers and that of black southerners for their civil rights. True, most textile workers were traditionally hostile to African American aspirations and resisted strenuously any suggestion that the mills be opened to blacks. With few exceptions, they embraced the cause of white supremacy. More than most southern workers, they came to learn that whiteness carried with it some economic rewards. Yet in their own struggles they were to rely on many of the institutions later crucial to the freedom fighters of the 1960s. They displayed similar strengths of local leadership, they drew on the same sources of biblical inspiration, they sang the same songs of defiance. Moreover, as the stories of Marion, Honea Path, and Orangeburg amply illustrate, they both faced the ferocious determination of the upwardly mobile white middle class to resist challenges from below, whether white or black. The determination, dignity, and bravery of those fighting for justice in the mills, or for an end to segregation, is one of the more positive aspects of these struggles, as was the belated involvement of the federal government in their resolution.

In exploring these specific continuities between the struggles of white southerners in the mills and black southerners for civil rights, this book breaks new ground. No other historians of the South have done so. It seemed pointless to try, given that the textile industry was closed to blacks. Yet as with the stories of Local 22, and other brief examples of class triumphing over race, mine, also, is a sad tale of what might have been. Southern workers in the mills and southern civil rights activists displayed similar characteristics: dignity, bravery, commitment to the struggle, even the strength to die for it. They held to their humanity, to their sense of self-worth, even as their opponents tried to strip them of it. Yet they waged their struggles apart, in the case of the mills, class never proved stronger than race, not even for the briefest of moments. Their enemies were the same, they were the victims of similar brutalities, as the following pages will clearly show. Yet they were also enemies to each other, and this was the greatest tragedy of all. Only after the Civil Rights Act of 1964 forced them to, did whites and blacks come together in the mills, and their struggles became conjoined. By then it was too late.

The purpose of this book is to explore these several continuities, to elaborate on this tragic irony. In so doing, we shall return to Marion, to Honea Path and to Orangeburg. But first we must briefly retell the story of these struggles.

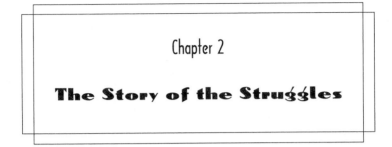

Chapter 2

The Story of the Struggles

The shooting started in Marion just after 7:00 a.m. on October 2, 1929. Earlier, workers at the troubled East Marion mill had resolved to resume their ongoing strike at midnight; consequently, quite a crowd had gathered at the mill gates as the day shift—or those workers willing to brave the taunts of union pickets—prepared to enter the mill. Also present were McDowell County sheriff Oscar Adkins and a troop of his deputies, all men who had spent the summer dealing with the volatile labor situation in the town. The tension, observers recalled, was electric.[1]

Sheriff Adkins twice ordered the strikers to disperse, an order they ignored, claiming the right as pickets to remain on the street, thus preventing free entry to the mill. The mill superintendent then spoke directly to the sheriff. Almost immediately he and his deputies discharged teargas into the angry crowd, and then the shooting began, "coming," as Douglas Eller of the *Asheville Citizen* wrote, "as a bolt from the mists of dawn." It was all over in a couple of minutes, he said, estimating that no more than seventy-five shots had been fired, but to deadly effect. "A scene of horror" awaited Eller and those like him who "dashed to the rescue." In all, thirty-six men and women were hurt by the volleys, many seriously, most hit in the back as they frantically tried to escape the carnage. Six lay dead or mortally wounded, including George Jonas, a crippled mill worker, sixty-five years old, who, enraged by the teargas, had first grappled with the sheriff. Now he lay dying, his hands locked together by Adkins's cuffs. All who had died, or were soon to do so, had been shot from behind. The year 1929 had been a violent one in the South's textile towns. The police chief, Orville Aderholt, and a local strike leader, Ella May Wiggins, had both died in Gastonia, North Carolina, during the long strike there, while in Elizabethton, Tennessee, strikers had been gassed and clubbed, and United Textile Workers official Alfred Hoffman and Edward McGrady of the American Federation of Labor were both kidnaped at gunpoint and driven to the North Carolina state line. In neither place, however, did the scale of violence approach that seen in Marion over the summer, culminating in the October 2 massacre. Indeed, it was the single most violent incident in the creation of the textile South.[2]

Cotton textiles had come much later to the South than what was initially the nation's textile center, New England. Not until the 1880s did the drive to transform the southern Piedmont begin in earnest, a drive pursued by southern community leaders with messianic zeal as a means of recovering from the economic, ecological, and psychological ravages of the Civil War. As Jacquelyn Hall and her colleagues expressed so eloquently, "Business and professional men tied their hopes for prosperity to the whirring of spindles and the beating of looms." Vital to the change was the destruction of the region's independent farmers. Merchants profited from the tenant and sharecropping systems that replaced farm ownership, and they used the money to build the hundreds of mills that soon dotted the landscape. Dispossessed white farmers, initially from the marginal land of the southern hill country, provided an ample labor force, the industry's fortuitously late start enabled it to benefit from numerous important technological advances, and the great transfer of the textile industry from its traditional centers in Massachusetts and Rhode Island to the southern Piedmont was underway. By 1933, it had been completed in all its sectors. The Southeast had become the world's greatest producer of cotton cloth.[3]

The twin keys to this spectacular rise were abundant cheap, white labor and the availability of local investment capital. To quote the industry's leading economic historian, Gavin Wright, "The spread in tenancy and the decline in farm size increased the number of farm families for whom factory work seemed an acceptable alternative. From the 1870s to the end of the century employment grew at nearly 10% a year with no detectable upward pressure on wages." To this could be added the marginality of upland farms. Herman Newton Truitt's grandfather was simply one of thousands who could no longer make a living from his hard mountain soil, and thus he came to Burlington, North Carolina, and the mills of Spencer Love. Whatever the reasons, by 1900 southern mill wage rates were more than 30 percent below those of New England. The mills were making money, and every community wanted one. Textile mills, in fact, became a matter of such intense civic pride that the bulk of the capital was raised locally, they were essentially community enterprises often managed by men whose experiences were limited, and who were thus bound to make mistakes. Yet without such local involvement, such civic boosterism, the industry may not have developed as rapidly as it did. The price of learning on the job, therefore, was worth paying.[4]

If their employers had much to learn about mill management, the workers had to make an even more difficult conversion, from the rhythms of the land to those of the whistle and the machine. Here, in the South, the key institution was the mill village, in James Hodges's words, the answer to "the practical problem of assembling a workforce in small towns and rural places." Soon, such company communities "dotted the Piedmont landscape," essential to the region's transformation, creations of managerial self-interest to be sure, but also providing essential space within which the change from farm to factory could be effected and a mill culture could develop. By the 1930s, this village system was in decline, and when social scientists and political activists alike surveyed them, they saw mainly misery, oppression, and squalor. These things certainly existed there, they always had, but so did neighborliness, spirituality, community, and, in time, a distinctive and sustaining culture.

Mill village culture, like the workplace itself, was white. If employers ever thought about using black southerners in the mills for economic reasons, except for the most menial of "outside" tasks, they quickly rejected the notion. White mill workers, though they soon developed the angry class consciousness which resulted in the violent confrontations of 1929 and 1934, never extended this analysis across the racial chasm. Broadly, they shared the white supremacist assumptions of their class antagonists, and this the employers were always ready to exploit, especially in the years after World War II, when some CIO organizers began to see that economic and racial justice were inseparable. But this lay in the future.[5]

In its initial decades, the mill workplace, repetitive and governed by rigid notions of time, bore little resemblance to the slower rhythms of agricultural life. Yet even these could be moderated to better suit these first workers. Often women could slip home to check on the children, there was always time to talk, to eat lunch in a leisured fashion, even to walk off the job to watch a parade or a baseball game or to vote. Moreover, management, being overwhelmingly local, was usually accessible. Workers knew who controlled them and could usually deal directly with them, to protest decisions considered harsh or unjust and even, at times, to influence factory policy. In such ways was the transfer from farm to factory rendered less harsh, while who could doubt the economic advantages, especially as the demand for labor soared.[6]

Times were particularly good during World War I. There was a heavy demand for cotton cloth, even more mills were built, and those already existing operated around the clock, increasing the demand for labor. Throughout the textile mill South, from Virginia to Alabama, but especially in the Piedmont, wages doubled, even tripled between 1915 and 1920. Those left on the land found the temptation too great, and there was a further move from the mountains to the mills.[7]

Booms never last, and this one ended dramatically in 1920. The textile industry started the long slide that would culminate in the Depression years. The reasons for this were several. Wartime overexpansion was one; it simply could not be sustained. Changes in fashion were another, as young women raised their hem to above the knee, greatly reducing the amount of fabric required in each garment and destroying the market for cotton stockings. The development of the industry in other parts of the world, especially India, was a third, while the Harding administration's protectionist tariff policies, which resulted in the loss of important foreign markets, was yet another. Thus boom quickly turned to bust.[8]

Mill management responded to the downturn by cutting costs, mainly by pulling back the wage gains of the wartime years. Their workers fought back, for heightened wages had bought both heightened expectations and increased financial responsibilities. Allied with this was the fact that the boom had altered the composition of the mills' work force. The family labor system, the moving of whole families from mountain to mill, and their integration into both the work force and the mill village was quickly being abandoned. Operatives were henceforth much more likely to be adult workers, young men and women, often living independently, and supporting themselves. They were the first generation to see mill work as permanent, not as a supplement to the farm and as a means of acquiring the promises of modernity. The attacks on their wages not only hurt their pockets but also impinged on their sense of self-worth.[9]

The institution through which textile workers attempted to preserve their standard of living was the "unlikely vehicle" of the United Textile

Workers of America, an AFL-affiliated union whose cautious philosophy and skilled worker bias had made it a minor player in the struggle to organize the nation's textile workers. As late as 1914 it represented only 2 percent of them, almost all in the declining New England sector. However, its president, British-born Thomas McMahon, knew that the future of textiles was in the South, and that the UTW must establish a beachhead there. Thus the union moved South; between 1917 and 1919, around 40,000 workers joined UTW locals in what Janet Irons has described as "the most successful union movement the southern mills had ever seen." The employers did not like it one bit, but desperate for labor and in the midst of the boom, they were, for once, at a disadvantage. It would not last.[10]

With the end of the good times, and the consequent assault on their wages, it was through these newly formed locals and union-led action that workers fought to preserve their incomes. Between 1919 and 1921, industrial strife rocked the Piedmont, for management was determined not to give an inch to union demands. There were strikes and there was violence in which management, always aided by friendly state power, quickly gained the upper hand. In North Carolina, for example, where the UTW had its strongest base, Governor Cameron Morrison did not hesitate using troops to drive striking workers back to their jobs. The postwar industrial strife was over by 1921, with management the victors due to the economic downturn which reduced the demand for labor, the inadequacies of the UTW organization, and the widespread use of state power against it. Peace returned to the textile South, but the mill managers had been profoundly shaken. For them, the legacy was twofold. Their hatred of unions had been reinforced, and they would henceforth fight ferociously to prevent their future formation. Second, they had learned that the drastic slashing of wages in order to cut costs and maintain profits was counterproductive and only to be used as a last resort. Throughout the 1920s, they would find other means to achieve this end.[11]

One of these was consolidation of ownership. Hard times led to bankruptcies and sale, and more and more mills fell into fewer hands. Men like J. Spencer Love of Burlington Industries became textile giants through taking over mills from their local ownership. Control of some plants, like Gastonia's Loray Mill and the Baldwin Mill in East Marion, passed outside the region, or as was the case of the Bemberg Glanzstoff rayon plant in Elizabethton, Tennessee, outside the country. This powerful new breed of owners and managers set about finding a permanent solution to the problems of declining profitability, and they quickly settled on the use of new technology and new productive techniques. Men and women were replaced by machines wherever possible, the number of operatives needed to perform particular tasks greatly reduced, and they would work much harder. The relaxed prewar pace of operation was over, the "customary patterns" negotiated in the first decades of the industry were no more, replaced by "time and motion" studies, by fast, labor-saving machinery, by shop-floor reconstruction, by the increased use of piecework, and by a new type of hard-edged, tough supervisor, all against a backdrop of such a massive labor surplus that there was no need to hang on to workers. Most mills abandoned or greatly reduced their welfare activities, others cut the cost of village maintenance and restricted entry to them. The result was obvious: both living and working standards drastically declined.[12]

The new management practices may have seemed both inevitable and overdue to those who introduced them, but to the workers it was the end of what had already become a customary way of life. The relatively relaxed workplace was now a site of tension. Men with more machines to tend now ran where they once strolled; women found time pieces—"hank-clocks" they called them—attached to the machinery they used; no longer could they make quick trips home to check on the children—they scarcely had time to chat to their neighbors. Even that most private of acts, a trip to the toilet, could be questioned by an aggressive supervisor. Their work, one former millhand recalled, had been so speeded up that "you was always in a hole, trying to catch up." Another compared the changed milieu to the plight of the children of Israel enslaved by the Egyptians. Tension, competition, and insecurity was the unwelcome aftermath of the boom years.[13]

Women, particularly those over thirty, had been hit especially hard. Besides losing their cherished flexibility, they were often transferred from wage to piecework rates, almost always with a significant drop in income. Furthermore, as managers ran their mill around the clock in a futile bid to gain competitive advantage, it was women who increasingly worked the night shift, caring for their families during the day. Male and female workers, alike, however, faced the ever-present threat of being laid off, for the speeding-up of one loom, or the increasing of responsibilities, inevitably meant that someone else was let go. Moreover, it was hard to find another job, especially for those suspected of union sympathies. The UTW, so buoyant in the South during the boom, was reduced to impotence by its collapse.[14]

Manufacturers called these new practices by various euphemisms and saw in them the industry's salvation. Workers came to refer to them collectively as "the stretch-out," and they loathed them. For the next two decades, indeed, until World War II brought a second war boom, the focus of their attention and agitation was simple: to end this bundle of practices which had so rapidly constricted their lives and their communities. In 1929, they first struck back, when despite their private fears, thousands of them throughout the Piedmont walked off the job, and stayed out. By the end of the year, South Carolina had recorded eighty-one such stoppages, most organized without union involvement. In North Carolina, the story was similar, less so in Georgia and Alabama, where the mills were newer and with better equipment, and thus the owners had less incentive to adopt stretch-out procedures. Still, their turn would also come, as workers tried to regain some control over their working lives.[15]

Most of the 1929 strikes were short, relatively quickly settled, and occurred without significant union involvement. Three, however, were violent, prolonged, and gained national attention, even passing into the mythology of American labor struggles. The workers of the Bemberg Glanzstoff rayon plant in Elizabethton, Tennessee, who, led by young women, walked out on March 12, not only signaled the start of a tumultuous year, but the involvement of both the UTW and the national guard in the succeeding weeks set a pattern to follow elsewhere. Moreover, the eventual settlement and its prompt abrogation by management was indicative of the relative powerlessness of the union. No one died in Elizabethton, but they did in Gastonia during the prolonged and violent strike at the South's largest plant, the giant Loray Mill. The strike there, led not by the UTW but by dedicated young members of the National Textile Workers Union (NTWU), an arm of the American Communist Party, cost the lives of both the town's chief of police and a local strike leader, attaining as a result both national and international attention. The successive trials of the young people deemed responsible for Chief Aderholt's death, because of their politics, elevated them to a symbolic status similar to the anarchist martyrs Sacco and Vanzetti. Yet it was in Marion, in North Carolina's McDowell County, that the biggest single act of violence occurred, with the shootings on October 2. Again, the combination of intransigent management, state and local power, the weakness of the UTW, and a hostile social environment would defeat those workers struggling against workplace conditions deplorable even by the South's lax standards. With the tragedy at Marion, the uprisings of 1929 came to a close. They had little effect.[16]

Strikes against the stretch-out continued, however, even as the industry slumped toward its economic nadir. The next year, in September, the UTW tried again, in Danville, Virginia. The union, having learned from its 1929 failures, sent Vice President Francis Gorman there to direct operations, together with a top female organizer, Matilda Lindsay. Again the strike failed. The combination of national guardsmen and local police quickly dealt with marching strikers and pickets as well as ensuring safe passage to non-union workers, while the UTW coffers could not sustain relief payments for any length of time, crucial as winter approached. After four months, in January 1931, the strike ended with, in labor journalist Tom Tippett's words, "the most tragic end of all the strikes" and with the complete capitulation of the UTW. "The strike was lost, of course, weeks before the official end," noted Tippett:

> The reasons for its failure were as obvious as its collapse. The strikers were hungry, cold and ill and there was no money to finance the struggle further. The mills were quickly filling up with disillusioned strikers and imported workers. The state stood its soldiers and Danville its police between the union pickets and the working force, so that all intercourse was cut off. The strikers could maintain their indoor meetings downtown, they could not carry on union activity where it was needed in the zone of the mills. There was nothing left for the union to do save call the strike off and release its faithful members from an obligation to remain with a quickly sinking ship.

Though its failure in Danville was complete, the UTW was to rise again in the South just four years later, as its mill folk challenged the men and the stretch-out procedures which so circumscribed their lives, this time under the banner of Franklin Roosevelt's New Deal.[17]

Textile workers danced in the streets of Greenwood, South Carolina, and in scores of similar mill towns on the evening of June 16, 1933, when news that the Cotton Textile Code, the first to be approved under the aegis of the National Industrial Recovery Act (NIRA), the New Deal's main weapon in the fight for industrial recovery, had been approved. The NIRA's driving philosophy was, through the suspension of federal anti-trust laws, to permit business leaders to draw up codes of fair competition, applicable throughout their industry, allowing them to set prices and control output. Organized labor's demands were met by Sections 7(a), (b) and (c), which ostensibly gave workers the right to bargain collectively through representatives of their own choosing, to join unions unhindered, and required employers to agree to provisions for maximum working hours and minimum wage rates. Provided these provisions were included in each code, business had in effect achieved self-rule within the administrative framework of the National Recovery Administration. Both the act itself, and the process of code making, were clear wins for industry, but for workers Section 7(a) seemed the answer to their dreams. Cotton mill people believed their travails had ended, they had won shorter hours, higher wages, the right to organize, and, above all, an end to the stretch-out. No wonder they danced and they sang, and as they did so, they gave thanks to the man who had thus transformed their lives, Franklin D. Roosevelt.[18]

For a few months their hopes seemed justified, particularly for cotton, as owners increased production, partly to beat the new processing taxes which were also part of the recovery structure. For a while, especially in the South, employers were hiring, not laying off, and new shifts were starting up, until by September, employment in the mills was at its highest in the nation's history. For the first time in years there was a spirit of optimism in the industry, of faith in the New Deal and in the future, and this was reflected in mushrooming union membership, as workers rushed to make good the presumed benefits of Section 7(a). The UTW's membership base in February 1933 was only 15,000; by June 1934, it was 250,000. The preponderance of these new members came from southern mills, something their employers had not anticipated when they signed the textile code, and which they deplored profoundly. Instead, locals were quickly chartered throughout the South. "Textile workers," said H. D. Lisk, a southern organizer, believed the NRA was something "God had sent them"—God and President Roosevelt. "I sure am proud . . . of our president as it is the first time the laboring class of people has had anyone to help them," declared one Alabama worker, a sentiment echoed by thousands in that heady summer of 1933.[19]

Within a few months, sadly, their faith was on the ebb, as it became obvious that mill owners had little intention of adhering to those elements of the Cotton Textile Code of which they disapproved, especially provisions protecting the rights of their workers. Moreover, the enforcement machinery was quickly shown to be ineffective. From all over the country, therefore, but especially from the South, workers wrote to their champion, the president, telling of their betrayal and seeking his intervention. The management at the Loray Mill, claimed Carl W. Welch of Gastonia, was "simply not abiding by the code." He had been working "full time three shifts," he said, despite the code's prohibition of three-shift days. Moreover, those who had "tried to organize a union" had been swiftly punished, either losing their jobs or having their hours reduced. In neighboring Bessemer City, the American Mills were "working women 12 hours a day and paying them $12 a week," thus thumbing their noses at the code's provisions and the local NRA authorities. Welch knew that the president could not have known this or he would have stopped it. "I know," he wrote, "and all the poor cotton mill people knew that you are doing everything in your power to help us." But the owners had not yet got the message. The president had to hit harder, on behalf of "the poor people" who loved him, for their situation was desperate.[20]

Mill people, in their disillusion, did more than contact the president; they put pressure on their recently elected UTW local leaders, and they walked out. In South Carolina's Horse Creek Valley, for example workers struck in October 1933, hoping to force local management to honor the Textile Code's provisions. "We are striking to have Roosevelt and his program incorporated in the operation of the mills," said local leader Paul Fuller. But Roosevelt could not help them. Instead, the South Carolina governor, Ibra C. Blackwood, sent special deputies, highway patrolmen, and a machine gun unit of the South Carolina National Guard "to keep the mills running." Strikers and their families were evicted from the mill villages in explicit defiance of Code provisions, and the owners continued to run their plants as they wished, despite Section 7(a).[21]

As their betrayal became obvious, textile workers increasingly sought national action under the banner of the UTW, even if it meant a general strike. The voices of southern workers were loudest, and indeed, it was in Alabama that the "precipitating event" occurred. Following minor strike eruptions in May and June 1934, in July, Alabama's textile workers took matters into their own hands. On July 16, they started to walk out, despite the opposition of the UTW's national leadership. Within a week about half the state's 40,000 millhands were out, and though the strike then stalled, it forced the union's leaders to stop equivocating. At a special convention held in New York in August, where beaten and bloodied Alabama strikers were prominently on display, UTW president McMahon called for a general strike to begin on September 1, unless the demands of the Alabama strikers—a minimum wage of twelve dollars for a thirty-hour week, reinstatement of workers dismissed for union activity, recognition of the UTW, and an end to the stretch-out—became accepted throughout the land. Further negotiations were futile, the president showed no disposition to intervene, and thus began, under the leadership of Francis Gorman, what remains the largest industry-wide conflict in the nation's history.[22]

Historians have not devoted much attention to the 1934 strike, and the few that have looked at it, like Janet Irons, have emphasized its southern aspect, understandable since its epicenter was clearly in the textile belt of the Carolina Piedmont, where it was to be won or lost. Though the strike's most violent battles occurred in Rhode Island, it was in the South that state oppression was most determined, through the use of special deputies and through state power in the widespread presence of the national guard. State governors were quick to build on what they had learned in 1929 in Elizabethton, Gastonia, and Marion. The most dramatic single example of this reaction occurred in Honea Path, in South Carolina, in the strike's first week. There, on the morning of September 6, special deputies hired by Sheriff W. A. Clamp of Anderson County and supplemented by 100 extra officers quickly sworn in by the owner of the Chiquola Mill, Dan Beecham, who doubled as Honea Path's mayor and chief of police, confronted a large group of strikers, singing hymns and waving American flags, at the mill gates. There were arguments and fist-fights as nonstrikers attempted to cross the lines. Then, in the words of an eyewitness, "all of a sudden you heard shooting." It only lasted, as in Marion, a minute or two, but when it stopped, seven were dead or dying and scores were wounded, mainly shot in the back as they fled frantically from the scene. Honea Path was the strike's single bloodiest incident. Sixty years later, a film team seeking eyewitnesses to the killings found some still so deeply traumatized that they could not speak of it. Certainly it deprived southern organizers of their most potent weapon, the "flying pickets" of motorized activists who sped from mill to mill, forcing them to close. In an atmosphere so charged, it was just too dangerous to keep them active, to risk them being "shot down like dogs," in southern strike leader John Peel's bitter phrase.[23]

Though the strike lines held firm in the South for another week, the Honea Path shooting was a body blow to the strike effort because of the sanction it gave state governors for widespread use of the national guard to maintain public order—and, incidentally, to keep the mills open if management so desired. But by week's end, the combination of intimidation, disillusion, and simple hunger were having a real effect. Local relief efforts were inadequate, workers needed to feed their families, and so they began drifting back to the mills. The strike ended officially on September 22, after a hastily mediated settlement which UTW leaders trumpeted as a victory. "The stretch-out is ended," declared the union's magazine, the *Textile Worker*. "The Union will grow stronger. The textile workers are at last free." In fact, it was a capitulation, and management took ferocious revenge on those who had stood briefly against them. The UTW was powerless to prevent this, and its influence was thus ended forever in the cotton mills. More important, so was the notion of organization as a means of achieving economic and social justice in the textile South.[24]

For a time, mill workers continued to believe that the New Deal was on their side, despite the government's seeming powerlessness to prevent the owners systematic blacklisting of returning strikers, though the September settlement supposedly prevented this. They continued to struggle against the stretch-out, using the various government agencies created as part of the 1934 settlement or in the wake of the NRA's demise. They welcomed the passage of the National Labor Relations Act of 1935 and duly filed complaints with the National Labor Relations Board, confidently expecting vindication. It never came. New Deal labor legislation, though crucial in altering the balances between capital and labor in the automobile factories of Detroit, the steel mills and the mines of Pennsylvania, had scant effect on the company towns of the South. Not even their entry into the state political arena in South Carolina changed the lives of the millworkers of Spartanburg, Greenville or Honea Path. The stretch-out, pronounced by Gorman as gone forever as a result of the 1934, was instead there to stay.[25]

By 1936, the UTW was effectively dead in most southern mill towns, and the main reason was the sense of betrayal strikers had felt in 1934, together with the savagery of the mill owners' vengeance. There were only fifteen members left in Burlington's local 1777, reported North

Carolina organizer Paul Christopher, and they were forced to meet entirely in secret. "Most of them are literally scared to death," he said, and it was the same throughout the South. Yet there was to be another attempt to organize textile workers during the 1930s, not by the UTW, or the AFL, but by the Textile Workers Organizing Committee (TWOC) of the new, rival labor organization, the CIO. Yet when the CIO drive got underway, and even after the foundation of the Textile Workers Union of America (TWUA) in 1939, it was toward the nonsouthern and noncotton sectors of the industry that most effort came to be directed. Indeed, TWOC chairman Sidney Hillman frankly stated that his decision to place most of his organizers outside the South was based on a realistic appraisal of the labor climate there. Those few TWOC organizers sent southward found the going very hard indeed, with hostile management and a work force desperate and disillusioned, many actively hostile to further organization and most unwilling, after 1934's bitter aftermath, to take the risk again. When the TWUA was eventually formed, more than 90 percent of its members were from northern or mid-Atlantic mills.[26]

As had happened two decades earlier, southern textile workers made some economic gains during the war boom years of 1942–45, while the TWUA also was able to establish a precarious foothold in the region. It was partly out of the optimism such progress engendered, but also from a desire to protect recently won northern bases from competition from the non-union South, that the CIO, through the TWUA, decided in 1946 to launch a massive organizing campaign in the region, targeting all major southern industries but focusing especially on the flagship industry, textiles. Men and money were to be poured into the campaign, named Operation Dixie, in a effort to end the region's low wage economy once and for all. Operation Dixie was to be headed by Van A. Bittner of the United Steelworkers, with the TWUA's George Baldanzi as his deputy. It would be, Bittner said in the optimism of its inception, "a great crusading movement on behalf of humanity," and it would surely succeed. "Nothing under God's sun is going to stop this mighty movement of ours from doing this job."[27]

As the first organizers moved South, few predicted failure. Yet failure is what eventually occurred, as once again the textile South blunted the hopes of organizers and those workers who supported them. There were many reasons for this. One was the unhappy legacy of 1934. The memory of defeat was still so fresh in the minds of thousands of workers, that they wanted nothing to do with unions thereafter. There was the question of race, an issue that had hardly mattered in the prewar drives, but in the postwar southern climate, with black southerners beginning to fight against the caste system which confined them, it was easy for mill owners to paint the TWUA, scarcely the most racially progressive of unions, as an agent for integration. Here the Ku Klux Klan, which had considerable influence among textile workers, was important. Many local Klan leaders had ties to mill management. Moreover, neither textile workers in their "whites only" industry, nor their organizers, had ever seen any disjunction between Klan and union membership. Now, for the first time, the incongruity became apparent, and the racial divide proved too wide to be bridged. Not only did the Klan attack the TWUA for its alleged race-mixing goals, but its rhetoric was also frankly anti-Semitic and often directed against the "foreign"-sounding national union leadership. Operation Dixie organizers had no effective counter to this type of attack, reinforced, as it often was, by fundamentalist preachers. "Every-time we have an NLRB election in the South, the race issue is used," complained a local union official. He was no doubt correct.[28]

Klan and anti-union venom also made much of the CIO's alleged communist connections, an effective strategy as the hope of world peace gave way to cold war fears. Again, fundamentalist clergy spread the message that the CIO had links with those who would undermine the nation's values, often linking their anticommunist message with southern white fears of racial strife for "the Communists have found their agitation is most effective among the Negro people." In vain did the national CIO cut itself free from all possibility of subversive political connections, in vain did Operation Dixie use committed Christians like Lucy Randolph Mason and John Ramsay to convince people, especially the mainstream clergy, otherwise. Postwar organizers found the political climate much more hostile than 1934, when they worked under the banner "The President wants you to join a union."[29]

As well as these and other negative factors, however, TWUA organizers were also hampered by postwar prosperity, or a version of it, that had trickled through to the textile mills. Wages were higher than they had ever been, especially in non-union mills, partly as a result of management conviction that better-paid workers would be more skeptical of TWUA recruiting promises. For the first time textile workers could accumulate a modicum of material wealth, a refrigerator, a television set, perhaps even an automobile, on credit of course, but real nonetheless. Moreover, some were even buying their own homes, as managers, deciding the mill village had had its day, began to sell them off to their former tenants. This modest entry to the good life seemed threatened, not enhanced, by industrial activity. Strikes, after all, meant loss of income, and with that, an end to this recently acquired modest level of comfort, dependent as it was on regular instalment payments. Increasingly, Operation Dixie foot soldiers were told, "We've never had it so good, what do we need a union for?"[30]

The symbolic end of Operation Dixie, and of more than token TWUA activity in the South, was the general textile strike of 1951. Called in desperation by the TWUA, aiming to break the nexus between union and non-union wage rates, it involved 42,000 workers in seven states and ended in the union's complete defeat. In state after state, workers simply disobeyed the strike call or quickly returned to their looms. None of the union's demands was met, and in the aftermath, most of the hard-won gains of previous years, such as the automatic checkoff of dues, were lost. Demoralized and wracked with internal dissent, the TWUA was finished in the textile mills of the South for the immediate future. Not until after the great social transformation of the 1960s, the civil rights revolution, which finally opened the mills to black southerners, would it rise again, albeit briefly, and then often under African American local leadership.[31]

The social and economic history of Marion, North Carolina, was in many ways the story of the cotton textile South in microcosm. Situated at the base of the Blue Ridge Mountains, surrounded by high pine-covered hills, its physical location could scarcely be surpassed. County seat of McDowell County, and about 40 miles by road from Asheville, Marion in 1929 was home to about 8,000 people and three cotton mills, all built when the booster spirit predominated. Two of them, the Clinchfield mills, were locally owned and operated, and the third, the East Marion mill, was owned, operated, and controlled by the Baldwin family of Baltimore, Maryland. In 1929, working conditions in the three mills were similar, however, and according to contemporary observers, at the lower end of the scale, with twelve-hour shifts, very low wages, much night work, the illegal use of child labor, and a particularly onerous stretch-out system. Assured of a plentiful supply of cheap white labor from the marginal farms of the Blue Ridge, owners could see little reason to change their practices.[32]

Marion at first glance was an attractive town, set amid breathtaking vistas, proud of its nickname, the Land of the Sky. Mill executives lived in well-wooded streets, in spacious, handsome houses, as, for that matter, did Sheriff Oscar Adkins. There was a neat little town square, dominated by the courthouse and the McDowell Hotel. Two miles away, obscured by the woods, was a very different Marion, for there stood the Clinchfield and East Marion, or Baldwin, villages separated only by a hard-surface road. Even allowing for the natural exaggeration of commentators like author Sinclair Lewis, profoundly sympathetic to the workers' cause, conditions in both villages were vile. Observers reported drab houses, most in poor repair, without running water or sewers and with several families forced to share filthy outside privies. Pellagra was "rampant" there, as was despair, with bootleg whiskey and frequent revival services providing only brief solace—that and sojourns back in the hills when it all got too much. The workers had little alternative but to use the company store for their shopping, and most were in permanent debt. When news of the disturbances in Elizabethton and Gastonia reached Marion, therefore, it was scarcely surprising that two local activists, Lawrence Hogan and Dan Elliot, angry at, rather than accepting of, their conditions should seek assistance in forming a union of their own.[33]

In June 1929, Alfred Hoffman of the Hosiery Workers Federation of the UTW was sent to help them. The 300–pound Hoffman, appropriately known as "Tiny," was a veteran of many a labor battle in Pennsylvania before being sent south in 1927. He had been run out of Tennessee at the height of the Elizabethton strike. His organizing skills were to be stretched to the limits as Marion's workers, driven to desperate measures by the wretchedness of their lives, signed up in droves. Less than a month after the official formation of the local, Hoffman led the Marion workers out on July 11, after the mill superintendent, to cover up a miscalculation, increased the twelve-hour shift by twenty minutes. Then followed three months of disorder, exacerbated by the Clinchfield workers' decision to go out as well, on August 13, which culminated in the October massacre. There was rioting, there was violence, there were arrests—148 strikers on August 28 alone charged with rioting and insurrection—the national guard came to town in late August to try to restore order, there were trials, there were even lulls in the storm before Adkins and his men opened fire on October 2. Then there were more trials, of the sheriff and his men for murder, of Hoffman and his associates for rioting and associated offences. By the end of the year, the strikers had been convicted and jailed, while those who had killed them had been set free, the familiar pattern of 1929.[34]

The mill people of Marion, like those of Elizabethton and Gastonia, had lost their battle. Yet in losing they had for a while discovered their voice. Night after night in July and August, they had stood up to their employers and even the national guard. At night they had paraded through the town, then stood in picket lines around campfires, singing old slave spirituals, now rewritten as labor songs. "Something is coming that will make us free—us mill people free men and women," they shouted. And, indeed, people did come to help as best they could, and to take inspiration from their faith and courage. Jack Herling, a UTW organizer, wrote in July that the picket line was "as strong as steel" and the strike parades were inspirational, involving the whole mill community, "kids barefoot" included. Once the parade had reached the courthouse, Herling wrote of the previous night's demonstration, "All the yelling singing, yipping and yapping we did until then, was nothing compared to what happened when we passed the court-house . . . the scene of injunction. . . . The crowd yelled itself hoarse and crazy, while some of the townsfolk cheered and others were contemptuous." But supportive or hostile, they were impressed by the strength of the message. "A whole delegation of teachers from Louise Leonard's Summer School came along," he reported, "and contributed a large amount of energy; I grew anxious about the dear girls." Despite the massacre, something positive had occurred in Marion, and we shall return to the town as we seek to understand the larger meaning of 1929.[35]

The union was beaten in Marion in 1929, but local leader Lawrence Hogan kept its spirit alive for a while. Only the prompt dispatch of troops to the town in 1934 prevented workers joining the national strike. Hogan's death in 1935 in a car smash was a decisive blow for the union cause in Marion. Operation Dixie passed it by, yet the mill people and the other town folk remained apart, still wary of one another. It was not until the 1970s, according to Sam Finley, a veteran of the 1929 strike, that folk "got to talking union talk" again, and that was in the changed world of the post–civil rights era South. By then the mills in Marion, as elsewhere, were integrated. "It was the law," said Sam Finley; blacks could no longer be "turned down on account of their race." Thus, with the return of "union talk" to Marion, the two great movements for economic and social justice in the twentieth century South had at last conjoined.[36]

When the South Carolina state police shot to kill at Orangeburg, they did so near the end of the most tumultuous decade in southern history since the Civil War. In a few short years, African American southerners, aided by dedicated and well-trained blacks from outside the region, and by idealistic whites, mostly young, mostly middle class and mostly from the nation's leading universities, had set out to transform the American South. The Civil Rights decade, as the 1960s is often called, was the culmination of a much longer period of social change, yet so swift did its pace become then, so encompassing its scale, so towering the individual leaders or symbols, that to focus on that one decade as embracing the most profound period of social change in the nation's history is scarcely surprising.

During that decade, the cleansing of the American South, and thus the nation, of the evils of segregation became a battle which moved from the nation's courts to the public spaces of the South, and then to the Congress of the United States. For the first time since the Civil War, the executive branch joined the fight. Presidents John F. Kennedy and Lyndon B. Johnson proposed national action in support of the right of African American citizens to the equal protection of the laws. Johnson even invoked the basic slogan of the movement, "We shall overcome," as he spoke eloquently on national television in defense of the right of all citizens to vote. As he watched the president's address on March 15, 1965, the man who had come to symbolize the spirit of the struggle, the Southern Baptist preacher Rev. Martin Luther King Jr., wept briefly, overcome by the emotion of the movement, as, for him, victory seemed at hand.[37]

In a recent article surveying the literature of the civil rights era, Charles W. Eagles, like many before him, has commented on the dominance of Martin Luther King in the movement's historiography, mirroring his preeminence in the actuality of the decade's most stirring events. King has come to tower above all other leaders of the time; along with Kennedy he is revered as the man who made civil rights the nation's most pressing national issue and invested it with an urgent moral dimension not susceptible to political compromise. From the bus boycott in Montgomery, Alabama, which first thrust him into national prominence and gave African Americans a leader whose magnificent biblical cadences exemplified their determination to wait no longer to realize on the promises of the first Reconstruction, Martin Luther King was black America's prime spokesperson—and the nation's moral conscience. In the first speech he gave as the boycott's leader, he struck the theme he was to make his own over the next decade. When he spoke of "raising the weapon of protest," nonviolent protest, protest in the name of Christian love; when he spoke of the Montgomery community's determination "to work and fight until justice runs down like water, and righteousness like a mighty stream," King, as one historian has written, "not only defined the rhetorical cadences of the civil rights struggle but the context within which it would be waged." That first speech, commented Taylor Branch, made the young King "forever a public person."[38]

Over the next few years, King increased his national stature, refined his message of nonviolent resistance in the name of Christian love, established his own civil rights organization, the Southern Christian Leadership Conference (SCLC), and suffered a deal of uncertainty, travail, and downright failure as he pondered on how best to move the conscience of his nation and its political leaders. Out of indecision, however, eventually came success. Leadership in the campaign to end segregation in the city of Birmingham, Alabama, brought a spell in jail, during which he wrote "A Letter from Birmingham Jail," his most famous tract, which exemplified the spirit of Christian nonviolence. It also brought out the ordinary black citizens of the city into the streets in their tens of thousands, and, eventually, even the president of the United States joined the struggle. On June 11, 1963, in his presidency's most important speech, President Kennedy reminded all Americans that the struggle exemplified by recent events in Birmingham was a moral one,

> as old as the scriptures and as clear as the American Constitution. The heart of the question is whether all Americans are to be afforded equal rights and equal opportunities, whether we are going to treat our fellow Americans as we want to be treated. If an American, because his skin is dark, cannot eat lunch in a restaurant open to the public, if he cannot send his children to the best schools available, if he cannot vote for the public officials who represent him, if, in short, he cannot enjoy the full and free life which all of us want, then who amongst us would be content to have the color of his skin changed and stand in his place?

Kennedy concluded by announcing that he would soon submit to Congress a comprehensive civil rights bill aimed at removing all these inequalities—the evils of segregation—permanently from American life.[39]

Martin Luther King was at the height of his national influence, dramatically confirmed two months later when, with the Lincoln Memorial as his backdrop, King outlined his dream to a jubilant crowd of 250,000 who had come to Washington to march in support of the civil rights bill and to a television audience of millions. "I have a dream," he shouted, departing from his prepared text,

> that my four little children will one day live in a nation where they will not be judged by the color of their skin but the content of their character. I have a dream today. . . .
>
> Let freedom ring. . . . When we let it ring from every village and every hamlet, from every state and every city, we will be able to speed up the day when all God's children, black men and white men, Jews and Gentiles, Protestants and Catholics, will be able to join hands and sing in the words of the old Negro spiritual, "Free at last! Free at last! Thank God almighty, we are free at last."

No single words of King's are better remembered than these, and for good reason. His prophetic vision had become, for a time, one that most Americans shared.[40]

Despite Kennedy's assassination in November 1963, the civil rights bill passed the following year, as did the Voting Rights Act of 1965, again after a national campaign led by King, and centered in Selma, Alabama. It was his last great triumph. He, too, was assassinated, in April 1968, after three years in which his attempt to move the civil rights movement outside the South met with scant success, while his growing opposition to the escalating war in Vietnam caused him to break with the nation's political leaders. His period of unquestioned national ascendancy was brief, but triumphant. He remains America's greatest African American prophet and moral advocate.[41]

Yet neither Martin Luther King nor his SCLC had ever been to Orangeburg, South Carolina, in the years before the massacre there, though in one of his last communications before his own death, he had warned Attorney General Ramsay Clark that the shootings "must not go unpunished" and demanded that the government "act now to bring to justice the perpetrators of the largest armed assault undertaken under color of law in recent southern history." Ironically, the civil disorder and then national anomie occasioned by King's death caused the investigation of the Orangeburg killings to drop off the urgent list. The struggle for civil rights had been waged historically in the town by the local branch of the NAACP before being given urgency by the arrival in 1963 of Reggie Robinson and the toughened young people of the SNCC. The SNCC, by this time, had developed considerable suspicion of King and the ministers who worked for him. Formed in the heady aftermath of the "sit-ins" of 1960, and largely the brainchild of the veteran activist Ella Baker, for a time an SCLC staffer, but who later became disillusioned with both the man and the organization, the SNCC provided the local shock-troops of the movement. Young activists, who in the main had dropped out of school to work full time in the South, usually in situations of extreme danger, they grew impatient with the emphasis on nonviolence and Christian love. After Selma, they broke completely with King and with the integration ideal itself.[42]

King did not take part in the "freedom rides" of 1961, except to encourage the participants. The plan to force the Department of Justice to enforce the laws against segregation in interstate travel by sending teams of riders into the South, deliberately to provoke arrest by southern authorities, was the creation of James Farmer, director of the Congress of Racial Equality (CORE). When the violence got out of hand and Farmer decided to abandon the challenge, it was the young men and women of the SNCC who enthusiastically took it up. Officials at CORE had kept King informed of their plans but had not sought to involve him actively. When the young people of the SNCC invited him to join them on the buses, he declined. Henceforth, SNCC and CORE representatives would often cooperate on local projects, especially in the savage battleground state of Mississippi. They were less likely to maintain detailed contact with the SCLC, while at the same time acknowledging, often reluctantly, King's preeminence as spokesperson for the civil rights cause.[43]

It was, of course, the oldest and most respectable of the civil rights organizations, the National Association for the Advancement of Colored People (NAACP), that had worked longest to make civil rights part of the national agenda. In particular, it had mounted from the 1930s a steady challenge to segregation through the nation's courts. Using the talents of a group of remarkable young lawyers, most trained by Charles H. Houston, dean of Howard University's law school, himself a brilliant advocate, the NAACP had by the late 1940s successfully chipped away at the legal walls of segregation, mainly in the areas of public education and voting rights. Then, in 1954 came the landmark decision in *Brown v. Board of Education of Topeka*, in which the United States Supreme Court ruled unanimously that in the field of public education the doctrine of "separate but equal has no place. Separate educational facilities are inherently unequal." This decision, striking as it did at the philosophical and legal heart of the southern caste system, is often taken as the symbolic beginning of the civil rights era, and certainly it marked the climax of the NAACP's long court campaign.[44]

There would be many more court appearances, however, for Thurgood Marshall, leader of the NAACP legal team and his staff as the white South bitterly resisted *Brown's* implementation. For the rest of the decade, and into the 1960s, school integration proposals were fiercely contested every step of the way, and it was the NAACP that bore the brunt of the struggle. At times, as in Little Rock, Arkansas, in 1957 or Oxford, Mississippi, in 1962, the law was eventually enforced by federal troops, but rarely did it come to that. Local NAACP leaders, for the most part, provided the vital leadership, and though they drew inspiration from the rhetoric of Martin King, the terms of their involvement were different.[45]

Thus to view the civil rights era entirely through the prism of Martin King's influence underestimates the contributions of other national groups such as CORE or SNCC. Furthermore, it ignores the significance of local leaders and of spontaneous, unplanned actions in the story. The "sit-in" movement of 1960, for example, developed not from any coordinated battle plan but from the determination of four freshmen at the Agricultural and Technical College in Greensboro, North Carolina, to challenge local segregation ordinances which permitted African Americans to shop in city stores, but not to eat at their lunch counters. Blacks in Fayette County, Tennessee, who in 1960 formed the Fayette County Civil and Welfare League and subsequently established a "tent city" there which briefly gained national attention, had no outside leader to guide them. Rather, they were responding to the extreme reaction of local whites at their attempts to register to vote, using the provisions of the 1957 Civil Rights Act. Evicted by their landlords, denied medical attention by local doctors and clinics, even refused gas by local pump attendants, these victims of extreme economic reprisal sought safety and support by forming their own community. Similarly, the forty evicted share-croppers who in January 1966 briefly occupied an abandoned air force barracks near Greenville, Mississippi, hanging a sign on the door reading, "This is our home—please knock before entering," did so not as part of a SNCC direct action project but out of extreme economic distress. "Now we're our own government—government by poor people," declared one of them, Mrs. Ida May Lawrence of Rosedale:

> You know, we ain't dumb, even if we are poor. We need jobs. We need food. We need houses. But even with the poverty program we ain't get nothing but needs. That's why we was pulled off that building that wasn't been used for anything. We is ignored by the government. The thing about property upset them, but the thing about poor people don't.

To focus unduly on national figures and action is to miss the crucial local dimension of this multifaceted movement.[46]

It is also to overlook the importance of local foot soldiers to the success of the movement. The fact that folk like Amzie Moore, Aaron Henry, and Fannie Lou Hamer of Mississippi, Daisy Bates of Little Rock, Arkansas, Diane Nash of Nashville, Tennessee, and, above all, Rosa Parks of Montgomery, Alabama, eventually became figures with some national recognition should not mask the fact that their contribution essentially occurred at the local level. Moreover, there were thousands whose names never gained even fleeting prominence but whose contribution to the struggle was crucial. In Orangeburg, Louise Cawley, a senior at South Carolina State in 1968 and a longtime activist, was in the student lines when the police opened fire. Unhurt, she subsequently courted death by repeatedly dragging those injured from the battleground. Stopped eventually by state police, she was so severely beaten that she required hospitalization, too late to save her unborn child. Georgia Reed of St. Augustine, Florida, a seamstress so badly crippled by polio that she needed braces and canes to move around, did not let her disability prevent her from leading freedom marches or sit-ins, nor from going to jail. Her example throughout the long and violent campaign there, her uncompromising courage, caused others to find theirs. Throughout the civil rights decades, hundreds, thousands of unknown men and women provided the very spine of the local movement which in turn made national action possible.[47]

It is important, too, to remember that though civil rights became the urgent national issue in the 1960s, the struggle against the southern caste system had begun much earlier. The NAACP had started its legal challenges in the 1930s, as the reform spirit of the New Deal, as well as causing white mill workers to confront the system that so circumscribed their lives, had the same effect on a few brave black southerners. The Southern Conference for Human Welfare (SCHW), founded in Birmingham, Alabama, in 1938, first brought liberal blacks and whites together in a pressure group for regional change and, as such, exemplified the New Deal's social democratic tendencies, as did Local 22 of the FTA a few years later in Winston-Salem. Earlier, the Southern Tenant Farmers Union (STFU), centered in Arkansas, had fused black and white southerners in a union of the dispossessed. The STFU leadership was avowedly socialist, and a few years earlier, at the height of the Depression, another sharecroppers union had been organized in Alabama by a few underground representatives of the American Communist Party. The Sharecroppers Union's membership was overwhelmingly, but not totally, African American. Confined to backward Tallapoosa County, it was no match for the local power structure, and by the end of 1932, most of its leaders were either dead or in jail after a bloody shootout at Reeltown. Yet the fact that its members were willing to meet violence with violence, even against hopeless odds, gives it a significance among the earliest challenges to the southern caste system.[48]

Local branches of the NAACP in the South, many organized by the charismatic James Weldon Johnson in the immediate post–World War I years but which had lain dormant through the reactionary twenties or, as in Alabama and Mississippi, had been largely destroyed by the ferocity of Klan violence, slowly rebuilt during the 1930s. Often the catalyst was support for federal antilynching legislation. Though successive administrations never supported such a bill, the campaign for it drew supporters back into the NAACP. Moreover, toward the end of the 1930s, the organization expanded its legal campaign into such areas as voting rights and police brutality, again issues which galvanized local activists. When Ella Baker became southern field secretary during World War II, the local branches were her primary focus, determined as she was to "challenge the elitist bias of the national NAACP leadership." Baker, says historian Patricia Sullivan, took "the NAACP to churches, schools, barbershops, bars and pool halls, she helped build chapters around the needs and concerns of individual communities and encouraged cooperation with labor unions and other progressive organizations. The NAACP, as the war drew to a close, was a serious presence in the South, ready to increase the tempo of the struggle.[49]

For black southerners, thousands of whom had fought against racism abroad, were no longer resigned to living with it at home. After 1945, the pace of the civil rights struggle quickened, as the NAACP continued to triumph in the courts, as brave individuals stood up for their rights, and as local groups and organizations enlarged the areas of battle. Some of these were interracial in composition. The SCHW, for example, set up state branches at war's end which tried to influence southern politics at the grass roots, as well as fighting the battle for an interracial labor movement, arguing that to keep white and black workers apart was fatal to the aspirations of both. In Chapel Hill, North Carolina, liberal students transformed a prewar discussion group, the Fellowship of Southern Churchman (FSC), into an active agency for social change, demonstrating through interracial community work projects that black and white southerners could live and work together. Bitterly opposed by the white power structure as they were, and easily transformed into political pariahs in the hardening cold war climate of the 1950s, their very existence symbolized the enlargement of the struggle. When Martin Luther King and the brave men and women of Montgomery dramatically raised civil rights stakes in 1956, they did so in the context of ten years or more of escalating local challenges.[50]

Not all of this activity was nonviolent. As Timothy Tyson has recently pointed out, the concentration on Martin King and his message of nonviolence has drawn attention away from the fact that there were always "black Southerners who stood prepared to defend home and family by force." The sharecroppers who shot it out with the sheriff and his deputies in Camp Hill were part of that tradition, as were the black citizens of Columbia, Tennessee, who in 1946 averted the lynching of one of their number, James Stephenson, shooting and severely wounding four white police officers in the process. Most notably, Tyson has brilliantly recovered the life of Robert Williams of Monroe, North Carolina, a war veteran no longer prepared to accept the second-class status the South insisted upon, who in 1957 led a group of disciplined marksmen against a Klan motorcade, turning it into a rout. Williams had no use for King's nonviolence, nor his insistence on the integrationist ideal. For him, as for the later Black Power advocates of the northern ghettoes, standing up to white supremacy meant using guns, as both a tactic and a means to self-respect. When the young activists of the SNCC started questioning non-violence in the late 1960s, it was often argued that they were betraying the civil rights movement's core philosophy. Rather, they were returning to a strain always present in the struggle, which King and his message had for a time suppressed.[51]

As well as looking back before King to understand the complexities of the civil rights struggle, it is also necessary to look beyond him, to the succeeding decades, when the legislative triumphs he more than anyone else made possible began to bite, transforming the southern political economic and social landscape. In particular, it is only after the 1964 Civil Rights Act that the two great twentieth-century struggles, for the right to organize and the right to equal citizenship, come together, especially in the mills. Southern owners and workers alike bitterly resisted the integration of the mills, but in the end the law proved too strong. By 1980, the mills were integrated, and the struggle to achieve a better life for those who worked in them was resumed, this time finally fought by black and white southerners under the one banner. It continues still against increasing odds.[52]

To focus primarily on the struggle of white textile workers to achieve social and economic justice tends to obscure the fact that the southern labor movement, even at the high point of segregation, was, as has already been noted, not exclusively white. Robin Kelley and others have shown how black southerners provided the backbone for Alabama's mining unions, and Michael Honey, in a series of studies, including a prize-winning book, has examined interracial unionism in Memphis, Tennessee, and effectively linked the two struggles. The fight to organize tobacco workers also brought black and white southerners together, while, as Tim Minchin has shown, in the paper industry, as in textiles, it was again the 1964 Civil Rights Act which provided the impetus for successful organization. Until then, the industry had been strictly segregated, the union locals likewise. The act's passage changed all that, despite initial resistance from executives and white workers alike. With an integrated industry, a united union came eventually, and with such unity came greater strength.[53]

Nevertheless, the textile industry was the South's flagship throughout the twentieth century, and the workers' struggle the longest, the most bitter, and the most easily witnessed through the prism of class conflict. Whether led by the Communists, as in Gastonia, the UTW, the TWUA, or their fellow workers, textile strikers faced the ferocious opposition of those who believed they had made the new South—the cotton mill owners, their managers, their bankers, their support staff, their floor walkers and supervisors, together with the people who depended on the mill for a living, and that could often be most of the town. They had a lot to lose, and they knew it. Their workers, kept segregated in their unincorporated mill villages, disenfranchised, economically bound to the mill, had everything to gain, and they knew that, too. Not all mill towns were like Honea Path, where the owner, Dan Beecham, was also the mayor, but most conformed to at least part of that pattern. Race was largely absent from that struggle, class was the determinant.

What of the struggle of black southerners for their civil rights? Is there a class element to be found here, albeit much less obviously so? In the first place, the most ferocious defenders of the racial status quo, the strategists of massive resistance, the wielders of private economic powers, the local councillors, the education board officials, the merchants, the lawyers, the Klan members, even the law enforcement officers, were of the middle class. Like everyone else in America, beneficiaries of the wartime boom and cold war prosperity, they at least had something to lose. Their recently won good life, they believed, was still precarious, their jobs, their new housing, their possessions threatened by upwardly mobile, increasingly impatient black southerners, the new working class. Thus, the ferocity of their resistance, in the face of what from hindsight now seems hopeless odds.

What of the old white working class, the textile workers, the tobacco farmers, the increasingly marginalized? Many, including textile workers, also benefited from postwar prosperity, often becoming the shock troops of resistance, thus joining the white middle class in their struggle. But many did not. Historian Pete Daniel, in a recent book, painted the 1950s as a decade of racial possibility in the South. At the level of popular culture, he argues, the shared traditions were joining, nowhere more obviously than in southern music. Working-class young people, black and white, were singing each other's songs, listening to each other's radio stations, even dancing in each other's juke joints. Elvis Presley of Tupelo, then Memphis, is the representative figure here. Similarly, another prime southern working-class recreation, stock car racing, was also becoming integrated at both the performance and spectator levels. Daniel believes that what white sympathy there was for black aspirations to equality is to be found at the working-class level, the country level, even the mill level, where the shared traditions had always been most obvious.[54]

In *The Color of the Law*, Gail O'Brien adds some dimension to that view. She tells the story of the race riot which rocked the small Tennessee town of Columbia in 1946. In the night of violence, what is significant is that it was the black southerners who shot first, and at police officers, wounding four of them. Retribution was ferocious: thirty-one blacks were eventually arrested and charged with an array of crimes, most carrying long jail sentences. A trial venue was selected in Lawrence County, a date set, and a jury empaneled in due time. Its members were all white. Yet for the first time since Reconstruction, a white jury found all but two of the defendants not guilty of crimes of violence against whites, and the two convicted were found guilty of relatively minor offences. O'Brien believes this happened primarily because the prosecution, in its thirst for vengeance, had not paid enough attention to jury selection. Thinking any white southerner would do the job required, they had permitted the selection of a jury full of poorer men, small farmers, and laborers, those in most danger of becoming marginalized. They listened to the evidence, to the posturings of the powerful—and they voted for acquittal.[55]

In the pages that follow, aspects of these two great movements for social and economic justice, these "southern struggles," will be examined, not to simply highlight what divided white and black southerners but also to draw attention to what united them, to continuities, to points of commonality between the two. Through exploring the intersection of class and race in the twentieth century South, through stressing the essential "southernness" of both movements, Charles Joyner's luminous contention that black and white southerners share aspects of a common past, that they come from "shared traditions," can once more be illustrated.

Chapter 3

Local Men, Local Women

Ella May Wiggins, or Ella May as she much preferred to be called, left her home in Bessemer City, North Carolina, on the morning of September 14, 1929, in a mood of somber determination. She joined a group of twenty-three local members of the Communist-affiliated National Textile Workers Union, and together they set out by truck for nearby Gastonia, there to join a rally of fellow unionists and strikers protesting the escalating climate of violence in the town in the bitter aftermath of the NTWU-led strike at the Loray Mill. Violence there had already cost the life of Gastonia's police chief, Orville Aderholt, and had provoked fierce reprisals. Indeed, the rally's Communist Party organizers, disturbed by the potentiality for further violence as armed bands of vigilantes patrolled the streets, decided to abandon the meeting, retreating ignominiously to the relative safety of Washington, D.C. No one, however, thought to warn those who planned to attend.[1]

Despite the seriousness of their purpose, Ella and her fellow unionists enjoyed the short trip along the highway. They stood on the truck's open bed, the full sun at their backs, the air crisp and clean. At Gastonia's outskirts, however, their journey came to an abrupt end. Armed vigilantes stopped the truck, angrily ordering its driver to turn around and go back to where he came. He was in no mood to argue, given the guns, but was terrified when the men followed behind in a convoy of cars. Just before reaching Bessemer City, they again stopped the truck. The details of what happened next will never be entirely clear, but what is certain is that as the unionists climbed down from the truck's bed, they were shot at. Ella May was hit by a single bullet, which destroyed the large aorta before lodging in her spine. Some reported hearing her say, "Lordy they have shot me" before collapsing. Certainly, she would have been dead before her lover, Charlie Shope, carried her from the truck. That bullet ensured Ella May's place in history, for she became a national symbol, the martyr not only of the Loray Mill strike but also of the whole year of violence in the southern Piedmont. Her grave in Bessemer City, for so long unmarked, now has a handsome memorial headstone dedicated in 1977 by Bill Brawley, president of North Carolina's Central Labor Council, in honor of this obscure woman who "probably had more impact on people's lives than all the statues in this blamed state." It was time, said Brawley, for North Carolina's labor movement to replicate her selflessness and her dedication.[2]

If Ella May's death in time made her a national symbol, her life was very much that of the southern white underclass. She was born on a farm near Sevierville, Tennessee, in 1900 but did not live there for long, as her family left the land, not for the mills but for the Appalachian logging camps. The Mays moved from camp to camp. During the day Ella and her mother did the loggers' washing, and in the evening Ella sang for them the songs of her mountain background, in that powerful raw voice that would later make her so prominent on the picket lines of Gastonia. Before she was out of her teens, however, she had married John Wiggins, an amiable drifter and a drinker, had borne the first of her nine children, and had left the mountains for the textile mills of the Piedmont.[3]

Ella's daughter recalled her mother once saying that she wanted "a life where she could be something or do something." She eventually was to find it in Gastonia, in the strike of 1929. Before then, she bore eight more children, losing four of them in infancy to childhood ailments, including pellagra, the "classic disease of Southern rural poverty." She was also the main breadwinner, for though Wiggins stayed with her until her eighth child came, he made no contribution to the family's support. The mills, therefore, kept her away from her infants even as they lay dying, and she hated them for that. Many of her best-known ballads reflect this hatred, with their theme of the separation of mothers from their children.[4]

When the NTWU came to Gastonia, Ella May quickly became caught up in the strike at the Loray Mill, even though she did not work there but in the American Number Two mill in Bessemer City. For her, the union, with its message of defiance and of a better future, soon became the focus of her life. She was a formidable figure on the picket lines, but it was at the evening strike rallies, the morale-boosting barbecues and dances, that became such a dominant presence. Fred Beal, the strike's leader, called her the "minstrel of the strike" and left a powerful recollection of her sig-nificance. "No evening passed without getting a new song from our Ella May," he remembered. "She would stand somewhere in a corner, chew-ing tobacco or snuff and fumbling over the notes of a new poem scribbled on the back of a union leaflet. Suddenly someone would call for her to sing and other voices would take up the suggestion. Then in a deep, reso-nant voice she would give us a simple ballad. Easily the favorite was 'Mill Mothers Lament.'" The opening verse starkly caught the bleak reality of the strikers' lives:

> We Leave our home in the morning
> We kiss our children goodbye
> While we slave for the bosses
> Our children scream and cry

But the final stanza looks to a future of economic justice triumphant:

> Now listen to the workers
> Both women and you men
> Let's win for them the victory
> I'm sure t'will be no sin.[5]

"Mill Mothers Lament" was sung at Ella May's funeral. By the time of her death, the union had surely given her life a larger purpose, as the Baltimore journalist but North Carolina native Gerald W. Johnson recog-nized more than most. "For a few weeks" he wrote in a moving, angry obituary, she "had lived," finding in the union "a light. . . . And she fol-lowed the gleam." She died "believing in something" bigger than herself, and this was a solemn warning to "the Christian gentlemen of North Carolina," who were behind her death. Her songs, her life, symbolized "the sense of justice of an outraged people, which cannot be murdered by mobs."[6]

More than thirty years later, another unknown, unlettered southern woman would, like Ella May, sing about justice and freedom for her people. From earliest childhood, Fannie Lou Hamer had a remarkable singing voice. Recognizing this, her mother, Lou Ella Townsend, the daughter of slave parents from Mississippi, sang to her constantly, us-ing music as a means both of socialization and instruction. As an adult, Fannie Lou herself used songs to teach and inspire her people, the ex-ploited African Americans of the Mississippi Delta. Long before she became a leader of local political protest, then a national figure, she had, like Ella May, become attuned to using her voice as a means of cultural resistance and a way of asserting "control and direction over one's life as the lives of one's community."[7]

On Sunday, June 9, 1963, Hamer and a group of local civil rights workers were probably singing hymns as the Greyhound bus on which they were traveling pulled into the bus station in Winona, Mississippi. They were returning from a voter registration workshop in Charleston, South Carolina, organized by SNCC and led by one of the movement's most dedicated activists, thirty-two-year-old Annell Ponder, a coordinator with Martin King's SCLC who had close ties also to SNCC. She was on the bus with Hamer and other local civil rights workers, on their way back to base in Greenwood, Mississippi. They had encountered nothing untoward on the way, except they had noticed that the bus driver disembarked at every stop to make a phone call. Still, though they had initially challenged his order that they sit in the back of the bus, in the end they had obeyed him. Thus, though wary, as all black bus riders habitually were in Mississippi, what happened in Winona took them by surprise.[8]

Five of the group, including Ponder, immediately alighted from the bus and made their way to the terminal lunch counter, where they demanded service in defiance of the state's segregation laws. They were immediately evicted by the police chief and returned to the bus, where Hamer awaited them. Ponder was unwilling to let it rest there, however, and began taking down the license numbers of the patrol cars, whereupon the five would-be diners were immediately arrested. Hamer, who had briefly alighted from the bus, prepared to continue her journey, hoping to get help, but before she could do so, a patrolman shouted, "Get that black son of a bitch, too! Bring her down in the other car." What followed became one of the civil rights movement's most celebrated incidents, as symbolic in its own way as the killing of Ella May.[9]

Once within the jail's walls, those arrested, including Hamer, were subjected to systematic beatings excessive even by the violent standards of the time and place. In later testimony, Hamer said that she was whipped by two young black prisoners as the police chief and several of his officers stood by. Using long blackjacks, they pulled up her dress, hitting her bare flesh until her entire body was bruised. By the time it was over, she could not walk, and her legs, one already weakened by a childhood bout of polio, simply did not work. Annell Ponder was similarly savagely attacked, as was sixteen-year-old Jim Johnson, whose left eye was permanently damaged. Hamer, too, never fully recovered from the outrage; her kidneys were weakened, and she lost the sight in her left eye. The other three arrested, mercifully, were left unharmed.[10]

Hamer was to describe the circumstances of her beating often, including the small acts of kindness she encountered amid the savagery. "We was there and we begged for cold water," she recalled,

> and the only thing that was kinda nice there—the jailer's wife and the jailer's daughter. We could tell when the jailer and the other men were out: they would bring us cold water, they would bring us ice. And I told 'em, I said "You are all nice. You must be Christian people." The jailer's wife told me she tried to live a Christian life and I told her I would like for her to read two scriptures in the Bible. And I told her to read the 26th chapter of Proverbs and the 26th verse and she taken it down on the paper. And then I told her to read the 17th chapter of Acts and the 26th verse and she's taken that down. She never did come back after that . . . I don't know what happened.[11]

On August 22, 1964, Hamer, by then vice chairperson of the Mississippi Freedom Democratic Party (MFDP) and already a well-known figure in national civil rights circles, vividly detailed her ordeal to the Credentials Committee of the Democratic Party at the National Convention carefully orchestrated to nominate Lyndon Baines Johnson. By challenging the right of the regular Mississippi convention delegates to their seats, the MFDP had both disrupted the smooth proceedings and angered the watching president. In eight minutes, Hamer not only reduced many of the convention delegates to tears, she had so transfixed a national television audience that the president felt constrained to hold a hastily convened press conference to lessen her statement's impact. Her transition from local activist to national symbol was complete.[12]

For Fannie Lou Hamer, as with Ella May, political involvement had given her life meaning. Before the civil rights movement, she had worked most of her life as a sharecropper near Ruleville in rural Mississippi, her husband farming land owned by W. D. Marlow. Intelligent but poorly educated, she long had a lively sense of the injustice of Delta race relations, but little sense of how to resist it, until a hot day in August 1962, when COFO representatives came to Ruleville to start a voting rights project. Fannie Lou Hamer, then forty-five years old, at last found larger meaning in her life and a way of fighting the injustices she had long experienced. She found in the young activists inspiration and conviction, they found in her the courageous local leader they needed—and one of the most powerful musical symbols of the movement. Attempting to register to vote may have cost her her job on Marlow's plantation, but it freed her to assume a key role in the local, then the state, and, finally, the national civil rights struggle.[13]

Unlike Ella May, Fannie Lou Hamer lived to see at least some of her larger goals achieved, some of her victories won. When she died in 1977, the year Ella May was finally memorialized, the tributes to her were immediate. Veterans of the civil rights struggle—Andrew Young, Ella Baker, Stokely Carmichael—spoke at her funeral. Earlier, several colleges had awarded her honorary degrees, she had even lectured at the nation's most prestigious institution, Harvard University. Yet she and Ella May remained alike in two key respects. Both of them used music, the songs of their class, their race, their background, as potent weapons of political struggle, and both, from positions of local involvement and leadership, became national symbols of southern struggles for social and economic justice.[14]

So much attention has been given to the great national agencies working for economic and social justice in the South—the UTW, the TWUA, the national civil rights organizations—that the importance of local leadership and grass-roots involvement has often been neglected. Yet these great national challenges were at one level merely the sum of thousands of locally led enterprises. Though the UTW eventually sent its most experienced southern organizer, Albert Hoffman, to Marion in 1929 to take charge of activities there, it was a local man, twenty-five-year-old Lawrence Hogan, who was behind the organizing of a local in opposition to the grinding stretch-out and eventually sought national assistance. Described by Tom Tippett as "a born leader" and "an outstanding figure all through the strike," Hogan eventually served time on a chain gang on trumped-up riot charges. Unlike the national UTW, Hogan did not abandon Marion after the strike's bloody failure. Instead, he worked with the survivors entirely on his own. He got the women working on rug-making projects, partly as therapy but also to earn some money. He taught classes, anything to keep the union spark alive. Hogan did what he could to draw Marion into the action in 1934, and when he died a year later in a car wreck, he was mourned as "one of the clearest-eyed leaders of federated workingmen in this section." Yet he had never sought a wider canvas for his work, preferring always the role of grass-roots organizer.[15]

In the general textile strike of 1934, though the appearance of national direction was maintained through the pronouncements and activities of strike director Francis Gorman, there was in fact very little central coordination, particularly in the South. There, local organizers, usually acting without sanction, determined its course. In Hogansville, Georgia, for example, in the Chattahoochee Valley, the local leader was Homer Welch, a former Methodist seminarian, now working in the Calloway Mill. Entirely on his own, Welch turned Hogansville into a potent center of strike activity, which spilled over into neighboring Newnan. Indeed, Welch's success in forcing the closure of Newnan's mills, using pickets from Hogansville, eventually forced Governor Eugene Talmadge to send in the national guard. Welch and his Hogansville supporters, most of whom were young women, were rounded up and transported to a hastily constructed detention center on Atlanta's outskirts, quickly dubbed the "concentration camp" by delighted members of the press. Like Hogan, Welch did not fade away upon the strike's failure. Instead, he remained in the South as a local UTW organizer, even as the union's support collapsed. Like Hogan, he was eventually to serve time in prison, convicted in 1936 of the first-degree manslaughter death of deputy sheriff Jim Bryant during a picket-line gun battle in Talladega, Alabama. Though no one contended he had fired the fatal shot, as the strike leader, the jury deemed him responsible for the officer's death. Decades later, former Hogansville workers interviewed for the documentary film *The Uprising of 1934* remembered Welch as a charismatic local leader, one who liked to "help other people, and a good Christian man" who started all union activities with a prayer. "People say that no one was for the union except trash," said Corrine Lindsay, but that simply was not so. "Homer Welch gave the lie to that," she asserted. He was a "fine man."[16]

No organizing effort in the South had more central direction than Operation Dixie, yet even there it was the local organizers who determined limited success or failure. As Tim Minchin has convincingly shown, among the many reasons the drive failed was the deep distrust textile workers felt for "foreign" organizers, those whose very surnames—Baldanzi, Bittner, Rieve—bespoke their immigrant origins. What success Operation Dixie achieved, both in building locals and in holding the line against management attempts to break them, was more the result of strong, determined local leadership than the result of national office support. The determination of strikers at the Hart Mill plant in Tarboro, North Carolina in 1949, who held out for nearly seven months against unequal odds, was because of the respect they had for their local leadership, and their consequent desire "to fight for their union." "We knew what we were fighting for," recalled Gerald Wornell. "It really wasn't that we wanted more money or anything, we wanted to be treated fair." Madelin Wells, too, remembered the strike clearly. It was a battle for "a better place to work," she said, and that could only be achieved through maintaining a strong local union. It was the Operation Dixie leadership, not the local strike leaders, who called off the strike for tactical reasons. As TWUA representative Lewis Conn, who made the decision to abandon the battle, admitted, the workers were still "holding firm" after more than six months and were unlikely to weaken. Conversely, the disastrous general strike of 1951, which destroyed the TWUA in the textile South, resulted from a national decision made largely to protect the terminally ill New England industry from further southern competition and was opposed by most of the local leadership, whose understanding of the prospects of success was grounded in reality.[17]

Finally, in the post–civil rights years, as the mills were slowly integrated and the TWUA returned to the textile South, success or failure was again determined by local factors, including the commitment of the new black workers and the strength of their leaders. At the Kenlon Mills, in Allendale, South Carolina, for example, "a 1970 election victory was attributed to the fact that the 'majority of workers were black and self-organized and the company could not crack their solidarity.'" Victories at Oneita Knitting Mills in Andrews, South Carolina, in 1973 and at the J. P. Stevens plant in Roanoke Rapids, North Carolina, in 1974 were similarly attributable to black militancy, focused by strong local leadership. There were many others, as union records amply show. Local organizers always knew that they could count on black support. "You could go into a plant and you'ld find out how many blacks was there, that give you a pretty good assurance," remembered one such organizer, Clyde Bush. "If you had fifty blacks that worked in that plant, you could count yourself fifty votes, automatic." Ironically, in view of the region's history, white workers, initially bitterly resistant to black organizers, frequently came to admire their sense of dedication—and even their militancy. In Carrboro,

North Carolina, in 1974, one white worker declared that she was now "glad" that the civil rights movement had happened, because it gave textile workers a new model through which they, too, could fight for their rights. She had become much more militant, she said, as a result of her association with local black labor leaders. All over the textile South it was the same. Nick Builder, a TWUA organizer throughout the seventies, claimed that whites often let blacks take the lead in union building because they were more militant. Whites would support the union once it was organized, he said, but they wanted blacks to "cook" it for them. This is not to say that the renewed organizing drive in the postsegregation textile South transformed the industry. It did not. What success there was, however, was again due to determined local leadership, often African American leadership.[18]

The title of John Dittmer's superb study of the civil rights movement in Mississippi, *Local People*, starkly states where he believes the emphasis in that story should lie. For all the national attention focused in the 1960s on the most segregated, and most violently resistant, of all the southern states, it was the perseverance and courage of local leaders and groups which ensured eventual victory. The story of Fanny Lou Hamer has already been told. There were many like her in Mississippi, local people who defied the terror. There was Aaron Henry, who led a boycott of downtown merchants in Clarksdale, Mississippi, the first use of a strategy that would soon become widespread in the state. Henry, who was also state president of the NAACP, suffered imprisonment, intimidation, and economic reprisal as a result, but he never wavered. There was Amzie Moore, one of the toughest of the state's activists. A Cleveland businessmen impatient with the court-based approach of the NAACP, Moore persuaded Robert Moses and his SNCC legions to come to Mississippi. Above all, there was Medgar Evers, the state NAACP's charismatic, courageous, and uncompromising field secretary, who would eventually pay for this activism with his life. These and scores like them are the people Dittmer identifies as the makers of change in Mississippi, not the federal troops and FBI agents who guarded James Meredith or who searched for the bodies of Michael Schwerner, Andrew Goodman, and James Chaney, nor the presidents who put them there.[19]

Of course, Hamer, Henry, Moore, and many other local people eventually achieved some national prominence, often due to the telling of their stories of struggle. But most in Mississippi and elsewhere did not. The names of Sarah Everett Small, Golden Frinks, and Mary Mobley are relatively well known only in Williamston, North Carolina, county seat of Martin County, in the heart of eastern North Carolina's black belt. In 1963, the ratio of blacks and whites was roughly equal in the town of about 7,000 people, but the opportunities available to each group were not. Williamston's blacks, like most in eastern North Carolina, lived in conditions not unlike those in the Mississippi Delta. The school system remained segregated nearly a decade after the *Brown* decision, job opportunities for blacks were limited to those traditionally reserved for them, and segregation barriers were rigidly enforced by law, and by violence. Only a few years earlier, a young local man, a college student, had been shot by a deputy sheriff, allegedly for resisting arrest, but the real reason was that he had dared to cross the sexual color line by making advances toward a white woman. Marches, sit-ins, and similar demonstrations may have been occurring in other parts of the state—in Greensboro, in Chapel Hill, in Raleigh—but Williamston's whites stood staunchly against the changing times.[20]

Yet Williamston would soon be transformed, due in large part to the efforts of Small, Frinks, and Mobley, and those who followed them. Sarah Small led direct action protests, boycotts of city stores, and voter registration drives. On July 4, Small and Frinks "sat in" at the lunch counter of the Shamrock Restaurant, which served only whites. When the manager locked the restaurant doors, Mobley, who worked in the kitchen, unlocked them, took off her apron, and walked out. From then on, as its historian, David Carter has aptly said, she "made the Williamston Freedom Movement her vocation." Frinks was eventually to be jailed as part of local white reprisals, but the movement continued. By July 1964, they had won crucial concessions; downtown stores were desegregated, as were most public facilities, including the town's sole movie theater. By then, national events had overtaken such local struggles, and the "foot soldiers" of Williamston, as they did elsewhere, returned to their homes and their communities, their phase of the struggle over. "Local people" they certainly were. "Williamston, for them," as Carter has concluded, "was not just a way station in a larger progression of civil rights struggles; it was the beginning and the ending, where they lived."[21]

So was the tent city movement in Fayette County, Tennessee. Located in the southwestern corner of the state, and with a black population in 1959 of 21,000—mainly sharecroppers and day laborers on the cotton plantations which dominated its economy—as opposed to 8,000 whites, Fayette County, like Williamston, resembled much more the Mississippi Delta's ambience than that of neighboring Memphis. Yet the civil rights movement was to arrive there with surprising swiftness, the catalyst being the unlikely vehicle of the 1957 Civil Rights Act. Scarcely the most radical of measures, it nevertheless stimulated a vigorous voter registration drive, led by a local service station operator and army veteran John McFerren. So successful was he that by the end of 1959, 4,900 out of the county's eligible voters were on the rolls, an extraordinary achievement given the high levels of intimidation they encountered.[22]

Organized white resistance, however, was not long in coming. By May the following year, McFerren found that his gas and oil supplies had completely dried up. Most companies refused to do business with him, and those that did, like Southern Oil of Memphis, had their trucks turned back by sheriff's deputies when they attempted to make deliveries. Most suppliers would not even talk with McFerren. A Texaco dealer in Somerville, Tennessee, simply said, "You know why" when asked the reason for his refusal to sell. Somerville's Esso representative confirmed that "he could not sell me any gas and didn't want to discuss it." A few were more direct, frankly admitting that there was a "gasoline squeeze on the Negroe's [sic] who have registered to vote in Fayette County" and that it had been organized by Rhuhe Rhea, who worked for Gulf Oil's Somerville plant. Local farmers, too, found that their gas supplies had also dried up. O. D. Maclin, who had been regularly supplied by Gulf, found that his account had been abruptly closed once he had registered to vote, even though he had never been late for a payment. Texaco removed the gas tank from Harpman Jameson's farm because he purchased less than 2,500 gallons annually from them, even though they knew full well that the state only allotted 1,800 gallons for tractors of his size. Amoco even refused to sell him gas, for cash, for his car and truck. Again, all this happened after he had become a registered voter in June 1959.[23]

Soon the economic repression had broadened far beyond gasoline sales. Blacks found their credit cut off, by their banks, by their feed and livestock suppliers, by their local stores. African American store owners, who might have helped out, were themselves subjected to such intense pressure that they themselves were forced to close their stores. The few white businessmen and farmers "who have refused to boycott Negro registrants, or have testified for them against the White Citizens Council persecution," one report alleged, were themselves "suffering right along with the Negroes," and they too faced complete economic ruin. Nevertheless, most of them could still pay for food, and a significant number of Fayette County's blacks, increasingly, could not. Whites, generally, did not lose access to health care, but there were no black doctors in the county, and white doctors would not treat "any Negro registrant in the County." Nor would the hospitals and clinics. The McFerrens lived only two miles from a health center, yet when their baby required emergency treatment, Mrs. McFerren had to make a forty-one-mile dash to a doctor she knew would treat the child, the local clinic having peremptorily turned her away.[24]

Then, inevitably, came the evictions. In Haywood County, 300 families were ordered to move by January 1, 1961, in Fayette County, 400, and of these, only 1 had not registered to vote. The initial reason given was that the mechanization of southern agriculture, even cotton growing, had so reduced the need for labor that such displacement was inevitable. In the larger sense, that was true, yet it does not mask the fact that those displaced, most of whom had "lived on their places many years" and some who had been "born there and have lived there all their lives," had all challenged white dominance by registering to vote, and this the local white power structure would not countenance. "If we don't get rid of these Negroes, you'll be seeing them sitting in office in the Court House," said one. "We'll go easy until the cotton crop is in and then we'll freeze them out." No amount of talk of mechanization, of the laziness and dishonesty of individual families and tenants could mask the fact that the act of registration was what had brought about the evictions.[25]

The black citizens of Fayette County fought back, initially under McFerren's leadership as chairman of the hastily formed Fayette County Civic and Welfare League. The league challenged the evictions in court and at the same time tried to relieve the worst privations of those displaced. Thus Freedom Village came into being, a potent symbol of local black resistance to white persecution. "Tent cities" were not new to the South. Striking textile workers evicted from their mill villages had sometimes sought refuge in temporary communities. The most symbolic was that established in Gastonia during the Loray Mill strike of 1929, where Ella May had sung her songs. In the Missouri boothill ten years later, displaced black sharecroppers had formed their own tent colony before some of them were more permanently resettled by the New Deal's Farm

Security Administration. Now, in 1960, Fayette County was to have its own tent community.[26]

Fortunately, there was a black landowner in the county, Shepard Toles, who refused to be intimidated by white pressure and was willing to rent three acres of his land to the Welfare League for $120 a year, and it was there that Freedom Village was established. By the end of 1960, seventy people, or eleven families, had moved in. The oldest inhabitant, Wyatt Williams, was sixty, and the youngest, Clara Jean Trotter, was just five weeks. They lived in hastily erected tents, each of about 100 square feet, sparsely furnished, with no flooring, the sole heating being a small, wood-burning stove. Sanitary facilities were tactfully described as "elementary," the wood stoves clearly presented a fire danger, and conditions were spartan in the extreme, yet one resident claimed that "the tents are warmer than the cabins from which she was evicted." Moreover, as the evictions continued despite court injunctions, the demand for accommodation there outstripped the resources of McFerren and his local supporters. This was one reason why the national office of the NAACP became involved in Fayette County.[27]

The other was to aid in food and clothing distribution, not only to the residents of Freedom Village but also to the hundreds more in Fayette and Haywood Counties who were in desperate need. As the situation there gained some national attention, donations of food, clothing, and money arrived in increasing volume, far more than McFerren could handle. He asked, therefore, for some assistance from the state and national offices, something he would soon regret, for with their involvement came bitter disagreement over control of the movement. McFerren naïvely presumed he would remain in charge, NAACP officials, while recognizing his courage and commitment, had real doubts as to his leadership capacity. "He is a nervous type individual," reported veteran branches director Gloster B. Current, "not unlike some others with whom we have dealt. In his zeal for this exciting cause he has little regard for objectivity and sometimes the truth." Before long the national office had taken over effective direction of the Fayette County enterprise, coordinating aid distribution, seeking further contributions, providing legal assistance in the court challenges, publicizing the situation, attempting to get the recently installed Kennedy administration involved. McFerren, who resisted such national direction and had assumed he would retain control of the local movement he had started, was instead peremptorily shunted aside, replaced as head of the Welfare League by a local minister, Rev. O. Odeneal.[28]

It is true that the movement he had started became too large for Mc-Ferren to control. Certainly the NAACP field report which spoke of his backyard as being "littered with donated shoes, simply strewn about open to the elements," and "cartons of food and clothes indiscriminately stacked against walls, with holes made in one carton or another and items pulled out and discarded if not of immediate use," is indicative of this. Moreover, once whites had discovered Freedom Village and had shot it up, wounding a resident, Early S. Williams, in the arm and narrowly missing his four sleeping children, it was time for the national publicity machine to take over, if only for the residents' protection. Yet John Mc-Ferren should not be lost to history. Like Robert Williams in Monroe, North Carolina, he had organized his community, and had first led them in resisting their oppressors.[29]

Gradually, tensions in Fayette County eased. There was no more reported violence, though individual acts of harassment continued. The oil companies and grocery stores started selling again, though not to McFerren; people drifted away from Freedom Village, some to new properties or to towns and cities, a few back to their old homes; and further evictions were successfully blocked in federal court, while those which had already occurred were under FBI investigation. Most important, President Kennedy in June authorized the sending of surplus food to Haywood and Fayette Counties to be given to "Negroes who had undergone `severe hardship' and had been compelled to leave the land because they had registered." At the same time, the Department of Justice announced that 100 landowners from the two counties would be facing civil rights suits. By year's end, only four families remained in the tent city, and the landowner, Shepard Toles, had asked them to move as soon as possible. The crisis in Fayette County was over, and the NAACP, rightly, claimed a victory of sorts. In all the justified self-congratulation, however, the name of John McFerren was never mentioned. It should have been, for he had made it possible. It was his local leadership, his determination to stand and fight, that gave the NAACP its chance.[30]

When, in November 1929, sixteen-year-old Miss Mouser English took the stand as a defense witness in the trial of UTW leader Hoffman and several other Marion strikers, all charged with riot, rebellion, and insurrection, press reports emphasized, along with her youth and her blonde, bobbed hair, the depth of her commitment to the strike cause. She had been, it seemed, a vocal presence on the picket line throughout the struggle, and by her own admission usually wielded a stick. Moreover, her incessant "cursing," incongruous as it seemed, coming from the diminutive "boyish-bobbed, brown-eyed mill worker," had certainly got under the skins of the sheriff's deputies, one of whom had eventually taken to her with his boots and fists. Mouser's friend, Annie Lee Wilson, described as "a small and rather vivacious woman," on one occasion took to the sheriff with her stick but missed. She was sorry about failing to connect, but not about the profanities she too had hurled at "them as deserved it," including "all the law." These two young women, textile workers and union activists, exemplified one of the most singular aspects of the 1929 strike wave, the active involvement of young women on the picket lines and in the local strike organization.[31]

Earlier in the year, it had been the young women of Elizabethton, Tennessee, who had sparked off the year's unrest by leading the walkout from the Bemberg Glanzstoff spinning plant, and then dominating the picketing. When the national guard came to town to restore order, and picketing was forbidden, rebel girls like Trixie Perry, a reeler in the Glanzstoff plant, and her friend "Texas Bill," draped themselves in American flags and paraded past the troops, forcing them, constantly, to present arms. Eventually charged with violating the injunction against picketing, they were both brought to trial. Trixie made herself a dress out of red, white and blue bunting for the occasion, her cap was a small American flag. "Texas Bill" was even more spectacularly attired. Forsaking her normal cowboy garb, she appeared in a "fashionable black picture hat and a black coat." Like Mouser English, she admitted to "cussing a little bit" at the guardsmen, especially after one had "stuck his gun in my face." These two "disorderly women," while scandalizing mill management and the local forces for order, provided marvelous theater for those in the courtroom and crucial moral support for the striking textile workers.[32]

A few weeks later, Gastonia, across the mountains, was to have its own "disorderly women." Once the strike at the Loray Mill had gained some national attention, journalists soon noted the vocal presence of young women on the picket lines, and at the strike rallies. Commenting on a mass meeting she had recently attended, Cora Harris of the *Charlotte Observer* wrote that most of those present were women, "dressed in their gay Easter frocks and a few with spring coats. I was particularly attracted," she said frothily, "by the popularity of silk stockings." Those present had more on their minds than fashion. One of these "well-dressed" young women caused wild cheering when she "jumped up to the platform screamed 'yes they put me in jail and I'm proud of it.'" She would go again, she affirmed, she would even "shed blood if it will help this 'ere Union." The radical journalist Mary Heaton Vorse, a frequent visitor to Gastonia, often commented on the resolution of the local women. They were much less inclined to waver than the men, she thought, much stronger in their determination to see the strike through, no matter what the cost, and this she much admired. Others were far less positive in their assessment of the local women's behavior. One outraged citizen wrote to the *Gastonia Daily Gazette,* strongly expressing his unease. "It isn't decent for a respectable lady to go on the streets," since the strike's beginning, he said. "I have seen young girls, I mean strikers, going up and down the street with old overalls on and men's caps, with the bills turned behind, cursing us, calling the cops all kinds of dirty things." Another complained, "What disgusts me is women mixing in this strike. A really to goodness women would not loiter around, and fight and curse like men. In all strikes, I think, the women ought to go home and leave the men to settle it." By 1929 all through the textile South, local young women were no longer willing to let men do the fighting, and for many, this was profoundly disturbing. In Ella May, the Gastonia strike produced the most potent symbol of what was a much more general characteristic of the year's disturbances. Trixie Perry, "Texas Bill," Mouser English, Annie Wilson—she was in all of them, and in hundreds more whose names are now lost.[33]

Five years later, when the general textile strike rocked the South, young women were again active participants. They picketed; they invaded plants along with their men, often as members of "flying squadrons"; they marched in the strike parades; they served on local strike committees; they were shot at; they went to jail; and they suffered in the strike's bitter aftermath. Take as just one example Gracie Pickard of Burlington, North Carolina. One of the most noisily active of the strike's local leaders, she was particularly hard on the national guardsmen sent to keep order, following them around town, baiting them loudly and obscenely, heedless of their increasingly angry warnings that women should go home and not become involved in the strike. As a final warning, they bundled her into a truck and drove her about the town, but she still "stood proud, knowing it was for the union." Eventually she was bayoneted in a scuffle, patched up, and taken to jail. There, the deputy sheriff assigned to guard her refused to acknowledge her femininity. "You know that thing that talked to you this morning?" he told a sympathetic friend. "Well she sure is on the inside looking out. She's down at the County jail."[34]

Etta Mae Zimmerman also went to jail in 1934, along with fifteen other young women, strikers from Hogansville, Georgia. Early on September 17, Homer Welch led them to neighboring Newnan and picket duty there. They were in good spirits, having sung the latest popular tunes on the truck ride to the East Newnan mill, but there they were arrested by heavily armed national guardsmen and transported to a hastily erected detention facility at Fort McPherson, near Atlanta, as Governor Herman Talmadge moved decisively to break the strike in Georgia. There they were held—112 men and 16 women in all—until the strike was settled. It was the women who received all the publicity, of course. They were asked about their grooming, their personal lives, and, only occasionally, about what had landed them in Fort McPherson. Etta Mae got off one good line when she allegedly told reporters that all the women would "feel more honored to go out with the national guard than with the scabs" of East Newnan Cotton Mill No. 1. Widely reported at the time, when interviewed fifty years later, she could not remember making the remark. One thing she did stress in that same interview, however, was that she had never felt the slightest shame about having been so incarcerated. She had done it for the union, she said, and she would do so again. Moreover, it was her local that she meant, not the national UTW, not Francis Gorman, not Thomas McMahon, not even Franklin D. Roosevelt. For her, the strike had always been about Homer Welch and the better life he had hoped for, and about "this community (Hogansville) and Newnan and La Grange." Etta Mae, probably, had never heard of Ella May, but she, too, had fought for the same cause.[35]

When the TWUA organizers came South as part of Operation Dixie, they were alarmed to find that the commitment which had so energized local women in the 1934 strike had dissipated. Staffers like Nancy Blaine, whose special assignment was to "crack the women," found this very hard to do. Women were very difficult to sign up, she said. They were afraid of their husbands, afraid of losing the economic gains the wartime boom had brought, and in particular, of not being able to keep up the payments on their houses. Moreover, their post-1934 suffering was still painfully fresh in the minds of most older women. Dorothy Daniel was sent to Elizabethton, where there had been so much female militancy in 1929, to try to revive the spirit of Trixie Perry and "Texas Bill." She had no chance. "These women are mice. . . . I have found practically no one with real leadership ability," she reported.[36]

Not every organizer's experience was quite as negative. Indeed, some reported that those women who did join their local were often its most active members, particularly during strikes, when they were often "at the heart of strike activity and violence." As in Gastonia in 1929, or Hogansville in 1934, their participation generated an amount of excited press comment. "Women Furnish Most Excitement in Textile Strike," ran one headline over an account of violence at Amazon Cotton Mill, Thomasville, North Carolina in 1947, which had largely involved women, though the reporter showed more interest in their grooming and general appearance than in their picket-line activity. Women were also prominent front-line participants in the 1951 Danville, Virginia, strike which proceeded the disastrous general strike of that year, again inviting comparison with 1934. In general, though, Operation Dixie was a male-oriented operation, and despite exceptions, the involvement of local textile women reflected this. Of course, the organizing drive, though focusing on textiles, was not exclusively mill-oriented. The Food, Tobacco, Agricultural and Allied Workers (FTA) employed a number of female organizers, most of whom were African American, one of whom, Moranda Smith of Winston-Salem, North Carolina, eventually became the FTA's southern regional director, and the highest-placed black women in the American labor movement at the time. The FTA picket lines were predominantly female and often integrated, as class solidarity asserted itself over the caste system. Historian Barbara Griffith reports an incident during a strike at the American Tobacco Company's Charleston, South Carolina, plant which made that point. During one minor confrontation, a white nonstriker spat on a black picketer, who retaliated by slapping the white woman. She was promptly arrested and charged with assault. At her hearing, however, the case was dismissed after white unionists appeared on her behalf. "I saw the whole thing," said one. "This scab spit in this sister's face, and she deserved every slap she got."[37]

Picket lines at the textile mills remained segregated throughout Operation Dixie, changing only after the 1964 Civil Rights Act eventually ended job discrimination in the industry. In the acclaimed 1979 movie *Norma Rae*, Sally Field won an Academy Award for her portrayal of the gallant, committed union maid, leading her black and white workmates to victory in a NLRB election. Norma Rae's real-life model, Crystal Lee Sutton, did in fact have such a moment of glory when she spearheaded the drive to organize the J. P. Stevens towel mill in Roanoke Rapids, North Carolina. Crystal Lee joined her TWUA local in 1973, and like Ella May more than forty years before, she soon found in it her "light." Working with organizers sent south by the national union, the fight against Stevens took over her life. She lost her job, her personal life was invaded, and her marriage foundered, but on August 23, 1974, the TWUA won an NLRB election, 1,685 votes to 1,448, with almost all Stevens' 700 black workers supporting the union. Crystal Lee herself was reinstated and awarded $13,436 back pay for her illegal dismissal. She worked a symbolic two days before returning to her new home in Burlington, North Carolina.[38]

Likewise, as Tim Minchin had demonstrated, there were many black "Norma Rae's" in the mills in the post-integration South determined to improve their workplace conditions and their lives, and in so doing to strike a blow against the twin barriers they had always faced—gender and race. One such was Laura Ann Pope, who "embodied the determination and spirited resistance that many African-American women brought to the textile mills." An NAACP member and community activist, she had taken a job at the Oneita Knitting Mills in Andrews, South Carolina, in 1970, primarily to help organize it. The plant's workforce was 85 percent women and 75 percent African American. After months of hard organizing, the TWUA decisively won an election in 1971, but the company simply refused to sign a contract. After more than a year stalling at fruitless negotiation, therefore, Pope and her fellow officials led Oneita workers out in January 1973. They stayed out for more than six months before the company capitulated signing a contract which conceded virtually every union demand. Leaders of the TWUA, astonished by the strike's success, attributed it "to the overwhelming support and militancy of the black women strikers." Pope put it another way. Comparing their victory to a failed strike ten years earlier, she said the failure was because "it wasn't enough black." Certainly, black women added militancy and commitment to union action in the post civil rights years. In Laura Pope, as in hundreds more, the "twin revolutions" of the 1960s, civil rights and the women's movement, connected. Again, one is forced to wonder how differently southern history might have unfolded if race had not kept white and black women workers apart for so long.[39]

Historians have often emphasized the youth of the women involved in the strike wave of 1929—Mouser English was just sixteen, after all—and even Ella May was only twenty-nine. Similarly, in 1934 Etta Mae Zimmerman and those who went to Fort McPherson with her were still in their teens or scarcely out of them. At thirty-three, Crystal Lee Sutton was a little older when she first joined the TWUA. Jacquelyn Hall and her colleagues were the first to point out the connection between the militancy of young women in 1929 and modernity. Unlike their mothers, they had no rural tradition to fall back on. For them, the mill and the mill community was their new world. "They did not see themselves as temporary sojourners," they write. "Their identities had been formed in the mill village." The story of women like Mouser English or Trixie Perry, even Gracie Pickard, those who "combined flirtation with fierceness on the picket line," was not only "firmly part of the female protest tradition; it was also clearly part of their particular quest for the liberating trappings of modernity." There was doubtless something of this spirit, too, in Crystal Lee Sutton.[40]

Yet when she wrote about the "disorderly women" of Gastonia, as well as commenting on their youth, and the smartness of their fashion, Cora Harris also noted that there were "some pathetic old women" in the crowd as well, "whose backs were bent with life's heavy burdens." Older women shared picket duties with the smart young girls there. Daisy McDonald, tall, dark, part Cherokee, and the sole breadwinner for her family of seven children and a disabled husband, organized the tent colony. One of the first strikers to be severely beaten by vigilantes was fifty-year-old Ada Howell, and more than forty years later, the leader of the Oneita strike, Laura Ann Pope, was a mother with two grown sons already working at the plant when she took her job there. Indeed, it was partly her distress at her boys' working conditions that sparked her determination to fight to end them. Older women struck in Gastonia in 1929 and Hogansville in 1934 for the same reason. They, too, hated the stretch-out, they had suffered disproportionately from it, and they wanted better working conditions and better lives, for themselves, for their husbands, and, most of all, for their children. Daisy McDonald, Ella May, Crystal Lee Sutton, herself a mother, and Laura Ann Pope, so separated by time, by context, and by race, had this in common.[41]

As Jo Ann Robinson worked feverishly throughout the night of December 2, 1955, cranking out thousands of leaflets describing the events surrounding the arrest of a local woman, Rosa Parks, for deliberately violating Montgomery, Alabama's segregation ordinances, and calling for a boycott of the city's buses, she could not possibly have known that she was now part of the symbolic beginning of the civil rights movement. The thirteen-month boycott which followed attracted national and international attention. It made its young leader, Rev. Martin Luther King, into a national spokesperson for all African Americans—and it ended, through eventual Supreme Court action, segregation on the city's bus lines. Yet it was essentially a local event, and the work of Jo Ann Robinson, at the time an instructor in English at Alabama State College and head of the Women's Political Council, the city's most active and assertive black civic organization, was central to its success. Robinson and her team had planned the boycott far in advance, and it was their tireless activity behind the scenes which sustained it. As such, she is representative of the thousands of southern women who, working at the local level, together made the civil rights movement.[42]

Like their counterparts in the drive to organize the textile mills, many of these women were young. This was particularly true of the next phase of the movement, the student-centered sit-ins and freedom rides. Young black men and women peacefully defied local ordinances which prevented them eating at the lunch counters in stores where they shopped or integrated the interstate bus lines and terminals as the Supreme Court had long conceded was their right—a right that was still denied them by the southern caste system. Young student leaders like Diane Nash of Fisk University moved from Nashville's sit-in campaign into a position of leadership in the freedom rides and finally into full-time civil rights work with the SNCC. Ruby Doris Smith, a student at Atlanta's prestigious Spelman College in 1960, became involved in the first sit-in movements in the city. She did not, however, attend the historic meeting at Shaw University in Raleigh, North Carolina, in the spring, which under Ella Baker's experienced tutelage led to the formation of the SNCC, preferring to stay in Atlanta and picket an A&P store with a large black clientele and a whites-only employment policy. A devout Methodist, she also took part in "kneel-ins" on Sundays. By the next year, however, she was caught up in the developing SNCC movement. She and Diane Nash had become the firm friends they were to remain for the rest of Smith's tragically short life. She had become a seasoned freedom rider, and she had spent time in jail, first in Rock Hill, South Carolina, then in Mississippi's notorious Parchman Penitentiary. Soon, like Nash, she left college life behind, become one of SNCC's few full-time female administrators, and was, in her biographer's words, "tough, committed and uncompromising in her devotion" to its cause. She died of cancer in 1967, only twenty-five years old but a veteran of the movement.[43]

In Mississippi and Alabama, young women stalwart in the cause abounded. Cynthia Washington moved alone into an Alabama county so dangerous that no civil rights worker had been there before. Deciding that she was too conspicuous driving around in her car, she did her work riding on the back of a mule. In 1965, reported Sara Evans, Annie Pearl Avery prevented a white policeman from beating her with his club by wresting it from him, shouting, "Now what are you going to do, mother-fucker," and then melting away in an enthused crowd of demonstrators. Annell Ponder, like Fannie Lou Hamer, was so brutally beaten in Winona, Mississippi, in 1963 that she could barely talk; nevertheless, she was able to whisper "Freedom" to her captors and supporters alike. Louise Cawley was twenty-seven at the time of the Orangeburg shootings, when her prompt action undoubtedly saved lives at the risk of her own. Like Mouser English and "Texas Bill," incidentally, she was not averse to swearing at the police, who eventually arrested and savagely beat her. In Williamston, North Carolina, Jackie Bond, a high school student of star-tling beauty, galvanized the town's teenagers into joining the Williams-ton freedom movement. Her "electrifying solo voice and level of fearless-ness," wrote David Carter, "inspired her followers, both physically in the marches and vocally in the freedom songs"—again echoes of Ella May all those years ago.[44]

Many of the women who helped make the civil rights revolution were not young, nor were they necessarily from the black colleges of the re-gion. Jo Ann Robinson, forty-three years old at the time of the Mont-gomery bus boycott, was a graduate and a college teacher, but Rosa Parks, whose defiant refusal to move to the back of the bus provided the precipi-tating event, was not. Rather, she was a seamstress at the Montgomery Fair department store and was on her way home from work when she was challenged. She was, however, much more than the simple black woman caught up in the vortex of great events, as some versions of the civil rights story attest, but had been a longtime activist for change, as secretary of the local NAACP chapter and as a state NAACP official.

Along with Martin Luther King, she had recently attended an interracial training session at the Highlander Folk School in Monteagle, Tennessee, long a target for white supremacist ire. The Montgomery bus boycott did not simply "happen"; rather, it was a well-planned, well-coordinated activity, certainly sustained by King's inspirational leadership but also by the endeavor and organizational skills of the Women's Political Council and those affiliated with it.[45]

As the fight to force the implementation of the 1954 *Brown* decision was joined, local women provided crucial support to the children who were in the battle's vanguard, and to their families. Easily the best known was Daisy Bates of Little Rock, Arkansas. Throughout the bruising events of 1957 and 1958, she was the black community's pillar. A long-time NAACP activist, she had recently been elected head of Arkansas' state chapters and was determined to resist the tide of white violence which followed the decision to integrate Central High. For most of that tumultuous school year, she was the nine students' guide, counselor, and resolute friend. They met at her home before school, and she counseled them after each school day. For this, she lived "under siege," forced to pay a private security firm for her protection in the face of vicious and increasingly frequent threats against her life. Her resolution throughout the crisis not only inspired the nine students to carry on the fight, it similarly uplifted the city's black community, and for this she has deservedly won her place in the pantheon of heroic women on whom the local struggle always depended. For there were similarly resolute people in hundreds of southern communities. In Tallahassee, Florida, Christene Knowles provided sustained support for the three teenagers selected to enter previously all-white Leon High in 1963—one of whom was her son, Harold—in the teeth of the sustained hostility of the school administrators, the white student body, and the wider community. Like Daisy Bates, Knowles's life was frequently threatened, but again like Daisy Bates and her nine charges, she and the students eventually prevailed.[46]

Tallahassee had its equivalents of Rosa Parks as well. When, on May 26, 1956, Wilhelmina Jakes and Carrie Patterson, both students at Florida A&M University, refused to move to the back of the bus when ordered by the driver to do so, they were promptly arrested and jailed, sparking a boycott of the city's transit system which rivaled in intensity that already occurring in Montgomery, if not in national attention. As with Jo Ann Robinson, local women played an active role in the Inter-Civil

Council, formed to coordinate the movement. Gladys Harrington was its secretary and was responsible for all press liaison, while Daisy Young provided the key link between student activists at Florida A&M and the boycott's male leadership, of whom the most prominent was a young Presbyterian minister, Rev. J. Metz Rollins. Middle-class African American women such as Daisy Bates, Jo Ann Robinson, or Daisy Young, and there were thousands like them throughout the South, had long been working together in black neighborhood community organizations, on school boards, on human relations councils, and increasingly frequently, within the framework of the NAACP. They possessed skills and experience easily transferable to the civil rights struggle.[47]

Likewise, Fanny Lou Hamer was neither young nor lettered when she transfixed the nation at the Democratic National Convention in 1964. Rather, she was forty-seven years old, with only the barest bones of an elementary school education. Yet she stands alongside Martin King and Malcolm X in the trinity of civil rights leadership, and alone as the symbol of the eventual commitment of the South's dispossessed to the struggle. Ella Baker, who more than anyone else provided the inspiration for the sit-in campaign, and whose importance to the general development of the movement has only recently been fully understood, had graduated from Shaw University in 1927 and had a career as an NAACP activist behind her by Easter 1960, when her influence at the Shaw University conference was decisive in the formation of the SNCC. Modjeska Simkins, longtime secretary of the South Carolina NAACP's state branch, did her most effective work in the 1950s, as a middle-aged woman. Like their sisters in the textile mill struggles, civil rights activism was not the sole prerogative of the young.[48]

Nowhere was this more obviously the case than in the battleground state of Mississippi. If Fanny Lou Hamer and Annell Ponder are the two symbolic figures, there were scores like them. The sociologist Charles Payne, in his rich analysis of the Mississippi movement, has shown that while male and female teenagers were likely to become involved in equal measure; in the "settle-aged" years between thirty to fifty, a pronounced gender imbalance occurred, with women three to four times more likely than men to become civil rights activists. Many reasons for this suggest themselves. The fact that rural black women have traditionally had to fulfil public roles, including those of confrontation, because they were less exposed to retaliatory violence or economic reprisal than their men, is one. The religious nature of the local movement, in a culture where women participated in church activities much more than men, is another. The growing importance of women as family heads, hence their increased likelihood to become caught up in the movement claiming the commitment of their children, is a third reason. There are elements of truth in all these reasons, as well as some real problems. The fact remains that in Mississippi at least, middle-aged and older women were much more likely than their menfolk to be involved in local civil rights activism. This may well prove to be true of other states in the South, once the research has been done, and yet the reasons may equally well remain elusive. Perhaps Zora Neale Hurston should have the last word. She called southern black women "the mules of the world." They did, she asserted, what needed doing. Certainly, in Mississippi at least, women like Fanny Lou Hamer bore out Hurston's adage. When civil rights "needed doing," they were there.[49]

Though Payne and most other historians have focused on the post-1945 years in their discussion of the civil rights activism of southern black women, it is worth noting that they have a much longer history of such involvement. In January 1926, Elizabeth Little, described as "a Negro welfare worker," was arrested in Birmingham, Alabama, after she had led a group of twenty blacks to the county registrar's office in a vain attempt to register to vote, a precursor to the drives of the 1960s. Earlier, in 1922, Mary White of Gadsden, Alabama, fought fiercely, though unsuccessfully, to save the life of her nephew, I. B. Berry, sentenced to hang for the murder of a white youth in the course of a quarrel. A New Orleans woman, Althea Hart, took on that city's police department in 1930, angered beyond endurance by the shooting of "a fourteen year old colored girl," Hattie McCary, by a white patrolman, Charles Guerand, after she had allegedly resisted Guerand's advances. "Far too many of our people have suffered the same injustices as this girl," she wrote W.E.B. Du Bois, "and the same thing will continue if our people doesn't stand behind us and fight for the best results." Guerand had claimed he had acted in self-defense, but all blacks knew better. "A lie for a white man is better than the truth for a black man. The victim was but a child," she protested, "and had been annoyed by this man for some time. He insulted the girl. She resisted him and in anger he shot her." Hart's persistence put her own life in danger but it eventually had the most remarkable result. The NAACP took up the case, and despite his protestations of innocence,

Guerand was arrested, tried, and eventually convicted of Hattie Mc-
Cary's murder. The crowded courtroom heard both the verdict and the
consequential death sentence in "stunned silence," for it was the first
time in "New Orleans' criminal history where a white man had been
sentenced to die for the slaying of a Negro." The NAACP legal team,
headed by Chandler C. Luzenberg, which had assisted the district attorney throughout, hailed the sentence as "a signal victory." It would not
have been won without Althea Hart's fearless determination to see justice prevail. In Atlanta, Ruby Blackburn's tireless activism as a black
community organizer eventually brought her to the notice of the white
power structure, including Mayor William Hartsfield, whose policies and
programs she was occasionally able to influence to the benefit of the
city's black citizens. The importance of Modjeska Simkins in South
Carolina's NAACP before the civil rights era has already been noted. Indeed, throughout the South in the depression years it was the regional
field staff, black and white, women like Daisy Lampkin and Mary White
Ovington, who kept local branches going, tirelessly traversing the region, stimulating activity, putting branches in touch with one another,
helping them raise money, organizing youth and women's auxiliaries.
Their work remains largely unheralded and unknown, but it was certainly not unimportant.[50]

Many of the white women, some southerners, some not, who worked
for SNCC, SCLC or CORE at the local level have subsequently written of
the importance local black women had as role models, and as sources of
inspiration. Sara Evans in particular described the experience vividly in
her path-breaking *Personal Politics*. "But the most important models for
the young volunteers," she wrote, "were the older black women in local
communities." Living in their homes, eating from their tables civil rights
workers often became temporary members of the family, even to the
point of being introduced to friends as "my adopted daughter." Volunteers knew that they brought danger to any black household in the Deep
South: "Our hostesses are brave women and their fear is not at all mixed
with resentment of us, but that makes it none the easier for them." In
addition to "their warmth and courage" in taking in civil rights workers,
she continued, these women were also the local movement's leaders.
Young civil rights volunteers, disoriented and often frightened in the
alien demimonde of rural Mississippi, were to find in these "mamas"
"vital examples of courage and leadership." Some, like Casey Hayden,

Mary King, and Constance Curry, were eventually to have their tensions with the young black women in the movement, but for the older local women who guided them, comforted them, and sustained them, their admiration remained undimmed. That Hamer has become their symbol is indeed fitting, but there were many of similar courage, resolution, and inspiration. Twenty-five years later, referring in particular to Mississippi local activist and MFDP delegate Victoria Gray, Summer Project volunteer Theresa Del Pozzo recalled that "when I was twenty-two years old, it was people like her who set an example and definition of values that framed my adult life."[51]

Thirty-five years earlier, young women who had come south to help the Gastonia strikers in their struggle had found similar resolution and courage in the local women they worked with. Sophie Melvin, a Young Communist League Activist from New York who had been sent to work with the striker's children, discovered in women like Daisy McDonald and Ella May sources of real strength. The radical journalist Mary Heaton Vorse, a frequent visitor to the tent colony, observed how Melvin and her companions, "so remote from home, so surrounded with the hate of the well-to-do," were initially all but overwhelmed by the hostility they encountered. As was to be the case for the Mississippi volunteers, however, it was "the affection of the workers," especially the women, who sustained them, who shared what little they had with them, who showed them the way to survive. They were there in the courtroom at the trial of those accused of murdering Sheriff Aderholt, still supporting those who had tried to help them. "A pathetic group," sniffed Cora Harris, especially the "flappers" in their "brief skirts, colorful blouses and chokers, bracelets and hats at jaunty angles," some there with their mothers, older women "with deep lined faces." She had missed the only important point: these two groups of women, so different in background, in experience, and in political perspectives, had come to share each other's worlds, as happened also to Sally Belfrage, Casey Hayden, and the other Mississippi volunteers more than three decades later. Then, it was seen as a way station in the revival of American feminism, but it is also one of the points of connection between these epic southern struggles.[52]

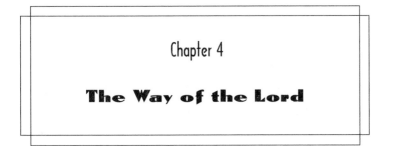

Chapter 4

The Way of the Lord

They buried their dead in Marion on Friday, October 4, 1929. The service was held in the open air, adjacent to the space where strike rallies had been held for the past two months, the gray-draped coffins in the center, in front of the speaker's stand. From early morning, however, mill workers had been bringing wild flowers to the site, until by midmorning the stand, the coffins, and the surrounding ground were a mass of blossoms. Each casket, too, bore a ribbon stating that the dead men had all been members of the United Textile Workers of America. By midmorning, the October sun had highlighted the magnificent fall coloring of the surrounding trees, which contrasted with the evergreen pines of the Blue Ridge chain. As journalist Tom Tippett commented, "The South often a paradox of beauty and ugliness, was certainly such on that October day."[1]

A huge crowd had gathered for the service, almost all from the mills. Francis Gorman, UTW vice president, was among them. He had been on a train in Georgia on his way back to New York when news of the shooting reached him but had immediately changed direction. So was state organizer John Peel. Marion's upper class, however, "remained aloof," according to Tippett, "a little shocked and inarticulate." Certainly none of the local clergy had visited the families of those slain to offer what consolation they could. Nevertheless, the message of the gospels permeated the proceedings. The gathering sang gospel music favorites, "Nearer My God to Thee" and "They Tell me of an Unclouded Day" were but two of them, then a union song set to a hymn tune. The Rev. James Myers of the Federal Council of the Churches of Christ, himself a former labor activist, gave the eulogy, pleading "with the workers to banish all hatred, bitterness and hard feeling from their hearts" as they renewed their struggle to be "relieved from serfdom." Others, including Gorman, expressed similar sentiments before the two-hour service ended "with a long prayer from a mountain preacher named Poole." And what a prayer it was. Cicero Poole was no trained theologian, but he knew his people and he knew how they had suffered. "Oh Lord Jesus Christ," he shouted,

> here are men in their coffins, blood of my blood, bone of my bone. I trust, O God, that these friends will go to a better place than this mill village or any other place in Carolina.
>
> O God, we know we are not in high society, but we know Jesus Christ loves us. The poor people have their rights too. For the work we do in this world, is this what we get if we demand our rights? Jesus Christ, your son, O God, was a working man. If He were to pass under these trees to-day, He would see these cold bodies lying here before us.
>
> O God, mend the broken hearts of these loved ones left behind. Dear God, do feed their children. Drive selfishness and cruelty out of your world. May these weeping wives and little children have a strong arm to lean on. Dear God—what would Jesus do if He were to come to Carolina?

When Poole had finished, the bodies were taken to different graveyards. As the procession moved past the Baldwin Mill, still protected by the national guard, one young soldier, in defiance of regulations, removed his hat and rested his rifle in a silent gesture of sympathy. There was no local minister at one of the graveyards to lay the bodies to rest. A. J. Muste, head of Brookwood Labor College, stepped forward. "We consecrate this worker's body to the earth from which it came," he said. "He has fought a good fight in a noble cause. He will rest in peace." Thus, as with Cicero Poole, labor's cause and the Christian message were conjoined as Marion's dead were laid to rest.[2]

Less than a month earlier, they had buried Ella May in Bessemer City. On September 17, the sun stayed away, rain poured down as she was lowered into the grave. The NTWU leaders had hoped to use the occasion to spark a nationwide strike against "the murderous terror of the bosses' black hundreds." The reality was rather different, as W. T. Bost of the *Greensboro Daily News* wrote. The funeral, he said, "was a battle between Karl Marx and John Wesley and John Wesley won." Ella May was given a Christian burial. True, her fellow unionists Dewey

Martin, Wes Williams, and C. D. Saylors all spoke of her work for the union, and how she had "given her life for the betterment of her fellow workers," but it was Rev. C. J. Black of First Baptist Church who had the last word. He read from John 14 and First Corinthians as the plain pine coffin was lowered into the red clay, inviting all present, including those from the Communist Party of America, to be "men and women who fear God" as he prayed for peace and for Ella May's orphaned children. "Brother Black," remarked Bost, had "buried a dead sister exactly as a Christian. And Roger Williams had registered a triumph over Karl Marx." Robert Thompson of Raleigh's *News and Observer* was more reflective. Ella May, he thought, "was no more a Communist than she was a capitalist." Rather, she had joined the union, as she had also joined the church, "in the hope that it would in some mysterious way, improve the lot of herself and her children." Again, the cause of Christ and of labor were brought together in the aftermath of death.[3]

It was to be the same in Honea Path five years later. More than 10,000 gathered there on September 8, 1934, to bury the victims of the shooting at the Chicquola Mill. There on a grassy bank outside the town, for again the mill churches had been denied them, they sang "In the Sweet Bye and Bye" and other gospel choruses, then watched George L. Goodge, the AFL's southern director display an American flag, its fabric torn by bullets. "See the bullet holes where they shot through the flag on the picket line," he shouted. "This can't go on." Once again, Rev. Myers preached his message of reconciliation. Those who had died, he said, had done so "for the rights of the hard-working man, who is close to God." They had died fighting for decent working conditions, a cause as old as the message of Jesus, who had taught that "we are all children of God and entitled to better things than we have had so far." Joining a union was, he argued "a test of Christian character," and thus the slain men were exemplars of "Christian unselfishness." There was hand clapping, there were frequent shouts of "Amen," as once more the connection between the cause of labor and that of Christ—Christ the working man—was well and truly made. As the mourners followed the coffins to the graveyard, most sang the old gospel hymn "Thou Art Gone." A few, however, chanted, "Remember Honea Path. Remember Honea Path."[4]

Thirty years later, at the funerals of slain civil rights activists, the same fusions of cause occurred. They, too, were usually buried as Christians, sometimes to the same gospel hymns and with the same calls to continue the struggle, but without hatred and bitterness. Not all were equal to the task. Dave Dennis, CORE field secretary, broke the conciliatory mode at the funeral of James Chaney in Meridian, Mississippi, in 1964. In one of the movement's most powerful orations, he eschewed such expressions of "agape," the all embracing love of which Martin Luther King often spoke. "I feel that he has got his freedom," he angrily said of Chaney, "and we are still fighting for it":

> But what I want to talk about right now is the living dead that we have right in our midst, not only here in Mississippi, but through-out the nation. Those are the people who don't care. . . . That in-cludes the president on down to the governor of the state of Missis-sippi. . . . I blame the people in Washington, D.C. and on down in the state of Mississippi for what happened just as much as I blame those who pulled the trigger.

> I don't grieve for James Chaney. He lived a fuller life than most of us will ever live. He's got his freedom and we're still fighting for ours. I'm sick and tired of going to the funerals of black men who have been murdered by white men. I've got vengeance in my heart tonight, and I ask you to feel angry with me.

> Don't just look at me and go back and tell folks you've been to a nice service. Your work is just beginning. If you go back home and take what these white men in Mississippi are doing to us. . . . Then God Damn your souls.[5]

Dennis's passionate outburst, captured forever by the television cam-eras, remains one of the angriest, most uncompromising of all the civil rights era's eulogies. It was also one of the most untypical. Most, includ-ing those delivered by King himself, while expressing anger and sorrow, also spoke of healing and redemption. In the fraught atmosphere in Bir-mingham, Alabama, in September 1963, in the wake of the horrific Klan-inspired bombing of the Sixteenth Street Baptist Church that killed four young girls, his eulogy at the funeral service for three of them, Cynthia Wesley, Denise McNair and Addie May Collins, was one of reconcilia-tion. To the strains of "We Shall Overcome," he spoke about redemptive suffering and the need for all to cleanse hate from their hearts. Angry SNCC volunteers had organized a protest march after the funeral but abandoned their plans following King's call. Even the fiery Rev. Fred

Shuttlesworth, who spoke at the funeral of the fourth victim, Carole Robertson, moderated his tone and spoke of her redemptive suffering. Innocent victim as she was, she had also been "a soldier killed in a great battle for justice." The message did not sit well with Diane Nash Bevel and her SNCC colleagues, but it was much more the tone of most civil rights funerals than was Dennis's angry outburst a year later.[6]

Of course, given the intense television coverage of the movement's drama and tragedies, King recognized the potentiality, through such funerals, to make a statement to the nation and used them whenever possible. For more than an hour he pleaded with Carole Robertson's grieving parents to allow their daughter to be eulogized with the other three girls because of the national impact a joint funeral would make. He could not shift them; indeed, they resented his efforts to force them into such a "grandstand play." "We realize Carole lost her life because of the movement," Mrs. Robertson said, "but we feel her loss was personal to us." Thus King delivered his moving eulogy over three, not four, coffins.[7]

A significant number of those murdered during the civil rights era were white, and were thus eulogized and buried far from where they died. The families of James Goodman and Michael Schwerner, killed with James Chaney in Neshoba County, Mississippi, wanted them both to be buried next to their comrade in Meridian's black cemetery, but the state's segregation ordinances prevented this. Instead, they were memorialized in New York City. The funeral of Viola Liuzzo, killed by Alabama Klansmen in 1965 during the triumphant march from Selma to Montgomery, was held on March 30 in Detroit's Immaculate Heart of Mary Parish. Jon Daniels, who, like Liuzzo, went South in 1965 as a civil rights volunteer, was also murdered on the road between Selma and Montgomery, in Haynesville, shot by Tom L. Coleman, a White Citizens Council activist and alleged Klan member. Grief-stricken civil rights workers wished to hold a memorial service in Selma's St Paul's Episcopal Church but were denied permission because of the tensions in the city. Instead, Daniels was buried in his home town of Keene, New Hampshire. There, in St. James Episcopal Church, those attending heard Professor William J. Wolf of Harvard's Episcopal Theological Seminary, where Daniels was a student, read a paper the young man had sent from Selma. The title, "Theological Reflections on My Experience in Selma," accurately reflected its content. Selma, Daniels said, had not weakened his faith; just the opposite: "Darkening coals have kindled. Faith has taken wing and flown with a song in its wings." He was in Selma, he now knew, "because the Holy Spirit had sent me there." He wrote, too, of those who shared this faith, "the beloved community in Cambridge"; of "black men and white men, with all of life, in Him. Whose Name is above all the names the races and nations shout. . . . We are indelibly, unspeakably one." There were hymns and prayers at Daniel's funeral, and as at the funerals of Viola Liuzzo and James Chaney, it ended with blacks and whites singing together "We Shall Overcome." Christ and social justice, again brought together by death.[8]

Nowhere was this point made more poignantly or profoundly than in the most famous, and televised, civil rights funeral of all, that of Martin Luther King himself. There, in his own Ebenezer Baptist Church, mourners for the last time heard him deliver the message. Mahalia Jackson sang, with a poignancy almost too much to bear, "Take My Hand Precious Lord"; Rev. Andrew Young, the presiding minister, tried unsuccessfully to hold back his tears as King's majestic cadences rang out in a eulogy he himself had preached only a few weeks earlier and which had been recorded. "I want you to say on that day," he had declared, "that I tried to love and serve humanity. . . . If you're going to say that I was a drum major, say that I was a drum major for justice. Say that I was a drum major for peace." Only a day or two before his death, he had spoken at the Masonic Temple in Memphis and expressed similar sentiments. "Like anybody, I would like to live a long life," he had shouted, "longevity has its place. But I'm not concerned about that now. I just want to do God's will. And he's allowed me to go up the mountain. And I've looked over. And I've seen the Promised Land. . . . Mine eyes have seen the glory of the coming of the Lord." These two self-eulogies, now part of the very fabric of the civil rights movement, along with Jon Daniels's own invocation, together exemplify the spirit of Christian love at the movement's core. It was there as well in the struggle of the textile workers. Southern Christianity infused both movements, and never more powerfully than in the commemoration of those who had died for the cause.[9]

Southern black churches in all their aspects were central to the story of the civil rights struggle. From the movement's beginnings, church buildings became the focal point of such activity, given their importance as centers of black community life. In February 1919, for example, when the Atlanta branch of the NAACP launched a massive voter registration drive on the centenary of Lincoln's birth, the church was at its center. It was to be the greatest drive ever seen in the city, "for never since the abolition days of old has there been a more righteous cause." The city's black churches were to be its main rallying points, "holding continuous meetings" in order "to keep alive the enthusiasm." Ministers were especially urged to devote their sermons to promoting the drive, to maintain "honor rolls" of those successfully registering, and to arouse the black community "to our civil racial duty even as the Abolitionists roused the Nation sixty years ago." It was a role churches and clergymen were to fill for the rest of the century.[10]

During the hard Depression years, what NAACP activity there was in the South frequently involved church people and property. In March 1934, Rev. L. G. Duncan, pastor of the Bethel AME Church in Mobile, Alabama, contributed the first dollar to the local NAACP's campaign to help raise $120,000 nationally "to fight the Negro's battles." Duncan, described as "one of the most prominent ministers of this state" and an active NAACP member, frequently permitted his church to be used for branch meetings and rallies. The Bethel AME Church in Camden, Arkansas, became in 1932 the site of several rallies in support of Louis and Elbert Blake, a father and son condemned to die in the electric chair on April 1, convicted for murdering two white men. Their deaths were never in doubt, but all the evidence clearly indicated that the white men had been killed breaking in to the Blake home with intent to kill, thus the defense claim of justifiable homicide. When NAACP national officers visited local branches, they used black churches for their public appearances. For example, when Mary White Ovington, the NAACP national treasurer, visited Atlanta in May 1933, her one public meeting was held at the Big Bethel AME Church and was integrated. Likewise, in 1931, when a group of Monroe, Louisiana's black citizens decided to revive branch activity there, their first task was to persuade the city's ministers to allow them the use of their pulpits to spread the news, and then to get the preachers to become involved themselves in the belief that their flocks would follow.[11]

As the pace of civil rights activity quickened in the postwar years, black churches and black clergymen continued to provide crucial leadership. The overarching importance of the movement's most significant figure, Rev. Martin Luther King, makes the point more cogently than anything else. King, a twenty-seven-year-old clergyman at the time, was catapulted into the leadership of an essentially local movement, the boycott of the city's buses in Montgomery, Alabama, in late 1955. Recently arrived in the city, his lack of roots there, of established friendships or enmities, were considered assets in holding the black community together in the hard months ahead. In his first speech to the Montgomery community, King, as earlier noted, not only "defined the rhetorical cadences" of the civil rights struggle—the gospels, as preached from the black pulpit, but also set the context within which it would be raised —nonviolent civil disobedience, again in Christ's name. "You know, my friends," he told the gathering in a packed local church, "there comes a time when people get tired of being trampled over by the iron feet of oppression." Then "the weapon of protest" had to be raised, but protest without violence, protest in Christ's name, and imbued with his all-encompassing love. In conclusion, he spoke of his and his community's determination to "work and fight until justice runs down like water, and righteousness like a mighty stream." That first speech, historian Taylor Branch has argued, made King "forever a public person."[12]

The success of the boycott and the courageous leadership he displayed throughout also made King America's best-known civil rights leader and a national figure. In 1960, he left Montgomery for his native Atlanta, as copastor, with his father, of the Ebenezer Baptist Church, the city's most prestigious black congregation. Atlanta also became henceforth the headquarters of the Southern Christian Leadership Conference, the civil rights organization which he had founded in the wake of the bus boycott, and which he was to head for the rest of his life. Nothing better exemplified the connection between the civil rights struggle and the black church than the SCLC. Alongside King, its leadership cadre, Ralph Abernathy, his loyal though sometimes envious deputy; executive director until 1964 Wyatt T. Walker and his successor Andrew Young; James Lawson; James Bevel; C. T. Vivian; Hosea Williams; and eventually the young Jesse Jackson were all ministers or theological students—with the exception of Williams, who called himself "Reverend" without a day's formal training. Ella Baker, who was SCLC's first executive director, had real difficulties with the leadership from the start. Resenting "the arrogance and egocentricity" of the ministers, including King, and used to the well-established bureaucracy of the NAACP for which she had formerly worked, Baker found "the haphazard informality of the Southern black church exasperating," and she soon left the organization. Yet through King and his deputies, SCLC provided a crucial national public face to the civil rights movement, constantly reinforcing the important connection between the church and peaceful social protest.[13]

Some local clergymen, civil rights leaders within their own communities, became more widely known because of the intersection between their local protests and the widening national struggle. One such was Rev. Joseph A. DeLaine of Summerton, South Carolina, the man most responsible for bringing the first of the five cases, all of which eventually became subsumed under the title case, *Brown v. Board of Education*, into court. DeLaine's name is not now commonly associated with the landmark 1954 decision, though it was so at the time. Summerton was in rural Clarendon County, which had a 75 percent black population in 1950 and a school population in which blacks outnumbered whites by more than five to one in 1949 (when Rev. DeLaine filed his suit); it nevertheless spent nearly 70 percent of its school budget on its white children. *Briggs v. Eliot*, it was called, despite DeLaine's activism, and by the time the Supreme Court had made its historic judgment, he had lost his livelihood and been forced to leave Clarendon County and South Carolina after whites shot at him. Ironically, he was officially declared to be a fugitive from justice. Years later, as pastor of the Calvary AME Church in Brooklyn, New York, DeLaine attempted to prod the NAACP executive into providing some financial assistance for Harry Briggs, whose name was on the original suit and who had also been driven north by white reprisals. Though he wished no recompense for himself, Rev. DeLaine did remind Roy Wilkins and his colleagues that he, too, had suffered as a result of working with the NAACP and confronting segregation head-on. The years 1949 and 1950 were the "bitterest" he ever had, he recalled, and had cost him and his family "our friendship, our happiness, our economic opportunities and generally ourselves and friends." He was, he knew, a "casualty from the legal battles which have made the NAACP great," yet he could not have acted otherwise. As a preacher, he had had a special obligation to do so.[14]

Rev. Fred Shuttlesworth of Birmingham, Alabama, also felt that obligation. Unlike King, with whose fight his was eventually to entwine, he was not of the African American middle class, but the son of an unemployed miner and small-time bootlegger and a devout mother. The family spent most of the Depression years living on welfare and the generosities of family and friends. Fred himself worked his way through Selma University, a Baptist school, and Alabama State College before answering a call to Birmingham's Bethel Baptist Church in 1953. An uncompromising, somewhat authoritarian man, he also joined the local NAACP branch and "quickly became an activist in that ossified chapter," as historian Glenn Eskew has commented. As the local struggle against segregation quickened, he became its acknowledged leader. He led a boycott against segregated seating on the city's buses, he confronted school authorities demanding that the *Brown* decision be enforced in the city, he was beaten up by vigilantes, his church and house were both bombed, yet he remained combative and unbowed, the city's most important black clergyman but also the African American community's political leader. When King and the SCLC leaders came to town in 1963 for the Birmingham campaign, the images of which finally forced the nation's leadership into action, Shuttlesworth was there to provide assistance—up to a point. The fact that he became a national figure due to his association with King has tended to mask the fact that there was often bitter disagreement between them over direction and tactics, and that their relations remained strained thereafter. Moreover, from 1961, when he accepted the pastorate of the Revelation Baptist Church in Cincinnati, his Birmingham activities had to be combined with his duties there, and for two years he effectively divided his time between the two locations. After the 1963 campaign, therefore, his civil rights activities were muted, yet he remains one of the most significant of all the pastors who combined their Christian convictions with local civil rights leadership, and who thus strode briefly on the national stage in the company of King. "Martin didn't make Birmingham," he was sometimes heard to say in later life. "I made Birmingham." There was some truth in his boast.[15]

Yet most of the pastors and preachers who provided their flock with political leadership during the civil rights era did so in their localities without hope or expectation of greater national involvement. The Rev. Mark Gilbert of Savannah, Georgia, was one of the earliest of such leaders. His name was "barely mentioned in the history books," according to historian Stephen Tuck, yet "during the early 1990's he was still remembered admiringly. . . . As the 'preacher' and the 'dramatist' who led a movement some fifty years previously." There was good reason for this. From his arrival in the city in 1942 to become pastor of First African Baptist Church, Gilbert waged an uncompromising battle against segregation, inspiring others to do likewise. He formed the city's NAACP branch and superintended its growth, he organized voter registration drives and direct action protests against the local white power structure. The refusal of Savannah State College students, inspired by Gilbert's example, to relinquish the front seats on a local bus predated Rosa Parks's "precipitating event" by more than a decade. He eventually became leader of the state NAACP, which again he transformed through his personal fearlessness and dynamism, to the extent that its activities and influence clearly declined following his resignation in 1949. Gilbert, like most such local leaders, acted at great personal risk, and even greater risk to the church property over which they maintained stewardship. Throughout the South, churches were burned and bombed as those who stood against change attempted to destroy the locations in which it was advocated so uncompromisingly, and where the voter education projects, the "freedom schools," and other local projects usually took place. Some clergymen even threatened to emulate their Buddhist colleagues in Vietnam, immolating themselves as witnesses for the cause. In February 1964, for example, Rev. Elton Cox of High Point, North Carolina, vowed to "burn himself in oil if a restaurant in his home town didn't desegregate." Several other ministers, hearing of this, agreed to join him in a mass suicide on the city hall steps. Fortunately, the restaurant changed its policy before their resolve could be tested.[16]

Such extreme gestures, however, were rare, though the dangers of death and property destruction were real. Both King and Shuttlesworth had their homes and churches bombed or burned. This made national news. But Rev. James Pike of the Roanoke Baptist Church in Hot Springs, Arkansas, in 1963, also had his church and home burned, as did Rev. A. R. Blake, pastor of the Morris Street Baptist Church in Charleston, South Carolina, and president of the local NAACP branch, in March 1964. Neither received any media coverage. In June, the Mt. Zion Church, just outside Philadelphia, Mississippi, which had been used for voter registration meetings, was burned to the ground by Klansmen after the pastor and other church leaders had been viciously assaulted. All over the South, in fact, churches were destroyed, usually without much public attention and certainly without local investigation. So vicious was the Klan activity in McComb, Mississippi, after the Freedom Summer campaign there that several black ministers with no civil rights connections had their homes and churches bombed. Of course, pastors were not the only victims of violence—far from it. In McComb, as the Klan ran riot, black teachers, storekeepers, mechanics, and farmers were the victims of the indiscriminate campaign of terror. Yet in general the churches and the clergy were targeted, for they had long been in the vanguard of the struggle. When the movement first came to Hattiesburg, Mississippi, in 1962, in the form of an SNCC voter registration drive, it was the Rev. L. P. Ponder of Palmers Crossing who opened the St. John's Methodist Church to the young activists. "That's really where the Hattiesburg movement started," recalled one parishioner proudly. "It started for all practical purposes in St. John's Church in Palmers Crossing." And so it was in small towns all over Mississippi, indeed, all over the South; the local pastor provided the crucial spark—and the local headquarters. In Williamston, North Carolina, it was first the Cornerstone Baptist Church, then the Green Memorial Church of Christ, a larger venue, needed as the movement grew. A simple white clapboard structure, to those involved this Holiness church soon became "a shrine."[17]

The involvement of local pastors in the movement varied. Some simply opened up their churches for civil rights workers to use, others became, like Rev. Cox, outspoken advocates and committed activists. The detailed instructions CORE head office issued to local staffers about to lead new voter education projects stressed above all the need to gain the cooperation of as many local ministers as possible. It was important just to have them on board, and if some wanted to be more actively involved, that was a bonus. Well recognizing the importance of the pulpit as a means of spreading information, one of the first aims of any project leader was to get the ministers to include project news in their regular announcements. Most, of course, were much more involved than that. In the final days of the Goldwater-Johnson presidential race, for example, most black ministers in North Florida followed the entreaty of Rev. Cox, now director of the North Florida Citizenship Education Project, to turn their churches into local branch offices for the Johnson campaign. "Tell all citizens to VOTE and to carry others to the polls," he advised, provided they promised to vote for Johnson, and asked them to stress this from the pulpit. Ministers all had cars, he knew. They should use them "to carry *all* you can to vote." "Lift an offering this Sunday," he further exhorted, "to assist in gas, food, many expenses since July to aid the Negroes and whites who have help [*sic*] to get over 5,000 new Negroes out to register. . . . Ministers can vote early and remain at the polls to give silent support for others. Ladies can bring them lunches." Finally, they should be prepared, he said, to use their church buildings for victory parties. "Let us join liberal whites in celebrating VICTORY on the evening of November 3 for Johnson and pray for the souls of Goldwater and Miller." Post-election reports showed clearly that most ministers within the Education Project's jurisdiction, which covered North Florida's Gadsden, Madison, Jefferson, Leon, Liberty, Lafayette, and Suwannee counties, had followed Cox's directions enthusiastically. Such activity, replicated throughout the South during the civil rights era, illustrates again the crucial role black churches and their pastors played at the local level. In one sense, King's national leadership was the embodiment, the symbol of hundreds of such local leaders.[18]

In contrast, thirty years earlier, those attempting to organize textile workers to fight for their rights seldom enjoyed the support of local clergy in their efforts, nor the use of church buildings as their headquarters. The owners and managers usually controlled village religious life as they did everything else, and ensured that the message from the pulpit was safely, often viciously, anti-union. Most of Gastonia's churches were opposed to the strike in 1929, the mill village pastors vehement in their defense of the system, the more so because of the Communist affiliations of the strike leadership. Never, commented Rev. James Myers, had he met such "a cold unresponsive" group as the Gastonia clergy, unwilling even to countenance relief efforts for the conflict's innocent victims, the strikers' wives and children. "Evidently they have not yet thought of any connection between the mind of Christ and low wages or night work for women or child labor," was his mordant judgment. Similarly, in Marion a few months later, most pastors used their pulpits to support the mill management, while George Waldrep has described the institutional church as remaining "a conservative social force in the textile South during the 1930's, no matter what workers believed true Christianity meant." For this reason, many labor activists severed formal connections with the churches of their childhoods, though not necessarily with their faith.[19]

There were exceptions. Both devout Christians, Dan Elliot and his wife Grace were members of East Marion Baptist Church in 1929, where Dan was a deacon and Grace taught Sunday school. But they were equally strong for the union and the strike. Dan was vice president of the UTW local, and Grace, a former student at Brookwood Labor College, headed the team of women who organized the strike rallies. Believing they had permission to do so, they even held a few such meetings in the church hall. For this they were bitterly attacked by antistrike forces and eventually called to judgment by the church moderator, S. G. McAbee, who summarily expelled them from the flock for "disregard for church discipline." The Elliots refused to buckle, and eventually the expulsions were reversed, though not before Mrs. Elliot had split the congregation. Her eyes "dimmed with tears," she led half the worshipers from the church one Sunday, only to conduct worship in the street outside. In Gastonia, most church halls were also closed to the strikers, though a few Holiness, or Pentecostal, preachers made what facilities they controlled available. Similarly, church halls were generally closed to strikers as locations for rallies and strategy sessions in 1934, as indeed they were during Operation Dixie, when the major denominations for the most part resolutely supported management. Not until after the passage of the Civil Rights Act of 1964, and the consequent integration of the textile mills, were church buildings sometimes used for union meetings or rallies. By then, the mill village system had been abandoned, and most of the churches were African American. Again the "southern struggles" were conjoined. In the film *Norma Rae,* the heroine is shown attending her first union meeting in a black church. Crystal Lee Sutton, the real "Norma Rae," had a similar experience.[20]

The fact that few of them made their churches available to union organizers, of course, did not mean that all ministers sided with management in the union battles. Holiness preachers or Pentecostals, most of whom did not have organized churches of their own, frequently addressed strike rallies in Gastonia in 1929. Cora Harris, reporting on one such in early April, was especially taken by the first speaker, "a tall, rather distinguished-looking elderly man with a large flowing moustache"—the "Billy Sunday of Loray," she dubbed him. He opened the rally with a hymn and then spoke to a text, Malachi 3:8, "Will a man rob God?" Denouncing the mill owners of Gaston County, he asserted that they "robbed God" every day of their lives. The young Communists of the NTWU were far from happy at having to share their platforms with such men of God, but in the South they had no choice. Similarly, in Marion the same year, Holiness preachers held open-air services for the strikers when they were denied access to the town's churches, and, of course, Rev. Poole was there to eulogize so movingly Marion's dead.[21]

In the national strike of 1934, it is not always appreciated how many of the local UTW organizers and strike leaders were either ordained ministers or had received theological training. In Georgia, for example, Hogans-ville's charismatic strike leader, Homer Welch, who eventually was in-terned in Camp McPherson, was a former pastor. Before leading his fol-lowers to the picket line, he always held a brief prayer service, reminding them of the seriousness of their purpose, and assuring them that God was on their side. Macon's young organizer, Ralph J. Gay, who also went to jail, had been ordained before joining the UTW. Paul Fuller, director of the AFL Education Department, had been working permanently in the South since 1930, having been active in both the Elizabethton and Marion strikes the previous year. By 1932 he was actively organizing in the Horse Creek Valley area, working out of Augusta, and in 1933 led the strikes there. Fuller, a northerner and a graduate of Brookwood Labor College, was also an ordained minister. The ubiquitous Rev. Myers of the Federal Council of the Churches of Christ was a constant presence in the picket lines in both 1929 and 1934 and also, poignantly, at the funerals of those slain. Obviously active clerical leadership was never as important in the prewar textile struggles as it was to become during the civil rights years, but it was a factor of some significance nonetheless.[22]

After World War II, the organizers of Operation Dixie came to realize that their job would be an easier one if they could win the support of at least some of the white South's ministers, especially those whose flock included large numbers of textile workers. This, they also knew, would be an extremely difficult task. Accordingly, they asked Lucy Randolph Ma-son, the CIO's southern public relations representative and a committed Christian, and John Gates Ramsay, director of church and community relations of the United Steelworkers and an ordained Presbyterian min-ister, to try to win them over. It was an impossible mission, and most ministers remained resolute in their antilabor stance. A few, however, showed some sympathy, notably the Reverend Lee C. Sheppard, a North Carolina Baptist, who issued a statement in 1948 denouncing as "un-American any ideal or movement which would hinder laboring men and women from organizing to secure decent wages and living condi-tions for themselves and those who follow them," and the Rev. James A. Crain of the Disciples of Christ, which had a strong following in the mill villages. Nevertheless, the tenor of the white pulpit remained strongly anti-union. If any of the local organizers had church connec-tions, they tended to keep them hidden. Black ministers were much more receptive to supporting union activity, especially during Operation Dixie.

Winston-Salem's clergy, for example, were right behind Local 22, even as it challenged the city's white political establishment. But no black ministers had textile workers for constituents because of the industry's all-white structure. Yet again, racial exclusivity kept southern workers apart.[23]

Both textile union leaders and civil rights advocates, throughout their campaigns, used the message, the imagery, the rhetoric and the cadences of the scriptures and the pulpit in the advocacy of their causes. In Charlotte, North Carolina, veteran UTW organizer H. D. Lisk heralded the beginning of the 1934 strike at a mass meeting of union delegates which, according to seasoned *New York Times* reporter Joseph Shaplen, soon turned into "an old time Southern camp meeting," complete with shouts and prayers. "God is with us," Lisk shouted. He would "help us in our battle for human justice . . . and no power on earth can stand up against those who battle for the right." Roy Lawrence, president of the North Carolina Federation of Labor, cried, "We fight for the Lord and for our families." The very first strike in history, he claimed, "was the strike in which Moses led the children of Israel out of Egypt. They, too, struck against intolerable conditions, and it took them forty years to win that strike." The deliverance of the children of Israel from slavery, an image the black community had used since the days of slavery with reference to their own condition, was thus invoked by white southerners in their struggle for justice. Thirty years later, civil rights leaders, including Martin Luther King, would again make use of it so often that it became a central image of the movement, as it has been for all struggles for human rights. Later in the strike, Paul Fuller articulated the other central image of 1934, again at a funeral. Speaking over the coffin of Norman Carroll, an Augusta, Georgia, striker killed in a gun battle with police, he reminded the 7,000 workers present that Jesus, too, "was a labor leader, and was crucified by the same reactionary forces that today are fighting the labor movement, a movement which is going through the same persecution as did Jesus, for each tried to free the people." Cicero Poole had made the same comparison five years earlier, over the seven flower-decked coffins in Marion.[24]

These two images—Moses as the deliverer of the children of Israel and Jesus the fighter against reaction and injustice—long part of African American religious belief, became so important and universal to the civil rights struggle that further comment is unnecessary. Martin King used them constantly, from his first speech in Montgomery. They underpinned "A Letter from a Birmingham Jail," the most famous of all his statements. "Was not Jesus an extremist for love?" he wrote. "Was not Amos an extremist for justice?" "Let justice roll down like waters and righteousness like an ever-flowing stream." Shadrach, Meshach, and Abednego are there too, refusing to obey the laws of Nebuchadnezzar, in the name of "a higher moral law." So are the early Christians "willing to face hungry lions and the excruciating pain of chopping blocks rather than submit to certain unjust laws of the Roman Empire." Rather surprisingly, Moses is not mentioned in King's famous jeremiad, but the story was one he referred to constantly, as he did to the prophet Amos. Indeed, Amos's ringing call for justice was the theme of his first Montgomery address, it was there in the "Letter," and again in his concluding address to the August 28, 1963, Washington march. Then, the crowd response to Amos's words was so emotional that it caused King to depart from his prepared text in favor of his extemporized, and triumphant, conclusion. The two images, Moses the deliverer and Jesus the fighter, central to civil rights rhetoric as they were, had been equally important to those who fought southern labor's battles. Again, the two struggles came together, in the language of the scriptures.[25]

They joined too, in the way they used gospel hymns, turning them into songs of protest and defiance. Sometimes they were the same songs. "We Shall Overcome," which became the anthem of the civil rights movement, had previously been sung at many union rallies, North and South. Originally, it had been a gospel tune, "I'll Overcome Someday." "We Shall not be Moved," a traditional African American sacred song, was frequently sung at strike rallies in 1934 and at later organizing drives, before passing into the civil rights repertoire. "Oh Freedom," a traditional slavery song, was also used, with appropriate changes in its lyrics, as a southern union song in the 1930s and 1940s, then becoming one of the most powerful of civil rights anthems. There were many others which served both movements equally well, once lyrics and musical styles had been altered. Most came from traditional gospel roots which the South's two cultures had once shared, and were to do so again.[26]

Striking textile workers much preferred to sing gospel hymns at their rallies than the labor songs deriving from union battles waged elsewhere. "The Ballad of Joe Hill" had little relevance to them, while "Solidarity Forever," sung to the tune of "John Brown's Body" was downright offensive. But "Tell Me of an Unclouded Day" did have meaning. Of course, they sang many other songs, those of the mountains they had but recently left, variations of "Barbara Allen" were particularly popular, even the latest hit tunes. At Gastonia's strike rallies, Ella May performed the ballads she herself wrote, one of which, "Mill Mother's Lament," soon became sufficiently well known to be sung throughout the South in 1934. Others adapted the words of traditional ballads to make them topical. "Up in Old Loray," for example, was sung to the tune of "On Top of Old Smoky." Yet it was the gospel tunes that sustained them the most, as they did elsewhere. Most strike rallies began, and ended, with a hymn.[27]

The same was true of the civil rights movement, when song was central to the cultural environment, indeed, became the "language that focused people's energy." There, given the traditions of African American sacred music, there was seldom need to alter the lyrics, so directly did most of them speak of the struggle for justice and freedom. "Go Tell It on the Mountain," "Leaning on the Everlasting Arms," "Come Bah Yah," "Been in the Storm So Long," "Wade in the Water"—a mere sample of the scores of African American gospel tunes, many dating back to the pre–Civil War era, which more than a century later became the anthems of the civil rights struggle.[28]

White southern textile workers and black southern civil rights activists both thought of their struggles in theological terms, as part of the struggle for justice and freedom which the Christian message promised. Moreover, they believed that God was on their side. Historian George Waldrep, writing of textile workers in Spartanburg County, South Carolina, in the 1920s and 1930s, has argued convincingly that the union movement's involvement in religion and politics "went beyond simple references to 'Jesus, the Rebel Carpenter of Nazareth,'" important as these were. Southern unionists came out of a culture with its roots deeply embedded in Protestant Christianity. To them, in Waldrep's telling words, "church and union stood for the same thing: the dignity and redemption of human beings." Jesus' earthly purpose, they believed, was to work "for the welfare of man," the purpose of organized labor was no different. "Organized labor," argued one Glendale worker, "is a right and a Christian's duty. A Christian is for better conditions as Christ was and still is." Christ himself was an organizer, look at his disciples and the unity they forged. "How can a Christian oppose an organization that stands for right?" Waldrep quotes a Pacolet unionist as saying. "Only the ignorant and the unsaved" was the obvious answer.[29]

Even the Lord's Prayer could be explained in terms of organized labor, as UTWA organizer Gordon Chastain noted in a 1936 radio broadcast. Mill owners did not provide the means necessary to secure "our daily bread," nor any of the other necessities of life that God proclaimed. It was, he continued, impossible to avoid temptation, when wages were inadequate to acquire such things honestly. Nor could "the power and the glory" be properly afforded Him, because of the selfishness, the greed and the "jealousness" of those in power over their lives. Only after they had striven "to make this world better than when we first knew it" could the Lord's Prayer have real meaning, and that was the true purpose of organized labor, to build a better, a more just community, one closer to God. Their struggle, in the words of Paul Fuller, was "a battle of righteousness if ever there was one." Though the battle continues still, it is no longer described in such theological terms. Indeed, since the failure of the textile strike of 1934, Jesus and his Kingdom have given way in the rhetoric to much more worldly concerns—and a greatly diminished sense of possibility.[30]

Civil rights activists, too, fought for a better community, one closer to God, expressing themselves in language remarkably similar to those of the union battles of the 1930s. None did so more clearly than the young idealists of SNCC's first years. Their beliefs, too, were deeply rooted in the Protestant tradition, most had come to civil rights activity through the church, and as they articulated their vision of a changed South, they, too, talked of it in terms of community, "the redemptive community," SNCC's initial statement of purpose called it. More often, they talked of the "beloved community," a vision of the future where "Black and White together" would "demonstrate to the world new possibilities for human relationships." It would be a community, ran the SNCC statement, where "courage displaces fear; love transforms hate. Acceptance dissipates prejudice; hope ends despair. Peace dominates war; faith reconciles doubt. Mutual regard cancels enmity. Justice for all overcomes injustice. The redemptive community supersedes systems of gross social immorality." Like the textile strikers of the 1930s, the young men and women of SNCC sought to establish a community closer to that of God. And if the brutal experiences of their southern struggles, again like the textile workers, eventually curbed their idealism, they never entirely lost the vision. It was a vision, of course, that most civil rights activists shared, including Martin Luther King, who gave it its most soaring exposition on August 28, 1963. Then he spoke of his dream, and of the day "when all God's children, black men and white men, Jews and Gentiles, Protestants and Catholics, will be able to join hands and sing in the words of that old Negro spiritual, 'Free at last! Free at last! Thank God almighty, we are free at last.'" That was King's "beloved community." For all the differences of race, location, and time, textile workers would have recognized its wellspring, for it was theirs as well, the religious culture that was common to all southerners.[31]

Both textile strikers and civil rights activists also made good use of the symbols and legends of American civil religion—commitment to the Constitution and those who made it, to the theorists of American liberties, and to freedom itself. King was particularly fond of doing so; the First Amendment, Abraham Lincoln, Thomas Jefferson—all three are used in "A Letter from a Birmingham Jail," for example, as they were throughout his speeches and writings. Similarly, when textile workers turned to politics, as they did in South Carolina in 1934 after the textile strike had failed, and helped elect one of their own, Olin P. Johnston to the governor's mansion, they believed they were part of a political tradition that connected Jefferson, the "modern day Moses," Franklin D. Roosevelt, and Johnston himself, "South Carolina's Roosevelt," some called him. Like the civil rights workers of the next generation, they, too, fashioned a political credo, and, again like them, rooted it firmly in the Declaration of Independence, the Bill of Rights, and the cardinal Jeffersonian belief in "life, liberty and the pursuit of happiness," though still limited to whites, of course. Jeffersonian liberties, in their case, included the right to join a union, free from managerial interference.[32]

Of particular significance was the way both textile strikers and civil rights activists used that most potent of symbols—the Stars and Stripes. Textile workers paraded down Gastonia's streets at the beginning of the 1934 strike, the flag proudly borne at the head of the parade. At the strike's end, workers returned to the mills in "victory parades," again with the American flag flying high, a potent symbol of their conviction. The flag accompanied the motorized "flying pickets" as they sped along the South's highways, closing mill after mill. It was there in South Carolina as strikers and guardsmen did battle in the streets of Greenville and at the mass funeral for those slain in Honea Path. In Greenville, a phalanx of women, all draped in flags, had confronted troops at the Woodside Mill with cries of "You ought to respect the flag" and "Get out of the way, the flag is here." At the funeral, George Goodge had dramatically displayed the bullet holes in the flag workers had been carrying when they were shot. "This can't go on," he cried. Five years earlier, Gastonia's and Eliza-bethton's strikers had carried the Stars and Stripes as they picketed the Loray and the Glanzstoff mills while "Texas Bill" and Trixie Perry, as has been noted, fashioned garments out of flags for their courtroom appear-ances. Of all the civic symbols mill workers used, the flag was the most important—signifying as it did the seriousness of their purpose.[33]

Civil rights workers too, marched under the Stars and Stripes, at no time more triumphantly than on the Selma-Montgomery highway in March 1965. Often they carried the flag in miniature as they picketed downtown stores and places of entertainment. Usually they did not have them for long. Even in Albany, Georgia, in 1962, where Police Chief Laurie Pritchett permitted picketing under strict conditions, he would not allow those so engaged to carry flags. Newsreel and television cam-eras clamored for shots of his men removing them, relatively gently, from demonstrators' hands. Usually the treatment was much rougher; the sight of the flag being used as a symbol of civil disobedience seem-ingly had an incendiary effect on most southern law-enforcement offic-ers. As at Honea Path, some activists eventually lay in flag-draped coffins. Medgar Evers, murdered in Jackson, Mississippi, in 1963, was one. Police in Jackson, furious at the decision to allow a memorial service there, could do little on that occasion about the flags on display, for Evers was an army veteran who had served in France during World War II. Eventually he was buried in Arlington National Cemetery. The flag was there. In their use of civic symbols, too, those who fought these southern struggles made common ground.[34]

1. Strikers in Marion display their reduced paychecks. Courtesy of *When Southern Labor Stirs,* by Tom Tippett (1931).

LABOR DEFENDER

Oct. 1929

10¢

ELLA MAY—
MARTYR FOR AN ORGANIZED SOUTH

2. Cover of *Labor Defender*'s memorial edition for Ella May. As originally published in *Labor Defender*.

3. Flying pickets in action, September 1934. Courtesy of Library of Congress, LC-USF33–020926–M3.

4. E. B. McKinney of the Southern Tenant Farmers Union and "friends." Courtesy of the Kester Papers.

5. Lucy Randolph Mason addressing a dawn rally during Operation Dixie. Courtesy of the Mason Papers, Perkins Library, Duke University.

6. Students at a Fellowship of Southern Churchmen work camp. Courtesy of the
Fellowship of Southern Churchmen Papers.

7. Martin Luther King Jr., August 28, 1963. Courtesy of the *Melbourne Age*.

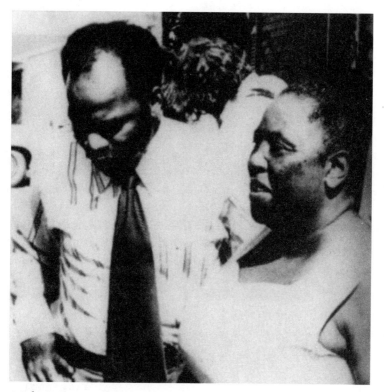

8. John L. Lewis and Fannie Lou Hamer. Courtesy of the *Melbourne Age*.

Chapter 5

Agitators

On August 15, 1964, a bomb destroyed a tavern in a black residential district of Natchez, Mississippi. According to SNCC worker Dorrie Ladner, it had clearly been meant for the house next door, a view confirmed by one of the firemen sent to deal with the blaze. "Those outside agitators are in that house," he reportedly said. "The bomb was set for that house." In the film *Norma Rae*, Norma's mentor, Reuben Warshawky, as played by actor Ron Leibman, is depicted as the quintessential "outside agitator" of southern demonology. He was portrayed, complained union official Howard Brown, as "a poetry-reading personality, who spouted 'Yiddishisms,' wears a denim jumpsuit unbuttoned to the waist, orders seltzer in a beer joint, and complains that the local hot dogs are not as good as northerners's [sic]." The real-life Reuben, veteran organizer Eli Zivkovich, even took to prime-time television to insist that he had been traduced in the film. "Sneakers I didn't wear," he complained, nor did he "happen to own a pair of jeans." As for Reuben's shoulder bag, he had never used such a device in his life. Indeed, he stayed "away from people who wear shoulder bags." White southern audiences, however, knew what he was, for they had had to deal with such people throughout their history, men and women from the north, their heads full of alien notions, determined to force changes to traditionally southern patterns of social and industrial order. Those who came to Gastonia in 1929 could clearly be seen to be of this ilk; so was John Dean, the tough Brooklyn-born organizer sent by the UTW to Alabama in 1934 to channel the anger of the textile workers there. As the pace of the civil rights revolution quickened in the 1960s, it was easy to brand the young volunteers who streamed southward to work with SNCC or SCLC similarly, and to blame them exclusively for the violence and disorder rocking the region.

This chapter, therefore, will consider the relevance and justice of such charges.[1]

At one level, of course, it has to be said that the white South was right. Since the days of Reconstruction, when the hated Carpetbaggers—more often than not men and women with high-minded ideals—had moved into the South, some admittedly to make a political or economic killing but most to do what they could to restore the Union and help bring political and social democracy to the region, "outside agitators" had continued to arrive, their targets always the South's hierarchical social and economic structure. Though most were driven by home-grown, often Christian, notions of equality of opportunity and the need to make the fourteenth and fifteenth amendments live, it was also true that occasionally such "agitators" were driven by non-American ideals and, more frequently, some also fitted the ethnic stereotype. They were foreign-born, and they were Jewish, and, as such, aliens, outsiders to be both feared and resisted by all available means.

Nowhere was this more obviously the case than in Gastonia in 1929. Formed in the aftermath of the October Revolution, the Communist Party of the United States, like many similar revolutionary cadres, had spent its first few years in underground factional bloodletting. By 1928, however, a dominant leadership group had emerged, committed to Joseph Stalin and world revolution. The party's industrial policy had also become clear. Henceforth there would be no more attempts to work within the framework of the increasingly hostile AFL; instead, it would build a new and revolutionary labor movement in America, one which would promote the class war and, eventually, overthrow capitalism itself. Thus was created the party's rival to the AFL, the Trade Union Unity League (TUUL), and, building on a strong constituency among textile workers established during the bitter strikes in Passaic, New Jersey, in 1926 and New Bedford, Massachusetts, in 1928, the TUUL's first affiliate was the National Textile Workers Union, created to challenge the UTW or any other union attempting to organize the mills.[2]

In 1929, the battle moved southward. The UTW planned an organizational drive in the mills, the NTWU had no choice but to follow, despite the complete absence of any party presence in the region, and total ignorance of its peculiarities. No matter, NTWU secretary Albert Weisbord decided in late 1928 to send an emissary there to organize a strike in a single mill and then extend it to other mills as circumstances allowed

until the South was subdued. This prime agent of change was to be Fred
E. Beal, a New Englander, an activist in the 1928 New Bedford strike, and
a party member of only a few month's standing. He arrived in North
Carolina on New Year's Day 1929 and soon found his mill, the giant
Loray complex in Gastonia. Working in secret, he quickly launched an
NTWU local there, and on April 1, after the dismissal of five workers, all
union members, had provided the precipitating moment, he launched the
strike.[3]

Beal certainly fitted the stereotype of the outside agitator and was
quickly branded as such by the local mill owners and their mouthpiece,
the *Gastonia Daily Gazette*. On April 3, the newspaper published the
first of a series of full-page advertisements—supposedly paid for by the
citizens of Gaston County—emphasizing this point. Beal was a Red, ran
the text, a Bolshevik who stood "against all American traditions and
American government." He was also an atheist, who "stood against all
religion of whatever kind," thus threatening "the very existence, the
happiness and the very way of life even, of every citizen of Gaston County.
. . . Shall men and women of the type of Beal and associates, with their
Bolshevik ideas, with their calls for violence and bloodshed, be permitted
to remain in Gaston County?" asked the paper. This question was to un-
derpin the whole strike story and its tragic aftermath. Indeed, it was to be
a constant theme throughout these southern struggles.[4]

Beal at least was American-born; some of those the party sent to help
him were not. Sophie Melvin of the Young Communist League, came to
work with the strikers' children. She had been born in the Ukraine in
1910 of Jewish parents but had fled her home in 1921 in the aftermath of
the Revolution. Amy Schechter, sent to organize the strikers' relief effort, was the daughter of Solomon Schechter, once a reader in Talmudic
studies at Cambridge University, and had been educated in prestigious
schools on both sides of the Atlantic. She had joined the British Communist Party in 1920, becoming a member of the CPUSA on arriving in
America the following year. Vera Buch, the strike's most important day-
to-day organizer, was American-born, as was her lover, NTWU general
secretary Albert Weisbord. Their ideas, however, were decidedly alien. In
1929, they were already dedicated long-term Communists, as well as veterans of the Passaic labor battles of 1926. Weisbord's frequent visits to
Gastonia particularly excercised the local leaders. On one occasion, after
he had urged Loray's workers to make the strike "a flame that will spread

from Charlotte to Atlanta and beyond. . . . So that we can have at least 200,000 workers on strike," a young mill worker turned cartoonist produced a huge drawing of a snake wound around an American flag under the heading "A Viper which must be smashed." The *Daily Gazette* devoted its whole front page to the drawing, above the caption "Communism in the South. Kill it." Finally, the party occasionally sent African American comrades, perhaps the most alien of all, to Gastonia to emphasize their solidarity with black southerners. Most, like central committee member Jack Johnstone, did not stay long. One sniff of southern air convinced him that New York was a much safer place to be. Nevertheless, their brief presence added immeasurably to the contention that these outside agitators, intent on the disruption of southern folkways and values, were a cancer in Gastonia's community and had to be rooted out.[5]

There were many reasons why the Loray strike ended tragically, and the ease with which its organizers so obviously fitted the outside agitator stereotype was but one of them. Nevertheless, it did convince the party that the South's white textile workers could not provide the revolutionary proletariat it was looking for. Henceforth its work would be primarily among black southerners. Though a few Gastonia veterans hung around on the fringes of Piedmont mill life, to reappear briefly and fruitlessly during the 1934 textile strike, what party activity there was in the 1930s took place mainly in Alabama. There, so-called outside agitators, white and black, like Tom Johnson, Harry Jackson, or Angelo Herndon, were sent to organize the sharecroppers of Tallapoosa County and the mine and steelworkers of Birmingham, working always with staunch local activists. In Tallapoosa County, they launched in 1931 the Croppers and Farm Workers Union (CFWU), members of which soon clashed violently with local law enforcement officers in July near the hamlet of Camp Hill. There Sheriff Kyle Young was shot in the stomach and several CFWU stalwarts were also wounded, including the union's local leader, Ralph Gray. Subsequently there was fierce revenge. More than fifty blacks were arrested as whites rampaged through the community, and dozens more were killed or wounded as rumors of armed blacks—"Negro Reds" as they were called—abounded. Roaming through the countryside they were, led by northern Communists, "searching for landlords to murder and white women to rape." How else could the "unnatural" armed resistance of sharecroppers and tenants be explained, or the ferocity of the whites' revenge?[6]

Yet the CFWU was not completely destroyed. Rather, the handful of members left after the rioting reformed as the Sharecroppers Union (SCU), establishing five locals in Tallapoosa County. Operating with only minimal direction from party central officers, the SCU slowly rebuilt its locals over the next fifteen months, until once again there was a shootout with the law, this time near Reeltown, about fifteen miles southwest of Camp Hill. There, on December 19, 1932, when deputy sheriff Cliff Elder came to seize the livestock of SCU member Clifford James as settlement of a debt allegedly owed his landlord, he found more than a dozen armed SCU members already on the scene, well prepared to resist him. Again there was violence, and when it was over, one unionist was dead, several wounded, and twenty or more were rounded up and jailed. Again, too, local whites took violent revenge, inflamed by the discovery of "Communistic literature" at the SCU headquarters. Eventually, nineteen SCU members were tried for assault with a deadly weapon and five were convicted, including Ned Cobb, whose autobiography, published in 1974 as *All God's Dangers: The Life of Nate Shaw,* became a best-seller and remains a moving testament to the triumph of the human spirit.[7]

The SCU was seriously damaged by the Reeltown shootout, but again it survived. By 1934 the party claimed 8,000 members. Yet it remained vulnerable, not only to the oppression of the landlords but also to the large-scale evictions resulting from New Deal agricultural policies. Moreover, it was an exclusively black organization. By December 1934 it had failed to recruit a single white member. Veteran white organizer, Clyde Johnson, was sent to redress this problem. He did his best, but the local power structure was always too strong. The SCU never had much strength outside Tallapoosa County, and, briefly in neighboring Lee and Chambers counties. Elsewhere, the violence meted out to the outside agitators, rendered more ferocious by the attempt to recruit whites, prevented any semblance of growth. Its merger with the Alabama Farmers Union in 1936, while necessary for its survival, curbed its radicalism, ended the influence of outside agitators in its leadership, and accelerated its passage into history. Its influence was entirely local, its successes pitifully few, but its example as an organization of the African American dispossessed who fought as fiercely as they could the forces and the people who oppressed them makes it important in the story of southern struggles, despite its lack of accomplishment.[8]

In Birmingham, too, the party's efforts among the miners and the steelworkers were similarly barren of accomplishment, due to the racism of white workers, which made interracial unionism almost impossible. Moreover, chauvinism existed within the party leadership itself, and, as always, there was the ferocity of local antilabor forces, often led by city commissioner Eugene "Bull" Connor. Connor was later to achieve national notoriety in the climactic summer of 1963, as he battled both Martin Luther King and the Birmingham Children's Crusade. There were local successes, of course, led by brave and dedicated outside agitators, white and black, but the battle lines were always uneven, and with the emergence of the CIO as an independent force, Alabama's Communist leaders, with relief, handed over the class battles to John L. Lewis, William Mitch, and the SWOC. There was no alternative.[9]

Of all the Communist Party's ventures in Alabama, however, none received wider publicity, nor greater obloquy, than the involvement of its legal arm, the International Labor Defense (ILD), in the trials of the nine young African Americans charged with raping two white women in Scottsboro in 1931. The long and depressing story of Scottsboro has become the stuff of American tragedy; indeed, its historian, Dan Carter, has so labeled it in his definitive account of the events. When the ILD's chief lawyer Joseph Brodsky and his deputy Allan Taub successfully seized control of the boys' defense from the NAACP's legal team, they opened the floodgates of anticommunist hysteria reminiscent of that in Gastonia two years earlier, when the ILD had similarly supplanted defense lawyers. Throughout the states, newspapers attacked these "outside agitators," while defending the resolution of local authorities in keeping the state calm. "It is difficult to speak with patience of the attitude of the International Labor Defense toward the trial at Scottsboro," complained the *Birmingham News* in April. Northerners should be grateful, not complaining, that local police had prevented a lynching and had observed "all the legal forms." The fact that Communist organizers had recently moved into Tallapoosa County confirmed the fear of outside agitators and further fanned local anger. In fact, the violence of white reaction to the Camp Hill shootings may well have been due to the fierce resentment the ILD presence at Scottsboro had already caused. In time, defense lawyer Samuel Leibowitz came to personify these fears. Born in Rumania, Jewish, flamboyant and politically on the left, he was the epitome of the outside agitator, the disseminator of foreign perspectives and ideology, alien, the quintessential "Red from New York." As such, he represented a stock figure in the demonology of the South.[10]

Nevertheless, one did not have to be a Communist to be labeled an outside agitator, an alien bent on destroying the southern way of life. UTW organizer Albert Hoffman found that out in 1929, first in Elizabethton and a few months later in Marion. Hoffman, originally from Pennsylvania, trained at the Brookwood Labor College in Katonah, New York, and, as noted earlier, nicknamed Tiny, was certainly no Communist but an authentic, home-grown American democrat. He had been quietly organizing in the South since 1927. Sent to Elizabethton in March by the AFL to take control of events there, he immediately became the prime focus of company and community enmity because of his "outsider" status. Indeed, on the night of April 3, this status was dramatically symbolized by mob action. An unruly group of men, allegedly organized by the town's business leaders, forced their way into Hoffman's hotel, took both Hoffman and AFL president William Green's personal representative to a nearby car, blindfolded them, and drove them to the North Carolina state line before letting them go, warning them they would be killed if they returned to Tennessee. Both men did return, but the symbolism was nevertheless clear. As outsiders, disturbers of the social order, they had to be expelled.[11]

A few months later, when trouble started in Marion, Sam Finley and Lawrence Hogan drove across the Blue Ridge Mountains to Elizabethton, looking for someone to help them organize. They returned with Tiny Hoffman. Under great difficulty, he ran the strike, was certainly its most visible personage, and, as in Elizabethton, the lightning rod for community hatred, all the more so as other outside agitators, including Brookwood-trained teachers from the Southern Summer School for Woman Workers, came to help where they could. Hoffman was not run out of Marion, however, but sent to jail instead, and he took no further part in the UTW's southern campaign. Other outsider agitators did, however. In 1930, they were in Danville, Virginia, or so H. R. Fitzgerald, president of the Riverside and Dan River Cotton Mills Company, constantly complained. Ironically, one of those he most angrily blasted, Matilda Lindsay, vice president of the National Women's Trade Union League, though a resident of New York, was actually a native Virginian. The other prime target of Fitzgerald's ire more accurately fitted the stereotype, for that was UTW vice president Francis Gorman. The British-born Gorman, who had come to the Rhode Island mills as a lad, cut his southern teeth in Danville. In 1934, he was to lead the UTW in the disastrous national struggle of that year.[12]

Hoffman's kidnapping and subsequent expulsion from Tennessee was something outside agitators frequently experienced. In Kings Mountain, North Carolina, Cleo Tesnair, an NTWU organizer and a northerner, thus doubly damned, was abducted from his home in September 1929, driven across the South Carolina border to Gaffney, taken to a heavily wooded enclave, and there flogged severely. His kidnappers warned him solemnly against returning to Kings Mountain. A few days earlier, Ben Wells, a Lancashire-born NTWU official, had experienced similar treatment. He and two colleagues had just sat down to dinner when a mob arrived at their Gastonia rooming house, surrounded it, burst into the old gospel hymn, "Praise God from Whom All Blessings Flow," then dragged Wells out the front door, draping him in a American flag before forcing into a waiting car. They then drove to a lonely spot in nearby Cabarrus County, where Wells was tied to a tree and beaten with ropes and tree branches. The perpetrators were discussing what to do next when they were surprised by a local hunting party. They fled, their task unfinished, but the point again made—an outside agitator had been expelled from their community.[13]

Throughout the 1930s, labor organizers were the victims of similar symbolic action. As noted, it happened to John Dean, sent to harness the anger of Alabama's textile workers in June 1934. In August, as the tensions which eventually led to the national textile strike grew, two men abducted him from his Huntsville hotel and drove him across the state line to Fayetteville, Tennessee, before releasing him. Ignoring the standard warning never to return, Dean was back in Huntsville two hours later, walking the streets to the cheers of a large crowd of supporters. The local American Legion post, allegedly, was behind his abduction, though no charges were ever laid. One of the first investigations that Lucy Randolph Mason became involved in as the CIO's southern public relations representative was that of the abduction of Charles (Jimmie) Cox. On April 15, 1938, Cox, a young textile union leader from Tupelo, Mississippi, was kidnaped by a group of local anti-unionists, driven out of town, and savagely beaten. As always, he was warned never to return. The most celebrated incident, however, involved Joseph Gelders, an outside agitator despite his Birmingham, Alabama, upbringing. But he was a Jew, he was northern-educated, his politics were to the far Left—and he supported labor unions and labor organizers. Even his appearance shouted outsider. He was, said British writer Cedric Belfrage, "a lanky, soft-voiced, academic-looking man" with "an odd dancing gait." In 1936, Gelders was actively engaged in a campaign to free a local communist leader and union activist, Bart Logan, who had been jailed on trumped-up charges. On the night of September 23, he was kidnaped by four men, taking to the city's outskirts, and beaten so severely that he came close to death. Local doctors refused to treat him and his attackers, though positively identified, were never prosecuted, but the circumstances of his beating became national news and part of continuing labor mythology, the ultimate symbol of how the South treated outsiders and their "alien" philosophies. Gelders himself never recovered from the attack. His heart had been permanently damaged. In 1936, a subcommittee of the Committee on Education and Labor, chaired by Wisconsin's Senator Robert M. La Follette, began its celebrated series of hearings into "violations of the right of free speech and assembly and interference with the right of labor to organize and bargain collectively." Though the La Follette Civil Liberties Committee, as it is most often called, was more concerned with such abuses in America's industrial heartland, it nevertheless heard enough from southern organizers as to be left in no doubt as to the dangers facing outside agitators in the region. The Gelders case was simply the most publicized of many such incidents.[14]

During World War II, attacks on union organizers moderated somewhat, partly because the more prominent of them, like North Carolina's Paul Christopher, were southern-born and trained. Throughout Operation Dixie, however, the outside agitator fear was a prime weapon used against the TWUA organizers. As historian Tim Minchin points out, managers "repeatedly emphasized the ethnicity of the TWUA's leadership and suggested that this in itself constituted a strong enough reason to stay away from the union." Much play was made with the names of the TWUA leadership. In one letter from management, for example, workers in Swepsonville, North Carolina's Virginia Cotton Mills's plant were asked, "Here are the names of some of the main leaders of the union —Reevie [sic], Baldanzie [sic], Schaufenbil, Unger, Chapka, Sganbato. Where do you think these men came from? Are their backgrounds, their beliefs, their faith and principles anything like yours and mine?" Baldanzi and his leadership team found such stereotyping impossible to combat, accompanied as it usually was by crude cartoons, depicting the CIO leaders as obviously aliens, outsiders with the eastern European's trademark "big, long nose."[15]

The prominent nose was the obscene symbol of the Jew, and much of the material attacking CIO organizers was blatantly anti-Semitic. "Ironically," says Minchin, such "literature was even circulated in campaigns where the mill-owners were Jewish, particularly in the mills of the Lowenstein and Cone families." At a Lowenstein mill in Anderson, South Carolina, for example, the plant manager urged workers to "keep the CIO kikes out of this county." Throughout the South, mill owners routinely distributed the *Trumpet*, edited by the fiercely antilabor "Parson Jack" Johnson, and *Militant Truth*, a well-produced newspaper with a large amount of right-wing money behind it. Both were ferocious in their attacks on the CIO, and both were equally fiercely anti-Semitic and made no bones about linking these twin evils. *Militant Truth*, in fact, was financially backed by Joe Kamp of the Constitutional Educational League, one of the nation's most ferocious anti-Semites, who before the war had been an enthusiastic supporter of numerous quasi-fascist enterprises, including the Silver Shirts and the German American Bund. Kamp had also spoken publicly of his admiration for Adolf Hitler and the "final solution." Small wonder Lucy Mason despaired when she discovered that the Cone family had approved the distribution of *Militant Truth* in their mills and that a rising young North Carolina evangelist, Reverend Billy Graham, was often featured in its columns.[16]

Closely linked, as always, to the outside agitator epithet was the charge of communism. Operation Dixie's southern foot soldiers were always vulnerable to the allegation that they were simply carrying out the alien political philosophies of their northern-based leaders. In the increasingly tense cold war climate, such charges had considerable impact, all the more so since, by expelling a number of left-wing unions in 1949–50, the CIO itself seemed to be acknowledging subversive infiltration. The TWUA, however, was staunchly anticommunist; there were few Communists in Operation Dixie, but this did not stop employers constantly alleging otherwise, all the more so because it be so easily connected to the race issue. "Everybody knew that a Communist was a Nigger lover," recalled Junius Scales, one of a handful of actual Communist Party members involved in the campaign. Thus to brand union organizers as "Reds" was also to accuse them of attacking the region's caste structure. Right-wing propagandists constantly linked the two. In *Communist Carpetbaggers in Operation Dixie*, for example, Joe Kamp argued that the world conspiracy had deliberately selected the South as its American battleground because of its large African American population. "Un-American" agitators, he concluded, aimed to incite not only "class war" but also "a bitter and vicious race war." Such arguments, however far-fetched, seriously weakened Operation Dixie's southern drive and showed in stark relief how durable, how potent was the "outside agitator" label. It was to remain so throughout the 1950s and 1960s, as the drive to cleanse the South of racial segregation made the region a battleground once more—and a new breed of outside agitator descended on Dixie.[17]

There were relatively few alleged Communist Party members in the ranks of the postwar civil rights activists. Martin Luther King had a couple on his SCLC team, close adviser Stanley Levison and his associate Jack O'Dell. Both had overt past associations with the party and, according to FBI director J. Edgar Hoover, were still clandestinely active members. Levison was allegedly a top Soviet espionage agent. When King was told of this, he refused at first to believe Hoover. President Kennedy, however, made the severing of all connection between the two men a condition of his continuing to give King primacy among civil rights leaders. King reluctantly went along, though Levison spared him the pain of formally cutting ties by resigning his position. Moreover, the two men kept up a secret relationship following their formal break. Bayard Rustin, too, briefly flirted with the party in the early 1930s, but by the time he joined King's team it was his homosexuality rather than his politics that was a potential cause of embarrassment. Otherwise, King's closest associates were all disciples of Jesus Christ, not Karl Marx.[18]

Robert Williams was of a different ilk, of course, but then he was not in the southern civil rights movement's mainstream. Born in Monroe, North Carolina, in 1925, Williams always seemed better connected to those who did battle in Camp Hill or Reeltown than to the nonviolent message of Martin Luther King. A veteran of World War II, during which he learned how to use guns and "decided that I just wasn't going to let any white man have that much authority over me," Williams returned to his home town in 1955, after some years in Detroit, where he wandered "along the edges of the American left," and in Durham, North Carolina, where he read "a lot of Communist stuff," often supplied by his friend

Junius Scales. Back in Monroe, he eventually became president of the local NAACP branch, which he turned into a militant symbol of resistance. In its newspaper, the *Crusader,* he urged blacks to fight back against oppression, with guns if necessary. He himself was usually armed, he organized community self-defense networks, and at times he and his followers used their weapons—against the Klan and others who menaced them. As such, he was a potent symbol of resistance, a growing source of concern to the FBI, and a challenge to Martin Luther King and his nonviolent message. In 1961, after a violent confrontation with Monroe's police and an FBI warrant for his arrest, Williams fled to Cuba, where for some years he broadcast his show *Radio Free Dixie* courtesy of Fidel Castro. The assumption was that Williams had become an avowed Marxist. Perhaps so, yet he was certainly no Stalinist, refusing to conform to the Soviet line on key issues of dogma. By 1965, he had relocated to Beijing, where Mao and the Chinese leadership gave him greater freedom to write as he liked. Yet Marxism, Chinese-style, soon proved equally unpalatable, and by 1970 he was back in the United States. He lived in Detroit for the rest of his life, though returning often to Monroe after 1976. By that time both the federal government and the state of North Carolina had dropped all charges against him. During the tension-filled 1960s, Robert Williams was comprehensively demonized as the violent revolutionary masquerading as civil rights leader, the Marxist who lurked behind the nonviolent facade. Certainly, he was a potent symbol for those opposed to King's message of "agape," and to that extent stood outside the current civil rights mainstream, but he did so rather as a symbol of an alternative southern black tradition—one of militant self-defense and of armed resistance to oppression—not of an "alien" ideology.[19]

The paucity of Communists in the postwar civil rights movement did not prevent those opposed to change from trawling aggressively for them. In particular, southern segregationist politicians were adept at using the investigative apparatus of the cold war as a means of rooting out those advocating racial change—under the guise of catching subversives. Throughout the cold war years, the House Committee on Un-American Activities and the Senate Internal Security Subcommittee were enthusiastically used for this purpose. Particular targets were organizations, created during the high tide of New Deal reformism and often with young southern idealists, now Washington-based public servants, in the vanguard, their regional origins conveniently obscured by their New Deal liberalism until they too became outside agitators. Of these, the most frequently scapegoated was the Southern Conference for Human Welfare (SCHW) and its successor, the Southern Conference Educational Fund (SCEF).[20]

The Southern Conference for Human Welfare had its origins in Franklin D. Roosevelt's failed attempt to realign southern politics along liberal-conservative lines and, in particular, from a conference held in Birmingham in 1938 to discuss the *Report on the Economic Conditions of the South,* a document produced by a number of southern New Dealers. Roosevelt, in fact, had used this report to justify his assertion that the South was "the nation's number one economic problem." At the Birmingham meeting which was attended by Eleanor Roosevelt; Supreme Court Justice Hugo Black; University of North Carolina president Frank Graham; leading southern New Dealers, black and white, like Clifford Durr, NYA chief Aubrey Williams, Mary McLeod Bethune, and Clark Foreman; nongovernment southern liberals like Lucy Randolph Mason and Virginia Durr; and Joseph Gelders and a few others equally far to the Left, it was decided to form a permanent organization dedicated to changing the South. Thus the SCHW was created.[21]

From its beginning the SCHW took direct aim at the southern caste system. It supported the first legal challenges to segregation in public education, while its long and eventually successful campaign to abolish the poll tax was aimed at removing the South's main barrier against the right of its black citizens to vote. It also advocated the creation of a strong, interracial labor movement in the South and supported those few fragile links between white and black workers. As such, the SCHW became the prime target of southern conservatives, and though it emerged from World War II seemingly energized by several small successes, by the establishment of solid state organizations, and by the general climate of democratic optimism in the wake of victory, such buoyancy was considerably misplaced. The optimism was soon replaced by a climate of frustration and fear, as peace became a chimera, replaced by the threat, then the actuality, of cold war. As the search for domestic scapegoats grew, the SCHW, which for a few years had harbored actual Communists in its ranks, was fatally wounded. Branded as early as May 1947 as a "deviously camoflaged [sic] communist-front organization" whose only aim was to serve the purposes of the Soviet Union, it was eventually deserted by the CIO, which was increasingly wary of crossing the racial divide, and by non-Communist liberals like Frank Graham and Lucy Randolph Mason. Under constant attack by mainstream southern politicians as a collection of outside agitators bent on subversion and internally riven by cold war politics, the SCHW disbanded in 1948. Only its education arm, SCEF, remained, with the staunchly non-Communist southerner and former New Dealer Aubrey Williams as its president and former Highlander Folk School staff director James Dombrowski as executive director.[22]

Neither Williams's prominent New Deal profile nor his southern background prevented SCEF being assailed throughout the 1950s as a communist organization bent on subverting core American values—a prime tool of outside agitators. The Senate Internal Security Subcommittee gave it a particularly savage grilling in March 1954, with Mississippi's arch-segregationist senator, James Eastland, in command. Williams, Virginia Durr, Dombrowski, and Myles Horton of the Highlander Folk School, all ironically southerners, were nevertheless branded as outsiders, servants of an alien ideology, accused by men like Paul Crouch, once genuine Communist Party members and now FBI and HUAC informers. State bodies like the Georgia Education Commission, the Mississippi Sovereignty Commission, and the Alabama Committee on Constitutional Government went over the same ground throughout the decade, but it was the two federal bodies, HUAC and SISS, that were the most active. Congressional committees held eight sets of hearings in the South between 1954 and 1958, even as the hunt for domestic subversives had run its course in the rest of the country. The reason was clear. Organizations such as SCEF provided an alternative vision of the South's future, including that of race relations, and had done so at least since the New Deal. As the southern political establishment prepared to combat the challenge to its way of life New Deal liberalism and the recent war had accelerated, and which the 1954 *Brown* decision so starkly symbolized, the branding of groups and individuals who supported such change as subversives as outside agitators, whatever their actual origin, was an essential weapon.[23]

In the 1960s, of course, came the realization of Senator Eastland's nightmare. Outside agitators in their hundreds, even thousands, poured into the region, far, far more than had ever appeared in Gastonia, Marion, Danville, or as part of Operation Dixie. They came from all over the country, as the pace of the civil rights movement quickened, to sit in at the lunch counters and soda fountains of Greensboro or Nashville, to picket fast food restaurants and downtown department stores, and, in 1961, to board the interstate buses as freedom riders. From the beginning, these outsiders were both white and black. Indeed, the televised bedside interviews with James Zwerg, a white student from Wisconsin, brutally beaten by segregationists at the Montgomery bus terminal in May 1961, were among the first to alert the nation to the dimensions of the coming struggle. Yet initially the agitators the South feared most were black, the young men and women of the Student Non-violent Coordinating Committee, who from its foundation in 1961 sent its youthful foot soldiers to the South, especially the "closed society" of Mississippi, there to work at the grass roots, conducting voter education schools and other community-based activities, living with their people, guiding them, sustaining them, and eventually, as in Albany, Georgia, leading scores of local challenges to segregation. Most of them, in fact, were southern-born and raised, but enough were from outside the region to give the familiar charge of outside agitator some credibility.[24]

Above all, there was Robert Moses. No one fitted the stereotype of southern demonology better. Born and raised in Harlem, Moses's intellectual gifts were recognized early. Educated at Stuyvesant High School, where he developed an interest in Chinese philosophy, and at Hamilton College in upstate New York, one of only three blacks in the whole student body, Moses chose to major in philosophy. He graduated in 1956 and was immediately accepted into Harvard's prestigious Ph.D. program. His ambivalence about academic discourse grew, fueled, ironically, by the disillusioning experience of taking Paul Tillich's classes. Tillich had been the subject of Martin Luther King's dissertation, but Moses was less than impressed. "It was all paltry," he believed, word playing, and he longed for content, for action. In 1958, Moses's mother died suddenly. The shock sent his father mad. He became convinced that he was the actor Gary Cooper and had to be institutionalized. His son used these twin tragedies as his excuse to leave Harvard and return to New York, ostensibly to care for his father. He taught mathematics at Horace Mann High School, read widely, and from 1960 followed through the newspapers the quickening pace of southern protest. Later in the year, on Ella Baker's recommendation, he moved South to work in King's Atlanta office, but within a year he had become SNCC's first field representative. It was not long before, as Taylor Branch aptly put it, he had "met his future" in the person of Amzie Moore of Cleveland, Mississippi, World War II veteran, local small businessman, and a longtime fighter for his civil rights. It was Moore who persuaded Moses to make Mississippi his particular battleground, and there he worked for the next four years, directing voter-education projects, leading public protests, always in danger, frequently beaten, often sent to prison—hated and reviled by the whites where he worked, revered by the blacks—the living embodiment of the outside agitator.[25]

There were others like him. The abrasive and flamboyant James Forman was from Chicago, but upon becoming SNCC executive secretary he had made the South his bailiwick. Always combative, and with "a taste for apocalyptic heroics" that the less-dramatic Moses found "amusing," Forman was a major irritant to the southern whites he often insulted and, in time, to many of his SNCC colleagues. He, too, obviously fit the outside agitator stereotype, as, later, did Stokely Carmichael. Less obviously, so did John Salter, a labor organizer from Arizona who inspired by the freedom rides, came with his wife, Eldri, to Mississippi in 1961, and began working in Jackson. Though his father was a Penobscot Indian, Salter was defined by Mississippians as white, and thus the subject of particular wrath. An outsider, he had also "crossed" the racial divide. Jane Stembridge was another white who had joined the civil rights movement early, arriving in Atlanta in 1961 to work with Ella Baker. Her outside agitator label was inaccurate, as she had grown up in the South, before enrolling at New York's Union Theological Seminary. Ivanhoe Donaldson and Ben Taylor also came early to the South. Black students from Michigan State University, they arrived in December 1962 with a truckload of supplies destined for SNCC projects in the Mississippi Delta. Arrested in Clarksdale and charged with narcotics possession once police had found aspirin and vitamin pills among their cargo, Taylor and Donaldson clearly fitted the stereotype, as did Charlie Cobb, a northern black who came from Howard University to work for SNCC in Greenwood. From 1961, white southerners, increasingly, watched these invaders and fought them with desperate ferocity.[26]

For a time, it was the northern-born SNCC foot soldiers like Donaldson, Cobb, and even Moses who were most outspoken in opposing using more white volunteers on SNCC local projects. There were reasons of security behind such opposition—whites and blacks working together in the Deep South were certain to attract threatening attention—as well as a disinclination to open their tight-knit circle, as John Dittmer explains, to "large numbers of people of a different race, class and culture," fearing what this would do to their organization. Yet after two years, they knew that as long as blacks were the only ones being brutalized in Mississippi and elsewhere, white America would pay little attention. While white volunteers would certainly bring visibility to the struggle, they might even bring protection, and this was the reason why, in 1963, Ivanhoe Donaldson symbolically suggested that "we bring down 5,000 whites and put 'em all in Belzoni." As young white volunteers came South, overwhelmingly from northern campuses, to work on SNCC's Mississippi projects, culminating in the Freedom Summer of 1964, but also in Alabama, Louisiana, South Carolina, and even in North Carolina's black belt, not only did the physical complexion of these latest outside agitators change, but so did their bearing and their assumptions. Their very presence was reminder to the white South of the perceived humiliation of Reconstruction, and once again they resisted—with a desperate ferocity.[27]

Michael "Mickey" Schwerner typified the new invader. Jewish, a Cornell graduate, and from New York, he and his wife Rita came to Meridian, Mississippi, in 1964 to organize a community center there under CORE's aegis. They were soon joined by a local movement worker, James Chaney, born and raised in Meridian's black community, and in June by a young summer project volunteer, Andrew Goodman, who, like Schwerner, was white, Jewish, and from New York. Their joint task was to establish further freedom schools and community centers in the heart of Mississippi's Klan country, Neshoba County. Instead, they were murdered by Klansmen, with the complicity of the county's law enforcement officers, in what Dittmer rightly describes as "the most depressingly familiar story of the Mississippi movement."[28]

As part of the fabric of the civil rights struggle, familiar the story certainly is. Singular it clearly was not. Jon Daniels from New England, shot on a lonely road near Hayneville, Alabama, in 1965, was also murdered for being an outside agitator; so was Viola Liuzzo and so was James Reeb. Many were lucky to escape a similar fate, as the white South resisted their invasion. But they continued to come, to Mississippi in 1964 and to Selma in 1965, the last great battleground. Moreover, the national concern at the disappearance of Schwerner, Chaney, and Goodman, the national manhunt that occurred, and the outcry that followed the discovery of their decomposing bodies forced the federal government to move more actively against the Klan. Outside agitators remained hated scapegoats in the South, yet the chances of surviving their task with nothing more serious than community antagonism had increased.[29]

Throughout the civil rights era, however, the South's prime "agitators" came not from the hostile North but from within. It had always been so; it was just now more obvious than ever before. The four young students from North Carolina Agricultural and Technical College in Greensboro who on January 31, 1960, sat at the bus terminal diner and asked for a hamburger were all local boys, friends since they had entered Dudley High together. True, they had read some of Martin Luther King's speeches, but their decision to put their bodies on the line arose much more from their sense of anger and frustration at the glacial pace of change since the *Brown* decision than from anything they had studied. Similarly, the thousands of young men and women who followed them throughout the South were also overwhelmingly local people. In Nashville, they were students from all-black Fisk University, in Raleigh, from Shaw, in Durham, from North Carolina College for Negroes. Those relatively few whites who took part, as in Nashville, where some Vanderbilt students joined Diane Nash and her colleagues, were also generally from the South.[30]

It was a similar story with the freedom rides in 1961. As is well known, the idea of testing Supreme Court decisions banning segregation on interstate bus travel had originated with CORE's James Farmer, himself somewhat of an outside agitator, despite his Texas ancestry, because of his northern upbringing, his upper-class status (as a boy he had even visited FDR in the White House), his aristocratic demeanor, and his interracial life-style. Indeed, CORE had sponsored such a journey as early as 1947, which eventually cost Bayard Rustin thirty days on a North Carolina chain gang. But once the CORE-sponsored expedition had been halted by a mob in Birmingham, it was the young men and women of the fledgling SNCC who took over. Twenty-one of them, all students from Atlanta or Nashville, all seasoned by the sit-in campaigns and all southern flew to Birmingham, persuaded a somewhat reluctant Farmer to stay with them, and continued the ride. In Montgomery they were beaten and brutalized; in Jackson, Mississippi they were jailed, but they finished the journey.

John Lewis was one of them. Born in rural Pike County, Alabama, so deep in the country, he later claimed, that he could not remember even seeing a white person as a child, gripped early with a religious fervor so extreme that he would preach for hours to the family chickens, he finished high school in 1957, the first of his family to do so. From there he went to Nashville's American Baptist Theological Seminary. There he first came under the spell of Martin Luther King's example and the nonviolent philosophies of Gandhi and Thoreau. Seasoned by involvement in the Nashville sit-in movement, then by the searing experience of the freedom rides, Lewis moved full time into SNCC work, the epitome of the black "inside agitator," to rework David Chappell's notion.[31]

Diane Nash was not actually on the bus when it reached Montgomery, though she had masterminded the ride's continuation and remained its focal point thereafter. Nash was a genuine outside agitator in that she had been raised in Chicago in a middle-class Catholic family. She was also sufficiently light-skinned to pass for white and had been a "Miss America" trialist. But she had moved South to attend Fisk University, becoming head of its student movement. During Nashville's sit-in campaign of 1960, she once confronted the city's mayor, Ben West, on the steps of city hall, forcing him to concede, before the television cameras, that he believed the city's lunch counters should be desegregated. The next year she led a widely publicized "jail-in" in Rock Hill, South Carolina, and then came her involvement with the freedom rides. When Rev. Shuttlesworth, himself by no means lacking in courage, attempted to convince her of the danger of further involvement with the question, "Young lady do you know that the Freedom Riders were almost killed?" her response became part of the movement's folklore: "Yes, that's exactly why the rides must not be stopped. If they stop us with violence, the movement is dead. We're coming, we just want to know if you can meet us." Nash, too, moved full-time into SNCC work, where her beauty, her courage, and her skills as a community organizer quickly made her, with Moses, its most recognizable figure. Nevertheless, the point remains that the bulk of those who came to work full time with the SNCC in those first dangerous years, as organizers, as teachers, and community leaders, were of the South, like Lewis, like Ruby Doris Smith, like Nash's eventual husband, Rev. James Bevel, like their white comrades Jane Stembridge and Robert Zellner. They were all "inside agitators."[32]

So, too, were the people, overwhelmingly women, who worked at the local level in the SCLC's Citizenship Education Program (CEP). The CEP is not well known amid the spectrum of civil rights activity in the 1960s, dominated as it is by the tales of confrontation eventually seen nightly on the television news, the clandestine murders, the brave children confronting mobs in Birmingham in 1963 or at schoolhouse doors throughout the region, the violence at bus terminals and public stores, and the soaring rhetoric of King. Yet the CEP functioned quietly and effectively for years throughout the South. Its prime purpose was once described by Wyatt T. Walker as community mobilization, "teaching people the techniques to organize themselves for action." Funded by the Field Foundation and initially directed by the veteran activist Septima Clark, the CEP trained volunteers, usually poorly educated rural blacks, in the workings of the American political system, with the ballot as the "unifying theme." For up to two weeks they learned about voter registration, how to prepare for the inevitable literacy tests, how to locate the registrars, and how to deal with their intransigence. Then, they went home, hopefully to start classes of their own.[33]

Throughout the decade, most of the CEP "graduates" did just that. In church halls, in school dining rooms, in private houses, these local people held their classes, hundreds of them, without pay, often without adequate materials. Their regular reports to CEP administrator Dorothy Cotton reveal, alongside some deficiencies in proper grammar, a level of dedication from teachers and students that at times becomes quite moving. "There are so many that wants [sic] to get into my first class," wrote Nan Warren from Birmingham in July 1963, "but I am only takeing [sic] 14." Clara N. Riggs of Emanuel County, Georgia, reported in 1962, "We have learned more about Social Security, the election laws, initiative, Negroes (Harriet Tubman, Truth, Attucks, Bethune, King etc). The freedom songs played an important part. We try to satisfy all problems that arise in class. We are working on our skit for a joint classing [sic] program." They were also planning a registration campaign, she said, "and area units of this organization are being set up."[34]

The age range of those attending these schools was infinitely variable, as was their gender, though women seemed in the majority. Sally Tuggle of Monticello, Georgia, had fourteen in her class in 1965, including Lillie Holloway, who was eighty-seven years old. Only one student was male, and he was sixty-eight. Three years earlier, Susie Green of Wadley, Georgia, was teaching eight men between the ages of eighteen and sixty-eight and seventeen women aged eighteen to sixty-four. In her 1963 class,

Magdalena Jackson of Richmond, Georgia, had eight men aged eighteen to seventy-three and seven women between the ages of twenty-one and sixty. Young or old, they all came to the Calvary Baptist Church out of a fierce desire, even a hunger, she said, "to get the education to learn how to speak for themselves, read and write plainly and save their own moneys, and work for a larger amount." Daisy Jones, a Savannah teacher, put it in a wider context. "Freedom is indivisible," she told Hosea Williams. "The cry for freedom around the world is so great, that the Congo is now free. If Africa stirs how can we prevent the 60,000 Negroes of Savannah" from also doing so. "The adult citizenship course is a cry for freedom through the ballot," she believed:

> We have a task which Jesus himself set before us. . . . Jesus gave the key. Your ballot is the key, not only does it protect the rights, but must inforce [sic] respect for law and order.

> Every negro who doesn't vote is lending his personal support to the most evil and destructive forces in our nation. He is, in effect deliberately hiring enemies of justice and true democracy.

Citizenship Education Project volunteers like Jones, and there were hundreds of them, all local people, were true inside agitators. As such they were key foot soldiers of the movement, and deserve their place in history, alongside their more celebrated and visible colleagues.[35]

What of those whose lives they touched, those who were inspired by SNCC workers in Mississippi, or by CEP teachers throughout the South? Some in turn achieved prominence themselves as inside agitators. Fannie Lou Hamer's life, as noted earlier, was transformed by her involvement with SNCC activists. She went on to become one herself and to appear as the Mississippi Freedom Democratic Party's spokesperson on national television. When she died in 1977, the whole civil rights establishment mourned, as did thousands of Americans throughout the land, and she remains a potent symbol of those tumultuous times. Ella May was not similarly mourned at the time of her murder in 1929, yet she too had had her life transformed by her involvement in the Gastonia strike. Moreover, she became revered in memory, first as a symbol of the American Left but later, with the growth of the women's movement in the 1970s, as the heroine of a half-forgotten struggle. In 1979, Vera Buch wrote the foreword to a pamphlet commemorating the fiftieth anniversary of Ella

May's death. In it she brought the two southern struggles together. Ella had been specially marked, she claimed, not only for her union activism but also for crossing the racial barrier, in that she lived close to Stumptown, Bessemer City's black district, and counted some of her black neighbors as her friends. "It was for this they killed you Ella Mae [sic]," she wrote. Possibly it was, though Bill Brawley, president of North Carolina's Central Labor Council, had made no mention of it two years earlier, as he unveiled a memorial on what had previously been her unmarked grave. Rather he spoke of her courage, her commitment, and the way she had moved from follower to local leader. "She probably had more impact on people's lives than all the statues in this blamed state," he declared, yet few there were who recognized her name. It was time, he said, for the labor movement not only to revere her memory, but to follow the example she had set.[36]

Most "local people," mill workers who followed the union's call, sharecroppers and laborers who acted on the civil rights message, did not become figures of similar consequence. Yet their lives, too, had been transformed—and they knew it. Often they showed it in their continued support for those who came to work with them, even as in Gastonia, when the strike failed, and management sought its revenge. When the trial of those accused of killing Sheriff Aderholt opened, many reporters commented in their first stories on the crowds of mill workers who had gathered to show solidarity with their former leaders. They were mainly folk, wrote one, with "the stamp of generations of poverty upon them," and exuding "the odor of long hours of toil." Tired and defeated they may have been, but there was no mistaking the warmth of their continued affection. Vera Buch was profoundly moved. "At every recess of the court they flocked around us and nearly ate us up in their joy at seeing us," she told her friend Mary Heaton Vorse. Similarly, when John Dean returned to Huntsville in August 1934, he marched down the main street in triumph, flanked by his cheering supporters. Civil rights workers, too, were constantly amazed at the level of support they received in their various "local" communities, given the real risks they put these people under. Fannie Lou Hamer once explained why. By coming, and by staying, they had showed they cared: "Nobody never came out into the country and talked to real farmers and things before. . . . They treated us like we were special and we loved 'em. . . . We trusted 'em, and I can tell the world those kids done their share in Mississippi." Amzie Moore concurred. "How they stood. . . . How gladly they got in front of that line . . . and went to jail. It didn't seem to bother 'em," he recalled. By their courage, the example of their actions, these "agitators," outside or inside, empowered the lives of those with whom they worked.[37]

Though most of the inside agitators who became civil rights activists were black, there were always some whites who stood apart from the rest of their race and class to support the aspirations of black southerners. Invariably they suffered severely for their stand. Juliette Morgan of Montgomery was one such. A quiet, almost reclusive city librarian, she was so moved by the dignity of those boycotting the buses in 1956 that she wrote to the local newspaper comparing the way taxis were being used to the "taxicab army" that saved Paris in 1916 by moving soldiers to the front. The boycotters had not only learned from Gandhi, she declared, but also from Thoreau, as she called on her fellow citizens to recognize that "history is being made in Montgomery." Morgan was unable to cope with the campaign of systematic harassment that followed publication of her letter. Just over a year later she killed herself. Claudia Thomas Sanders did not lose her life as a result of her particular stand, but she could easily have done. Fifty-six years old in 1957 and the wife of a prominent Gaffney, South Carolina, physician, she had contributed an essay to a pamphlet *South Carolinians Speak: A Moderate Approach to Race Relations*, in which she had argued, as a Christian, for gradual compliance with the *Brown* decision. For this, she and her family were ostracized, and on November 18, the Klan attempted to bomb their home. Luckily, the fuse was faulty, yet the partial explosion was sufficient to indicate that the family was fortunate indeed to be alive, so great was the damage. The culprits were soon arrested, tried and acquitted—despite ample evidence of their complicity. No one defended Sanders or her family; most of her friends, in fact, had long since ceased speaking to her. Soon she left Gaffney for good.[38]

Virginia and Clifford Durr, who had returned to Alabama after the New Deal years, were not forced out of Montgomery because of the ostracism resulting from their stand as inside agitators, but Clifford Durr's ability to earn a living as a lawyer was all but ruined. Aubrey Williams, too, found his business opportunities in Montgomery progressively curtailed, and his prospects for simple social exchange similarly blunted because of his stand against segregation. Worn out by the cumulative experience, exacerbated as it was by the constant and unwelcome attention of the various committees seeking to smoke out domestic communists, due to his SCEF connection, he eventually returned to Washington. Then there was Robert Zellner, again of Alabama. He was a Methodist minister's son whom SCEF hired in 1961 and then sent to SNCC as a field representative to work on white southern campuses. For the next four years Zellner was the prototype white inside agitator, working bravely in Mississippi and Georgia throughout the heat of the battle, until, ironically, SNCC's sad decision to purge itself of all connections with whites.[39]

White inside agitators during the movement years were often connected through their involvement in the great agencies of change, especially SNCC. Those of earlier generations, too, similarly came together in organizations dedicated to sweeping away the South's reactionary economic and social systems. Durr and Williams, for example, were charter members of the SCHW, perhaps the best-known, and eventually the most notorious, of these. But there were others, many of them almost lost to history. Of these, one of the most "respectable" was the Fellowship of the Concerned, founded in Atlanta 1949 by Dorothy Tilly. The deeply religious Tilly, wife of a prominent Atlanta businessman, had a long history as an inside agitator fighting for equal justice, so much so that she was the only southern woman appointed to President Truman's Commission on Civil Rights. It was her experience in 1947, however, of sitting alone in a courtroom in Greenville, South Carolina, as a silent witness against injustice, during the trial of thirty-one taxi drivers charged with the lynching of a local black man, Willie Earle, that convinced her of the limitations of individual action. It had left a "special kind of mark on her," she later reported, "to see the defendants and the jury making a brazen mockery of the trial, openly talking and cracking jokes back and forth." People needed to know about such enormity, she thought. "If they did, they would stop it." If "good people" filled the courtrooms, "just their presence" would stop such injustices as that she had recently seen in Greenville.[40]

Thus was born the Fellowship of the Concerned, so named, Tilly explained, "because it was built on our concern about the state of justice in Southern courts." The idea was simple: groups of women would attend trials, as she had done, as observers for justice. There was no constitution, there were no dues, all Fellowship members had to do was to pledge to "sit in the courts" to "learn how justice operates in my community" and "to work with others in times of tension to see the rights of all are protected." Tilly coordinated this all-women network entirely on her own from a tiny Atlanta office.[41]

Her ambitious aim was to recruit a membership which covered every county seat in the South. This was never achieved, but she did establish working networks in twelve southern states. Most of Georgia was covered, as were half the counties in Kentucky, fourteen in South Carolina, eight in North Carolina, and seven in Tennessee. More than 3,000 women had their names on the books, and before long they had expanded their activities from court watching to poll watching, making sure that black voters were treated equally. In Louisville, Kentucky, Fellowship women ran a roster at the local hospital on Saturday nights, looking for signs of discrimination in emergency room procedures. After the *Brown* decision, they were active workers for peaceful integration of their local schools. In Montgomery during the bus boycott, these white, middle-class ladies, unlikely inside agitators, provided quiet support for the black women most actively involved. "Islands of healing in a land of hurt," Jo Ann Robinson once called Tilly and her Fellowship women. She was right. Thoroughly respectable middle-class women though they were, imbued with the spirit of Christian love, pillars of their communities, they were also part of the movement to change them.[42]

Another group of inside agitators also motivated by the spirit of Christian love and similarly almost lost to history was the Fellowship of Southern Churchmen. Founded in 1934, it was described by historian Robert F. Martin as "a loosely knit interdenominational and interracial association of Southern Christians who were determined to change their region's economic and social structure." Initially, the FSC was little more than a like-minded study and prayer group which came together intermittently for community sustenance rather than to pursue an activist social agenda. For a few years immediately after World War II, however, under the direction of Christian activist Nelle Morton, it broadened its structure and entered the ranks of those grass-roots groups actively fighting against segregation. Members of the FSC, too, became inside agitators.[43]

Morton's first decision upon taking over the FSC was to move its office from remote Black Mountain, North Carolina, to the university town of Chapel Hill. There her plan was to build on the postwar democratic idealism and mood for change which she discerned in the student body, channeling it, through her organization of committed Christians, into uncompromising activity for social and racial justice. She was particularly hopeful that the work camp idea, popular in Europe since World War I, could be adapted to suit southern needs. The work camp philosophy was simple: bring together Christian young people to live in selected communities and there "work with their hands without pay, on some useful project" designed to help individuals, families, the whole community, in a practical way. Morton believed this idea could be used to break down racial segregation. By living together interracially, young southern Christians would not only lose their own prejudices but also provide examples for the communities in which they worked.[44]

Initially, her idealism seemed justified. The first FSC work camp, held in July 1945 in eastern Tennessee, went off without incident, but it was the only one to do so. Certainly the young idealists of the FSC had no trouble living interracially, but those in the communities they had hoped to influence were far from impressed. There was trouble with local whites at the Big Lick camp in eastern Tennessee in 1946, while the following year all the members of an FSC project were driven out of Tyrell County in North Carolina's eastern "black belt." The group of ten, including one African American, had gone there to help build a community store for local blacks to use but from the start were regarded with such suspicion by the white community that even the blacks, fearful of trouble, wanted them gone. Eventually after an interracial group of FSC workers from nearby Phoebus, Virginia, including three white women, came for a visit, and all the young folk went for a swim in the river, the townsfolk had had enough. A mob of 300 armed men invaded their camp that night and ran them off the property. They decided not to return; the reality of white southern determination had checked the idealism of this particular group of inside agitators. Though Morton decided to persist with the work camp idea, she conceded that henceforth rural locations would have to be off limits. A 1948 project, located in Atlanta, also went awry, with police raiding an interracial social event. For Nelle Morton, it was the end of a dream of using the camps to attack segregation by example. Though FSC inside agitators had done some fine work in other areas—assisting Bayard Rustin and his fellow freedom riders in 1947, for example, and arranging an interracial concert for the black mezzo-soprano Dorothy Maynor—Morton took little solace from them. She left office in 1949, and with her departure the FSC's days as an active agency for social change had ended. It limped along as a discussion and support group for a while, again based in the remote North Carolina mountains. In 1963, its remaining members voted it out of existence. For a few years, however, it had provided some young inside agitators a means of working at the cutting edge of social change.[45]

Some inside agitators formed permanent communities, within which they attempted to live their ideals rather than come together for limited periods of time. The Koinonia Farm community, south west of Americus in Georgia, was one such. Founded in 1942, Koinonia Farm was an interracial Christian cooperative where, in the words of its historian, "young white Southerners took their religious beliefs and concern for African-Americans further into social action than most Southern white Christians or liberals would go." These particular inside agitators, rather than seek social change through legislative and court action, attempted to provide an example of regional harmony "through economic cooperation and building an interracial community where white and blacks would live and work together." The work camps of the FSC were similarly motivated, but at Koinonia the commitment was permanent. There, white and black southerners, overwhelmingly Baptist, formed their version of the "beloved community." There they farmed cooperatively, sometimes in partnership with blacks and whites from the local community, attempted to involve themselves in other community enterprises, to teach agricultural techniques, especially to African American farmers, to minister to their spiritual needs, and, above all, to maintain a constant Christian interracial witness. Inevitably, therefore, Koinonia became caught up in the vortex of the quickening civil rights movement. From the late 1950s, Koinonians were "the target of violence, legal harassment, intimidation and economic boycott" from the local community because of the farm's interracial stance, until its continued existence was at risk. And yet it survived, it still does, though in a more corporatized form. These inside agitators, too, are thus part of the narrative of the southern struggles.[46]

The Koinonia leadership always tried to work closely with other communities of like-minded "agitators." Of these, the most important and best known was the Highlander Folk School, their "blood cousins" as the Koinonians called them. Highlander, in fact, spans the "southern struggles" story. Very much the result of the vision of its cofounder, Myles Horton, himself a white inside agitator, it was established on a property near Monteagle, Tennessee, its model the folk schools of Denmark, which Horton had recently visited. The other cofounder, Don West, fell out with

Horton within a year and disappeared, leaving him in sole command. Initially, Horton insisted that Highlander's prime purpose was to assist the white industrial and rural workers of southern Appalachia in their struggles for a better life. From its beginning, it was particularly concerned to reach out to local union activists, primarily from textile mills trying to give them the organizational and educational tools necessary to win their fight. In 1937, Highlander and the CIO signed an affiliation agreement, and for the next few years its influence was considerable. Under the CIO's aegis, its workers education program, as historian Patricia Sullivan put it, "aimed to enable workers and union leaders to understand the world in which they lived while envisioning their role in changing it." Local union leaders were taught history, the intricacies of labor legislation, economics, and organizational techniques. By 1944, Highlander representatives were conducting extension programs for the CIO in every southern state; its alumni could be found in positions of influence at all levels of the industrial union movement.[47]

With the end of the war, and in the brief spirit of optimism that followed, Horton and his staff expected Highlander's influence to increase, the more so as Operation Dixie became a reality. It was not to be. Cold war realities caught up with the folk school, as it did with most inside agitators. The CIO excluded it from a role in the southern drive because of its leftist and interracialist reputation and in 1947 severed the connection completely, thus depriving Highlander of the bulk of its financial support. Like SCHW, with which it was always closely allied, Highlander and its leaders, too, became the quarry of those federal and state committees and agencies desperate to root out domestic subversives. Horton, initially, had not been particularly interested in using Highlander as an agency for interracialism; indeed, its function as a training school for white textile unionists precluded this. Eventually, he, like others came to see the absurdity of helping only one group of southerners, that to ignore black workers was no solution at all. Rather, it enabled employers to continue to exploit all workers, white as well as black. When the CIO had cut Highlander off, however, its emphasis shifted, and civil rights became its principal focus. Throughout the 1950s, Highlander staff ran interracial training programs for inside agitators, black and white. Rosa Parks had attended one of these a few weeks before her decision not to vacate her seat precipitated the Montgomery bus boycott; Martin Luther King was there in 1957, sitting with Aubrey Williams; and the young SNCC leaders John Lewis, Diane Nash, and Bernard Lafayette took part in a workshop in 1961 before joining the freedom rides. Throughout the early civil rights era, too, Highlander-trained staff had gone into hundreds of rural communities in the South to conduct Citizenship Schools, precursors of the vital SNCC and SCLC programs of the 1960s. Indeed, Septima Clark was appointed director of the CEP program in part because of her years of experience with Highlander. Horton's vision then, became an important source of inspiration both for the struggle of white southern mill workers for economic justice, and African American southerners for social and political equality.[48]

The Highlander Folk School did not survive unscathed the constant attacks of those most resistant to southern change, the more so as its civil rights focus grew in intensity. The SISS worked it over in New Orleans in 1954, and the Internal Revenue Service revoked its tax-exempt status in 1957. But it was the Tennessee legislature that struck the fiercest blow when it authorized an investigation into charges that it was, among many iniquities, "a finishing school for communists." The resulting inquiry concluded, predictably, that it was and that its charter should be revoked. The legislature soon found various technicalities which enabled this to happen. When, on April 5 1961, the state supreme court upheld a lower court ruling agreeing to revocation, it seemed all over for an organization which for thirty years had sustained both white and black inside agitators in their southern struggles. And yet it survived even the closing of its doors and exists still, as the Highlander Research and Education Center, different in form but fighting the same battles, connecting white and black southerners in their aspirations for social decency and economic justice.[49]

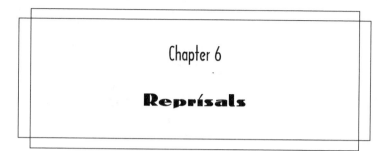

Chapter 6

Reprísals

On April 22, 1929, Ada Howell, a fifty-year-old Gastonia striker, was on her way to the relief store set up by the National Textile Workers Union when she met sheriff's deputy G. B. Prather. Without warning, he attacked her furiously, severely bruising her head and face, blackening both her eyes, then cutting her with his bayonet. Newspapermen found her wandering the streets, her clothing "spattered with blood." When it was suggested that her blood-soaked dress should be kept as evidence, without cleaning it, she dismissed the idea as impossible. "I didn't have enough dresses to lay these clothes away," she told Mary Heaton Vorse. She could not understand why she had been so violently attacked, as she was not part of any demonstration, nor had she baited Prather in any way. He had just "acted like crazy," she thought; there was no other explanation.[1]

More than thirty-five years later, another middle-aged southern woman was savagely beaten by a local deputy, this time at the state fair ground in Jackson, Mississippi. Her name was Julia Small, she was from Canton, Mississippi, and she taught a CEP school there. She, too, could not understand why the officer had attacked her, for she had said nothing to him. It took her a time even to tell anyone about her ordeal. "We were treated so bad," she eventually wrote Septima Clark, "its too much to write." Moreover, since the beating there had been further harassment, not only of her but also of her brother and sister, who had intervened on her behalf. "Our Lives as been treaten," she stated. "We kint res in Peace. Matter fack I nobody reasing." Howell and Small, both southerners, one white, one black, may have been middle-aged and of no physical danger to anyone, but to their assailants they represented a major threat to the social order, a challenge to the southern class and caste systems. Thus, more than three decades apart, and in vastly different contexts, they both suffered savage and unprovoked beatings from those sworn to uphold the law. As such, their histories conjoin.[2]

Beating by police was a common, in fact, routine, means of reprisal against such challenges. Union leaders and civil rights activists often bore the scars of such usage. Fanny Lou Hamer and Annell Ponder were two victims of savage beatings by Mississippi police whose ordeals eventually became widely known, as did that of Joseph Gelders thirty years earlier, but most suffered in relative silence. When Maggie Gordon of Holmes County, Mississippi, was beaten by local police, two FBI agents witnessed the whole event without lifting a finger to help her. She did not blame them, she later stated; there were "only two of them," after all, "against a roomful" of local and state police officers. In Greenwood in 1964, Willis Wright was brutally beaten by police after he had attempted to vote. If that was not enough, he also lost his job. When Lt. Emanuel D. Schreiber of the United States Army was violently attacked in Jackson in March 1964, his assailants, again policemen, told him he had it coming. It was because he was married to a "wooly bugaboo Nigger girl," they said. Schreiber fought back, with both words and fists. He was based in Mississippi, he responded, before leaving for Vietnam to risk his life in defense of the United States. Where were they? Moreover, his wife, though admittedly African American, was nevertheless a demonstrably finer person than they were. Still, the incident shook him profoundly. Mississippi's police, he thought, were merely the most obvious leaders in a "mania for intimidation," of violent resistance to change, which had infected the whole state.[3]

The "mania," of course, reached far wider than the Magnolia State. It came to infect the region as a whole, and everywhere, local and state police led the way. In Somerville, Tennessee, although the tensions engendered by the "tent city" protests of 1960 and 1961 had eased somewhat, they remained, volatile, below the surface. They again erupted in 1963, when the Fayette County Sheriff broke up a peaceful demonstration led by high school students. Completely out of control, Sheriff Pattat rushed at the young demonstrators, who by this time were kneeling in prayer, allegedly shouting, "Run Nigger, Run." He then threw teargas at them, before directing his men into attack. Five of the students were burned as a result of his action. Many more were cut or bruised by police batons.[4]

In Alabama, too, police routinely attacked peaceful demonstrators.

Perhaps the best-known incident took place on the Edmund Pettus bridge in Selma, where, on March 1965, during the escalating campaign for voting rights, 600 marchers on their way to Montgomery were halted by the combined forces of Selma's volatile and violent sheriff, Jim Clark, and a hundred state troopers commanded by Maj. John Cloud. Without warning, they were savagely attacked, with teargas, chains, cattle prods, batons, and charging horsemen. It was the most savage "police riot" of the whole civil rights era, as the officers attacked the marchers without regard for age, gender, or physical condition. The country watched, aghast, on national television. Two years earlier, they had watched the police of Birmingham similarly run riot, during the massive demonstrations there. On May 3, the nation saw children attacked by dogs, doused by jets of water with sufficient velocity to tear the skin, and beaten by police batons. On both occasions, Americans were shocked into support for the victims, and thus public beatings would often rebound against the perpetrators.[5]

Of course, most police beatings were not public, usually occurring in police interview rooms or other restricted places, far from the camera's scrutinizing eye. In Shreveport, Louisiana, when police beat the NAACP branch president, Rev. Harry Blake, after arresting him on a minor traffic violation, they did so in the vestibule of Blake's church. Indeed, so anxious were the police to do him damage, Blake later said, that they "got into their own way while trying to beat him," inflicting injuries on themselves as well as the intended victim. Thoroughly aroused, the officers then moved on to the Booker T. Washington High School, bursting into classrooms and assaulting students indiscriminately. In Mobile, Alabama, in April 1958, local police, enraged at the effrontery of two African Americans whom they caught in the act of trying to burn two crosses in the yard of a white church, beat them on the spot, then again when they got them back to the station.[6] Prominent NAACP officials were particularly fair game. Clarence Mitchell, director of the Washington Bureau, was promptly arrested in Florence, South Carolina, in February 1956, when he inadvertently sat in the whites-only section of the railway station waiting room, and was charged with resisting arrest. Though the charges were soon dropped, and indeed Chief of Police Julian Price expressed regret for the misunderstanding, in the interim Mitchell was given a thorough working over by the arresting officers. Police beatings, routine in Mississippi as a means of social control, were actually endemic to the whole region. Directed toward African Americans as they undoubtedly were, they were also used as a means of deterring whites from challenging the social order, as Howell had discovered in Gastonia.[7]

More often than not, though, those who struck most fiercely were not the police, though they might have worked behind the scenes, but local vigilante groups, some organized, others acting spontaneously. Ester Lee Groover found this out the hard way in the wake of the national textile strike of 1934. Testifying before the famous Subcommittee of the Committee on Education and Labor, chaired by Senator Robert La Follette of Wisconsin, and charged with investigating violations of free speech and interference with the rights of labor to organize and bargain collectively, he described in graphic detail what happened in Lanett, Alabama. Groover ran a dry-cleaning plant in the town, and though not a union member, he was sympathetic to the UTW cause and often said so. Moreover, he refused to sign a petition drawn up by the town's professional people, its doctors, merchants, teachers, and even its ministers, pledging to refuse service to any who joined the strike. The teachers, Groover told an incredulous La Follette, agreed to toss unionists' children out of school, the preachers, "to close the church" to union members. For his opposition, Groover was lured to a room in a local boardinghouse and there accused by two men, both with machine guns, of "doing a lot of labor agitating." They then threatened to "blow your damn brains out," accused him, probably accurately, of turning his business into the "headquarters for these agitators around here," and then "knocked hell out of me." When he reported what had happened to the police, they "laughed about it" and refused to take any action. Questioned by La Follette, Groover agreed that his assailants were not local people, that they had freely identified themselves as F. B. Hager and Legare Ansel, and were employed by a Pennsylvania strikebreaking company, Pennsylvania Industrial Services. Anyone who supported the union was likely to feel their anger. The town doctor had his car shot up on one occasion, and union organizer J. R. Hamby was severely beaten once local police had identified him to Ansel. "These machine-gun men were riding all over Troup County and Chambers County" during the strike, Groover asserted, brought there by the West Point Manufacturing Company, which owned the Lanett mill.[8]

In Birmingham the following year, Blaine Owen, a union organizer who also provided copy for the *Southern Worker*, was snatched from the street one summer evening, again after having been identified by a police patrol, and systematically tortured in the back seat of a car as it cruised the city's streets. As they rained blow after blow on him, Owen's assailants catalogued his crimes. He was a union agitator—that was bad enough —but he was also involved in "putting out a god damn Red paper," he had "too much hair," and was a "god damn nigger lover." Eventually the kidnappers left the city behind and Owen felt "the cool air blow off the mountain." Finally the car stopped, and he was dragged out, but the kicks and blows continued, even more painfully now as knotted ropes were brought into service. Soon Owen was completely covered in blood, blinded, and unable to breathe. Only then did they stop, his attackers believing they had killed him. Away they drove, leaving him for dead. Miraculously he survived, though, like Joseph Gelders, permanently damaged by the ordeal. The La Follette committee, though its focus was firmly upon the nation's great industrial heartland, uncovered enough southern stories such as that of Owen to leave no doubt as to the violence union organizers faced every minute of the day, as southerners protected both their industrial order and their caste system. Owen was punished for working to undermine both.[9]

Civil rights workers were also routinely beaten by vigilante groups, often working with the police. When the bodies of the three civil rights workers murdered in Neshoba County in 1964 were discovered, forensic examination showed that James Chaney had been savagely assaulted before being shot. By then, Robert Moses had lost count of the beatings he had suffered in Mississippi during his years there, and most of his SNCC colleagues were the same. Fanny Lou Hamer's vicious bashing by Winona police soon became part of the civil rights movement's iconography, and the stuff of a national television broadcast, but she had received plenty of blows before that from Ruleville residents incensed at her empowerment. And, of course, there were thousands of local people whose assaults went unpunished, usually unrecorded. Though known to be a civil rights activist who had previously been arrested for attempting to swim at a whites-only beach, Gilbert R. Mason, a black physician from Biloxi, Mississippi, was actually on an errand of mercy when he was violently assaulted on April 24, 1960. He had gone "to render medical aid to an individual lying prostrate in the neutral ground of US Highway 90, who was being beaten by a group of whites and within twenty-five yards of County Patrolman Merritt Brunies." These "ruffians" turned their attention to Mason, attacking him with pool cues. Though severely injured, he managed to return to his car and drive to the local hospital, the mob in pursuit. As racial tension increased throughout the 1960s, so did the incidence of random assaults, in Mississippi and elsewhere, until only the most vicious or bizarre gained any attention at all, so endemic had the violence become. Gloria Laverne Floyd was simply walking down her street in Jackson when some white youths in a convertible passed her, slowed down, and then "lassoed" her. She was dragged some distance, her head and shoulders severely gashed, her neck burned and lacerated by the wire "lasso," before she was let go, her assailants giving the rebel yell as they drove off. Gloria was only nine years old.[10]

Of course, blacks had always been routinely beaten in the South, for reasons unrelated to civil rights activity, and this practice continued. The NAACP was particularly angered by the treatment of Eddie Mayberry of Baxter, Arkansas, even though they were soon convinced that Mayberry was not linked to any specific civil rights activity. Nevertheless, the sequence of events starkly highlighted the violence endemic in the caste system, and, as such, bore comparison with that Frederick Douglass so graphically described in his various accounts of his life as a slave. Mayberry, twenty-eight years old in 1957, married with six children, worked as a farm laborer on the property of Jack Mehrans, at Panther Brake, five miles south of Baxter. On the morning of June 6, Mehrans called Mayberry into a small room, locked the door, and, after accusing him of filching gasoline, proceeded to beat him over the head and back, first with a plow handle, then with a lariat. Unable to escape through the locked door, Mayberry could do little to prevent these attacks, given that Mehrans was armed with a pistol, clearly visible in his belt. The beating continued for two hours, with an intermission while Mehrans paused for breath. "Get up and sit down over there and rest," he directed Mayberry at one stage. "I'm not through with you." When it was over, he was ordered back to work, despite his pain and his bleeding, and was forced to eat his dinner "in Mr Mehrans' yard and remain in his sight." Thus, Mayberry's many wounds remained untreated until the next day, when a chance visit to the farm by the local sheriff resulted in Mehrans driving him to a doctor, on Sheriff Tyler's orders. Mehrans alleged the injuries had occurred when "a caterpillar turned over" on Mayberry, something the victim did not then dispute, given the gravity of his condition. Moreover, Mehrans had warned him that any attempt to tell his story would result in even more severe treatment: "The beating I gave you is nothing compared to what I will give you next time. I'll rest on you four or five times— I'll beat you and sit down and rest and get up and beat you some more." Not only that, he would get Mayberry's family, he vowed, "just like he got me," and would ensure that he would be "put in the penitentiary for ten or twenty years if I left his place." Mehrans had good economic reasons for insisting he stay. Mayberry's wage for a six-day week was thirty dollars, much of which was withheld for unspecified debts. The comparison with the slave breaker Coffey, Frederick Douglass's eventual nemesis, is irresistible.

Like Douglass, Mayberry was empowered by his mistreatment. "I picked my chance to get away," he later stated, and on June 9 he left for Little Rock by train, "bringing with me my wife, six children and two grandchildren." There Arkansas state NAACP president L. C. Bates, soon, with his wife, to be embroiled in the fight to integrate Central High, attempted to seek redress. They healed his wounds and found him work, but they never found him justice. Mehrans went unpunished, but Mayberry had the last word. Explaining why he had risked his life and that of his family by fleeing the farm, his simple response was, "I decided I could not live under these conditions of slavery." He may not have been an activist in the usual sense, but in finally taking this stand, Eddie Mayberry too became part of the civil rights struggle.[11]

Inevitably, both police and the local mobs they were close to in their extralegal violence crossed the line. With tension always in the air, violent action sometimes ended in death. Who killed Ella May will never be known for sure, but what is certain is that the climate of fear and violence in Gastonia made her death unsurprising. Similarly, in Marion or Honea Path, the sheriff's deputies who fired the fatal shots were all members of the local community, violently opposed to the UTW and the perceived disruption of their social order and unsettled by the weeks of tension which preceded the killings, and the same could be said of the local police who gave way in Orangeburg. They, too, were extremely jittery after weeks of escalating tension. In Neshoba County, the law enforcement officers complicit in handing over Chaney, Schwerner, and Goodman to their killers did so knowing full well what would happen. Indeed, they had a common belief that they were foot soldiers in a race war, defending their southern way of life, and their very genes, against forces bent on their destruction. Many racial killings could never be sheeted home. In

1965, Freddie Lee Thomas, a voter registration worker in Sidon, Mississippi, was found dead by the side of the road on the outskirts of town. His body showed all the signs of having sustained a fearful beating, yet his death was recorded as resulting from a "hit and run" incident, with no racial connotation. He was but one of many so categorized. One of the most dramatic chronicles of the frequency of routine beatings, during the civil rights years appeared in the biographical sketches supplied by the Mississippi Freedom Democratic Party delegation to the 1964 Democratic National Convention. Every one of them had been beaten during the past decade in retaliation for their activism, and most had also spent time in jail. It was stark testimony, but scarcely surprising.[12]

Attacks on the property of those challenging the southern economic and social order were commonplace throughout the struggles. In Gastonia, strike leaders had rented a small wooden shack on West Gastonia's main street, not far from the mill which became the strike headquarters. When the need for more space became apparent, mainly to organize the distribution of food relief, they were fortunate in obtaining the use of an adjacent brick warehouse that had recently been abandoned, and there the strikers were able to collect their food supplies. At about 1:00 a.m. on April 18, however, a mob of masked men, variously estimated at between 50 to 200 strong, invaded these facilities, overpowered the 10 strikers who were sleeping there, and literally hacked the wooden headquarters to pieces, turning it into "a mass of kindling wood." They found the brick relief center somewhat more resistant to their sledgehammers, so they destroyed its contents instead, ripping open bags of flour and grinding up eggs and vegetables until nothing usable was left, before melting back into the night. Though a grand jury eventually convened to investigate the violence, no one was ever prosecuted or even identified as having been involved. The strikers rebuilt their headquarters and found other ways of distributing relief supplies, yet the destruction of their building and their food was a blow to the strike effort as well as a symbolic statement of the vulnerability of their position in a situation in which community violence was endemic. As such, it bears comparison with the church burnings and bombings of the civil rights years. The purpose was the same: destruction of the perceived centers of disorder.[13]

Of course, some bombings occurred not simply to destroy property but to kill people and could thus be considered acts of terror. The infamous bombing of Birmingham's Sixteenth Street Baptist church in 1963, which killed the four young girls, was obviously one such bombing. The church was destroyed, not as most were, in the dead of night, but at a time when it was most likely to be packed with people, during the annual Youth Day service on Sunday, September 15. Moreover, though members of the congregation had been involved in civil rights activity, it was certainly not a center of organized resistance. Similarly, the botched attack on the Natchez tavern in August 1964 was also clearly meant to kill, as the attending firemen confirmed. When Rev. Shuttlesworth's house was bombed to destruction on Christmas Day 1956, it was with the obvious purpose of destroying him as well. Attending police officers were amazed that the perpetrators had not succeeded. At least eight sticks of dynamite had gone off within three feet of his head, one marveled, even as he advised the fiery clergymen to leave town for his own safety. Shuttlesworth would have none of it. God had saved him, he told the officer, "so you go back and tell your Klan brethren that if God could keep me through all this, then I'm here for the duration." Attacks on property, then, were also often designed to kill people.[14]

Whites who advocated an end to segregation were prime targets for attack. Since 1942, the Koinonia Farm community coexisted reasonably well with the local community, but with the quickening of the civil rights drive this changed abruptly. From the late 1950s, the collective was subjected to a constant campaign of harassment and fear. On the night of January 14, 1957, their roadside market was completely destroyed by a "terrific charge of dynamite," an explosion so powerful that debris was later found nearly 100 yards away. There had been three previous attacks on the market, all of which had caused only minor damage. Three days later, after an anonymous telephone call, one of the farm homes was deliberately set alight and completely destroyed. On several occasions shots were fired into other farm dwellings. On January 29, 1957, for example, "a speeding car raked the house nearest the highway with what seemed to be machine gun fire" before firing a burst into the car in which Harry Atkinson, a Koinonia resident, was sitting on guard duty. It missed him by inches. There were frequent Klan rallies and cross burnings on the property, while Koinonia's neighbors were also harassed, particularly those who had had business dealings with the community. Jack Singletory and his family, who lived six miles from Koinonia, and had had what was described as "a warm relationship" with the community, had their barn burned as a result, as did another white neighbor, J. D. Clements, who lost all his heavy machinery as a consequence. Another neighbor, who had simply helped pick Koinonia's corn, was immediately "beset by all kinds of physical and legal harassments" to the extent that he decided to sell up and move from the district. On all occasions the sheriff and his men made no attempt to investigate the incidents. Indeed, often they did not even bother to respond to calls. The ordeal of the Koinonia community was repeated hundreds of times during the civil rights years.[15]

The presence of the Klan at Koinonia cross burnings, its responsibility for the Birmingham church bombing of 1963, the murder of Schwerner, Chaney, and Goodman the following year, in fact, its centrality to much of the violence of the whole civil rights era, opens up the question of how much of the beatings and the murders were well organized, not only in the 1960s but also during the period of union struggle. Certainly in Gastonia in 1929 there was a presumption among the strikers that they were opposed not simply by angered townspeople but by an organized conspiracy, put together by Loray mill management, which became "the focal point for acts of violence against the strikers." They called it the Committee of One Hundred, or sometimes the Black Hundred, and claimed it was responsible for all the acts of violence in Gastonia starting with the destruction of the strike headquarters on April 18. Quickly it became part of the demonology of the strike sympathizers. "The day the soldiers left Gastonia," wrote Tom Tippett, "the Loray Mill organized its own force into a Committee of 100, most of whom were deputized as sheriffs or special policemen," who embarked on a "reign of terror." The Committee of One Hundred, then, orchestrated the violence which had the unexpected consequence of the death of police chief Orville Aderholt, it was behind the night of violence on September 9, following the declaration of a mistrial in the case of those accused of conspiring his death. A few days later, Committee members had their revenge, when they killed Ella May. There is no doubt that the committee existed; so many people knew of it that denial was simply not possible. Instead, mill management admitted as much but denied that it was a vigilante group. They claimed they had appointed "a committee of one hundred . . . made up of workers from all departments of the mill" with the designated duty "to pass upon the acceptability of those strikers who might apply for their former places in the mill."[16]

Few were fooled by this explanation. Most knew the committee for what it was, an organized vigilante group, and they knew who led it. He was Maj. A. L. Bulwinkle, a local lawyer who had represented the district in Congress between 1920 and 1928, before being swept from office in the Hoover landslide of that year. Shattered by this unexpected defeat, he was offered some solace by Loray management, who hired him as the mill's legal counsel. Equally important, he threw himself into the task of strengthening the Gastonia post of the American Legion, which he had helped organize in 1929 and of which he was now president. It was Bulwinkle who successfully lobbied Governor Max Gardner to replace some of the national guardsmen assigned to protect the mill by a "picked body of deputies chosen from the ranks of the American Legion as former servicemen." Bulwinkle, thereafter, was their "man on the white horse," a shadowy but central figure throughout 1929, pivotal both to mill management's legal opposition to the strike, and to the illegal vigilantism which accompanied it.[17]

The American Legion could often be found defending communities against "outside agitators." In Anderson, South Carolina, during the 1934 strike, the town became an armed camp, as its residents awaited the arrival of the feared "flying squadrons." Its only recreation space, a park in the center of town, was taken over by the sheriff's office, becoming the headquarters for a force of "six hundred specially deputized mill workers and ex-servicemen, all armed to the hilt." E. E. Epting, president of the local American Legion post and commander of the force, believed their current call was just as vital to the country's interests as the one they had answered in 1917 since once again "foreigners" menaced their community. When the main force was disbanded, the veterans of the American legion were kept together under the command of Ben Cleveland, a decorated survivor of the French battlefields. Their intelligence wing, using radio equipment, hoped to monitor the striker's planning sessions, and then, using "pre-arranged signals," would mobilize the whole "protective force within a few minutes" if necessary. In the interwar years, veterans could usually be mobilized to defend the social order against outsiders, often under their old wartime commanders. This was not the case during the Operation Dixie crusade, as Minchin points out. Many veterans who returned to the mills came back as union sympathizers, he argues, and thus harder to mobilize against the TWUA organizers, who were often themselves veterans. Most violence now occurred between strikers and nonstrikers rather than being inflicted on workers by mill management and their auxiliaries, which, he says, marked a sharp break from prewar textile strikes, especially the general strike of 1934.[18]

Nevertheless, there was some organized and extralegal opposition to Operation Dixie, and there was some vigilantism, often directed by the Klu Klux Klan, working with mill management. Yet it rarely took the form of attacks on persons or property; instead, the race issue was raised during local organizing drives. Even then, attacks had to be tempered by the fact that many union members were also Klan supporters and saw no contradiction in this. This was certainly the case in the interwar years, when the mills were almost entirely white and Klan membership was never an issue. Sam Finley, secretary of the UTW local during the Marion strike in 1929, laughed off any suggestion that the forces of the Klan had been arrayed against them. He had been a Klan member himself in 1929, as had most of the union activists. The Klan had done "a lot of good" then, he said, crusading as it did against "wife beaters" and "child abusers." As for the "colored people," they had had nothing to do with the 1929 strike, as "they didn't work in the mill," and the Klan, therefore, had no interest in them. But for the "up town folk," mill management, the town's lawyers, and its merchants, it was different. They all held mill stock, and it was they, not the Klan, who were most violently opposed to the strike and who, in his view, were directly responsible for the shootings in October.[19]

That is not to say that the Klu Klux Klan did not involve itself in anti-labor activity during the interwar period. Glenn Feldman's recent study of the Klan in Alabama makes it clear that much of the violence directed against CIO organizers in Alabama's steel plants and rubber factories was Klan-inspired. Moreover, there is some evidence that the Klan was active in Huntsville during the 1934 textile strike. Nevertheless, it is true that before Operation Dixie, the organization had not marked textile unions for ferocious retribution. Too many people were members of both. Again, it is worth reflecting on the ultimate tragedy of this fact. White textile workers and black fighters for civil rights may have had common enemies, but this did not make them allies, because of the racial gulf between them. Textile unionists, themselves often the victims of violence and terror, could at the same time be its perpetrators against their fellow southern workers.[20]

The Klan was certainly behind much of the violence that took place during the civil rights era. One of the first NAACP officials to be murdered in the postwar years was Florida state secretary Harry T. Moore, killed, with his wife Harriet, when their home in Mims was bombed on Christmas night 1951, their twenty-fifth wedding anniversary. No one was ever indicted for the killing, even though the man who had made the bomb allegedly confessed, but few doubted that the Klan was behind it. Stetson Kennedy, the outspoken southern liberal journalist who had once infiltrated the Klan as an undercover agent for the Georgia State Bureau of Investigation and was a friend of Moore's, attempted to provide state police with a full list of those behind the crime, but they were simply "not interested." And from the symbolic *Brown* decision of 1954, NAACP field officers consistently reported a steady increase in Klan activity throughout the South, something a Southern Regional Council survey confirmed in 1956. The investigation, conducted over three months, concluded that "during the past several months there has been a conspicuous flurry of public activity by the Klan. Public meetings, usually of an impressive size, have been held in North Carolina, South Carolina, Georgia, Tennessee, Florida, Alabama, Louisiana, and Texas." In all these states, new and streamlined administrative structures had been put in place, and "financing has been injected" far superior to any previous time in the Klan's violent history. Of all the mushrooming organizations committed to the defense of segregation, it was the Klan "which most commands attention in the near future," concluded the report. Even in Miami, not usually regarded as a Deep South city, there was a huge increase in Klan activity, inflamed by black pressure on white residential neighborhoods. As early as 1946, Klan billboards adorned the highways leading into the city, while "dozens of cross burnings, and even a few house burnings, lit up Miami's night skies over the next few years."[21]

And, indeed, the Klan continued to grow in the years ahead, despite the eventually successful FBI attempts to infiltrate its ranks. Because it operated in secret, much of what is known about Klan activity during the civil rights struggle has come from informers or infiltrators, and there is much that will remain forever hidden. Klan members set the bombs which killed the children in the Sixteenth Street Baptist church; they killed Schwerner, Chaney, and Goodman; and Byron de la Beckwith, the murderer of Medgar Evers, had close ties with Klansmen. Throughout the civil rights struggle in Mississippi the Klan was there, beating, bombing, and murdering. Though it was bankrolled by some of the state's richest men, Mississippi Klan members were overwhelmingly from the less affluent white community, as, indeed, was the case throughout the South.

"Impatient and angry," wrote John Dittmer, and "consumed by anxiety over the future," poorer whites flocked to the fiery cross throughout the 1960s, the more so as they came to believe that "the battle for white supremacy was being lost," that the middle-class segregationists, the professionals on whom they had depended, had failed them. "Southern white leaders," wrote Pete Daniel, in the end depended on the Klan as enforcers. They needed men "who would intimidate or kill anyone who showed softness on segregation."[22]

Other segregationist groups, more acceptable than the Klan, could nevertheless be pushed into extralegal violence from time to time. The Patriots of North Carolina was one such. Headed by W. C. George of the University of North Carolina Medical School, and with a membership list of 20,000 in 1956, including several state legislators, it presented itself as the respectable, if uncompromising face of segregation in the state, and as such, said the Winston-Salem *Journal and Sentinel*, was "more than a scrubbed-face revival of the Ku Klux Klan in new haberdashery." Yet Patriots could resort to dark and violent deeds, if pressed, often through their Klan auxiliaries. Tennessee had its Society to Maintain Segregation, headed by Arthur A. Canada, who had made his reputation fighting organized labor, Louisiana its Southern Gentlemen, Virginia its Defenders of State Sovereignty and Individual Liberty, all militant symbols of "the counter-attack against racial integration" and all with close ties to each other and to global white supremacist organizations, including the Apartheid Bund of South Africa.[23]

Above all, they were all linked to the symbol of middle-class resistance to integration in the South, the White Citizens Councils (WCCs). Born in Mississippi in the wake of the *Brown* decision, the Citizens Council movement fanned out throughout the South in the following decade, providing the engine room of white resistance. Citizens Council members could be found on school boards and in boardrooms, in banks, in businesses of every description, in police headquarters and patrol cars, in local government offices, in state legislatures, and, as in the case of Mississippi's Ross Barnett, in the governor's mansion itself. Strongest in Mississippi and Alabama, which had 80,000 members by November 1956, but with a substantial presence elsewhere—South Carolina had 30,000 members by 1956, for example, Louisiana about 50,000—the Councils' original targets were blacks supportive of school integration, who were mainly from the small and vulnerable middle class. Next came those who had registered or tried to register to vote, and increasingly, those who were members of the NAACP. Indeed, the NAACP itself became a target of WCC activity, as it waged, through state legislatures and the various state antisubversive bodies, a systematic campaign to have it banned throughout the region.[24]

The Citizens Councils, as the voice of "respectable" opposition to integration, always disavowed the use of violence in its campaigns, while helping create the climate which made such illegalities commonplace. Its twin weapons were economic retaliation and simple intimidation. Wesley W. Law was a mail carrier in Savannah, Georgia, with an exemplary record of service. However, when he became president of the Georgia State Conference of NAACP branches, his employment was promptly terminated, following various charges of dereliction of duty filed by R. S. Fisher, a postal inspector and WCC member. Lawyers for the NAACP described the charges as "picayune" in the extreme, and they were right, given that they involved technicalities such as having stated on March 7, 1961, that "you had four (4) Forms 3579 to complete, when you had only one such form to complete," having taken sixteen minutes too long "to deliver 663 pieces of mail" on the same day, and most serious of all, having on March 4, 1959, been observed "urinating on the lawn at 1109 Lexington Ave., in view of a lady resident of the vicinity, who observed your actions." Presumably the woman in question was so shocked at what she had seen that it had taken two years before she had recovered sufficiently to report the incident. The NAACP vigorously represented Law, and in October he was reinstated, with back pay, yet his case, as Clarence Mitchell stated, was "similar to the pattern of economic sanctions being used by private employers to curtail and stifle the aspirations of colored Americans who are seeking equal treatment under the law." Law was fortunate that a department of the federal government was involved. Most victims of such economic intimidation were not so lucky.[25]

W. D. Burgess of Snow Hill, North Carolina, became president of the local NAACP branch in 1960. Immediately, his son and his wife, both teachers at the local black high school, lost their jobs. An investigation showed that they had both counseled parents thinking of making "an assignment for their children to go to an all white school," sufficient in the eyes of the authorities to brand them as activists. The WCC tactics, of course, were often successful. Writing from New Bern, North Carolina in 1957, Mrs. L. E. Jarma, a local NAACP member, said that "teachers that use to attend meetings no longer do, afraid of losing their jobs" because of WCC pressure. In rural Humphreys County, Mississippi, most of the 400 African Americans registered to vote there had torn up their poll tax receipts by April 1955. They were sharecroppers and had been threatened with eviction if they failed to do so.[26]

A particularly effective means of intimidation was the cutting off of credit or the foreclosure of mortgages and bank loans. For years, Moses Forbes and Theodore Edwards, both farmers from Snow Hill, North Carolina, had routinely borrowed from the Mechanics and Farmers Bank of Durham, North Carolina, in order make their crops. The crop was their security, and they had always met the terms of their agreements. But once it was discovered that they had joined the NAACP, all further loan applications were refused and the bank demanded immediate repayment of existing loans long before the agreed repayment date had been reached. Both the NAACP's state and national offices intervened, but to no avail, and eventually National Executive Secretary Roy Wilkins himself was forced to arrange refinancing for both men in order to prevent them losing not only their crops but also their land and livelihood. Again, Forbes and Edwards were fortunate that their plight did prompt national action. Most who found themselves in similar positions were unable to be similarly aided.[27]

From all over the South came similar stories of economic intimidation and reprisal, usually coordinated by the WCC local branch. In Elloree, South Carolina, for example, every known member of the local NAACP chapter had been "victimized economically, and subjected to various forms [sic] indignities." There had been, wrote I. DeQuincey Newman, the state NAACP president, "a systematic program of economic pressure foisted against Negroes who have been a part of school desegregation and NAACP activity in and around Elloree" which had begun in 1955 and had persisted thereafter. As a result, most local farmers had lost their crops, had "no source of credit due to economic reprisals," and were living in conditions of "hunger and general want." In nearby Clarendon County, where one of the suits leading to the *Brown* decision was first filed, the economic reprisals had been similarly vicious and persistent, directed especially against "the Negro parents that served as plaintiffs in this action and all known members of the NAACP." In 1959, the Citizens Council was as intense as ever, but the challenge had been met by equally committed activity. Blacks had organized the Clarendon County Improvement Association, and with the help of outside funds had been able to provide "necessary goods and services to the people that were suffering at the hands of the White Citizens Councils." Billie S. Fleming, the association's president, told a Senate subcommittee in 1959, "We are supplying fertilizer, seed, insecticides, cash loans and other services they could not get elsewhere." But it was a desperately hard business, and not every community could muster the monetary and human resources which helped Clarendon County's blacks to survive. A long report by Margaret Price, commissioned by various civil rights groups, starkly showed how successful the WCC's campaign of intimidation had been. She had investigated 417 "cases of violence, reprisal and intimidation" reported in the eleven states of the old Confederacy between January 1, 1955, and May 1, 1958. Most had resulted in the severe restriction of civil rights activity, particularly in pressing for school integration. White sympathizers with black aspirations also suffered economically as a consequence of their beliefs. Both Aubrey Williams and the Durr family in Montgomery, Alabama, had their businesses ruined through white boycott, while their social lives, their ability to interact with the community was also severely restricted. For the gregarious Williams, this was particularly hard to bear. "I like to play poker and golf, meeting with other men for bull sessions," he once wrote. His opposition to segregation ended all that, and eventually he returned to Washington to live, lonely and dispirited.[28]

Thirty years earlier, striking textile workers had also suffered economic reprisal, though on a much narrower scale. Most obvious was the refusal to rehire them once the strike was over, as happened in Gastonia and Marion in 1929 and, in particular, after the 1934 general strike, despite the specific provisions of the settlement prohibiting such discrimination. Strikers were usually evicted from the mill villages, their credit at the company stores abruptly cut off, while community pressure ensured that they were denied such assistance elsewhere. In Gastonia, journalist Mary Heaton Vorse tried to organize a milk fund, to which she assumed some of the town's more socially conscious women would contribute and which would at least mean that the strikers' infants would get some proper nourishment. The vehemence of their refusal, the hatred these middle-class women displayed toward the strikers, was what finally brought home to her the chasm that existed between them and the millhands. Economic retaliation then, had long been a handy weapon for those most resistant to social and economic change in the South.[29]

While local WCC chapters and other like-minded groups were usually male-dominated, white women also combined to resist social change, especially in the struggle to prevent school desegregation. In Little Rock in 1957, the Mothers League of Central High School was formed specifically to provide the sort of support to the segregationist forces that Daisy Bates and the NAACP were giving to the nine students and their families. The Mothers League was always closely tied to the Citizens' Council, while the outspoken activism of its members was used by Governor Faubus and other segregationist leaders as compelling evidence that their cause was not only just but respectable. The Little Rock Mothers League was a model for segregationist women in southern towns and cities as the fight for school integration intensified.[30]

Those who opposed southern change usually had the law on their side; it was there to be used to their advantage. Most obviously, this meant that those who did the beatings and the killings, even if accused, which was rare, invariably went unpunished. This was the case with Ella May's killers, with the sheriff's deputies in Marion, with those who fired the shots at Honea Path. Local juries acquitted them, despite the evidence, while sentencing the perceived disrupters of the social order savagely, often on trumped-up charges, or the most cursory of evidence. Those accused in Gastonia of murdering Sheriff Aderholt, for example, were tried not so much for their alleged crime, as for their alien beliefs. Prosecuting Solicitor John Carpenter perfectly summed up the mood in the courtroom, and of the whole trial in his closing address. After excoriating the defendants as "a traitorous crowd coming from hell," he asked the jury if they believed "in the flag of your country, floating in the breeze, kissing the sunlight, singing the song of freedom. Do you believe in North Carolina? Do you believe in good roads, the good roads of North Carolina on which the heaven-bannered hosts could walk as far as San Francisco." Into this peaceful land had come the outside agitators, Fred Beal and the men and women of the NTWU, "fiends incarnate, stripped of their hoop and horns," bringing "bloodshed and death." But now these evil invaders stood at the bar of justice. There was only one answer the people could give. "Do your duty men," Carpenter urged the jury. "Do your duty."[31]

Southern juries were similarly urged to do their duty throughout the civil rights era, either to convict those accused of disrupting the social order, or to acquit those who were simply defending their traditional way of life. The killers of Emmett Till in Money, Mississippi, were found not guilty in 1955 after such an appeal by defense counsel John C. Whitten. In his closing address, he expressed his confidence that "every last Anglo-Saxon one of you has the courage to do it," to strike a blow against "people in the United States who want to destroy the customs of southern people"—exactly the same argument as Carpenter's in Gastonia, except for the racial dimension. Little matter that the evidence against the accused, Roy Bryant and J. W. Milam, was overwhelming and courageously presented by the prosecution. It was the specter of "the outsider," the threat to the social order Till posed, that was the jury's sole concern. Ironically, Milan and Bryant admitted a few months later that they had indeed killed the boy when they sold their story to *Look* magazine for $4,000.[32]

The Till trial prefigured many subsequent courtroom dramas during the 1960s. Juries initially acquitted or declined to prosecute the murderers of Medgar Evers, the bombers of Birmingham, even those responsible for the deaths of Schwerner, Goodman, and Chaney in Neshoba County. Eventually some were brought to justice, often under the aegis of federal, not state, law, as was the case of the killers of these three young men. Seven Klansmen were jailed for the violation of their civil rights, a federal crime. The Birmingham bombers, too, were eventually brought to justice, in one case nearly forty years after the event when the South had been transformed. Similarly, justice eventually caught up with Medgar Evers's killer, again after a delay of thirty years. Nevertheless, at the time it was most needed, southern justice failed the crucial test of impartiality. It let killers go free while it sent thousands of American citizens to jail simply for asserting their basic rights.[33]

What of those who fired the shots in Orangeburg? Like the deputies in Marion or Honea Path, they too were cleared of blame. Defending the nine patrolmen charged in federal court with violating the slain students' civil rights, defense attorney J. C. Coleman declared that the patrolmen were in no way to blame for what happened. Rather, it was with the "outside agitator" Cleveland Sellers and his "burn, kill, power group" that responsibility lay. The patrolmen, he claimed, had fired only as a last resort, to prevent "frenzied" students from "getting out into the city of Orangeburg, burning, doing God knows what." Coleman's partner Frank Taylor, asked the defendants to stand and face the court. "Look at them," he implored the jury. "In your own mind, picture—could you find nine finer looking southern gentlemen." The jury of ten whites and two blacks evidently agreed. It took them less than two hours to find them not guilty on all counts. As for the arch-villain, Sellers, though indicted on several charges arising out of the Orangeburg shootings, he was never brought to trial. In 1970, he was accepted as a graduate student by Harvard University's faculty of education.[34]

In 1963, Guy Guess, a longtime resident of Lexington, Mississippi, had employed for the past twenty years a black woman, Pearl Bruce, as his housekeeper, apparently without anybody evincing the least concern. However, it then became known that not only had Bruce joined the local NAACP, but her sister-in-law, Anna Mae Weems, had once been president of the Waterloo, Iowa, branch. That was enough for Lexington's law enforcement officers—and the WCC. On June 8, 1963, both Guess and his housekeeper were arrested and charged with "illegal cohabitation," the only evidence being that witnesses had seen her in Guess's car as he drove her to the store—something he had done every day for the past two decades. He was released on $2,500 bond and strongly advised to quit the state—advice he heeded—but Bruce was not permitted bail, nor was she brought to trial. When the NAACP eventually heard of her situation, she had been in the Holmes County Jail for more than eight months, a bizarre example of the way localities used the law against those perceived to challenge the social order.[35]

Hazel Brannon Smith was a rarity in Mississippi during the civil rights years, a white liberal with the courage to oppose publicly the ruling orthodoxy. Like Pearl Bruce, she lived in Lexington, in Holmes County, but unlike her she had a ready voice, being the editor and publisher of the town's newspaper, the *Lexington Advertiser*. Her opposition to the WCC, her exposure of patterns of brutality among the local police, and her bitter contempt for the Klan, made her a prime target for harassment. The WCC ensured that her advertising revenue dried up, commercial job printing contracts were denied her, but eventually her fate, too, was decided in the courts. Members of the WCC, including two local policemen, brought a series of libel suits against her. She simply could not afford to keep fighting them, and in 1963 she ceased publication. The next year the bombers struck as well. The NAACP and the Eleanor Roosevelt Foundation had helped her start a small suburban paper in Jackson, the *Northside Reporter*, but on October 4 its office was destroyed.[36]

In Baton Rouge, Louisiana, three African American women, Pearl George, the local NAACP branch secretary, Willie Lee Harris, and Laura Harns, decided to sit on the white side of the courtroom during the trial of a fellow member. Without warning they were arrested, sentenced to ten days jail for contempt of court, and fined $100. When they refused to pay the fine, their jail term was increased by thirty days. Applications for bail proved fruitless; not until NAACP lawyers appealed directly to the U.S. Supreme Court were they released. Even then the Louisiana courts moved so slowly that they had already spent twenty days in prison on charges that could not possibly be sustained and were thus never to be heard. Similarly, physician Clinton C. Battle of Indianola, Mississippi, who had provided medical testimony to NAACP lawyers in 1956, found himself in jail as a consequence on trumped up "DWI charges." It was, he alleged, "part of a vicious smear campaign of the Citizens Councils," as retribution for his NAACP connection. All over the South, the courts were too often active agents of the segregationists, who were eager to use them as an effective means of punishing their challengers.[37]

Organizations sympathetic to the civil rights struggle found themselves under continuous legal scrutiny as the battle lines hardened, over and above the harassment of the federal and state investigative committees already discussed. SCHW's successor, the Southern Conference Educational Fund, which under Aubrey Williams was uncompromising in its support for an integrated South, found its tax exempt status increasingly threatened, while Williams, other members of his family, and SCEF officers were often in court defending themselves from patently absurd charges. The legal campaign against the Highlander Folk School eventually caused its doors to close and forced it to move its office to Knoxville. The Koinonia Farm community, as well as having to deal with bombings and burnings, also had to defend itself in court, including a full-scale grand jury investigation in the wake of the 1957 violence. Scarcely surprisingly, the Sumter County jury, among many charges, found Koinonia to have "a strong filial connection with the Communist Party," and "that they themselves (Koinonia Farm members) may be actual members thereof." In particular, the jury stressed that "one Miles [sic] Horton. . . . Known to be a member of the Communist Party. . . . Has visited Koinonia Farms Inc. . . . Where his views must have been favorably received." As if that were not enough, the jury revealed that Clarence Jordan, Koinonia's secretary-treasurer, had admitted under oath that he was a director of

SCEF, another allegedly communist organization. Koinonia's mailing list was full of "so-called friends and sympathizers" who were "known Communists." Indeed, the community was so clearly not what it purported to be that any tax advantages it received should be immediately removed. Koinonia's directors vigorously protested the "biased and unfair investigation," organized as it had been by Georgia's solicitor general, Charles Burgamy, an outspoken segregationist and Klan supporter, pointing out that the jury had found no evidence of Koinonia having broken the law. But that was beside the point. The presiding judge congratulated the jurors for "an outstanding job in the direction towards perhaps a rapid solution to this problem, which was revealing the linkage between civil rights advocacy and Communist belief." The Koinonia investigation was just another example of the way the South's judicial system had been mobilized in defense of its caste system.[38]

Civil rights leaders, as well as their organizations, were routinely subjected to personal legal harassment. Not even Martin Luther King was immune. The circumstances surrounding his imprisonment in Albany in 1962 and Birmingham in 1963 have become part of civil rights history, but they were the last in a long line of arrests and jailings which began in Montgomery. At the height of the bus boycott, he was jailed on a trumped-up speeding charge, the first of many such attempts to intimidate him, the most serious being in Atlanta in 1960, after a sit-in at the snack bar of Rich's department store. Already on probation following a suspended jail sentence for driving without a Georgia license—itself the result of harassment—King was ordered to serve four months on a state road gang, a savage sentence which prompted the intervention of presidential candidate John F. Kennedy and his brother. Quickly they secured King's release, a bold action which may have provided the margin of Kennedy's narrow election victory. Traffic violation, tax evasion, and perjury, King was charged with all these and more as the white South grew more desperate.[39]

Ella Baker, King's supporter turned critic and rival, faced similar harassment on a trip to Louisiana in 1960 to work with black students anxious to start direct action projects. Her presence, and the enthusiasm with which she was received, disturbed both black school administrators and the white power structure. On March 16, while making a left turn on a busy New Orleans street, she was stopped by a police patrol vehicle which had followed her for several blocks, charged with "careless and wreckless [sic] driving" and taken to jail, where she was held for two days before a judge dismissed all the counts against her. Her brief incarceration had, she believed, a clear political intent, and as such had disturbed her profoundly, even though she had used her time behind bars to investigate the conditions of her fellow prisoners. Such intimidatory practices became routine as the civil rights movement gathered speed.[40]

Of course, the organization which suffered most from legal harassment during the civil rights years was the NAACP itself. Some states tried to prevent its operation altogether, as a subversive institution, and NAACP members were the main targets of segregationist attack and intimidation. Particularly vulnerable were those lawyers who accepted NAACP work. Otto L. Tucker of Alexandria, Virginia, was one such. He had appeared for the organization in a number of school desegregation suits in Arlington, Alexandria, and Fairfax, during which he had gained a reputation as a skilled and persuasive advocate. For that reason, members of the Virginia Bar Association sought systematically over several years to have him disbarred, the first attempt anywhere, according to the NAACP, "to disbar an NAACP lawyer for participating in civil rights cases." In 1959, it was the Seventh District Committee of the Virginia State Bar's turn. Members accused Tucker of soliciting business, in that he offered to "represent Buford Kibler . . . one of two white youths accused with four Negroes in an assault case" in which Tucker was already representing the other five. A three-judge circuit court found the charge proven and reprimanded the lawyer, but to the anger of the bar association, refused to disbar or suspend him. The next year it was the turn of the Bar's Fourth District, and again the charges were soliciting business, in that "on or about the 3rd day of January, 1950, you did appear before the Circuit Court of Greenville County, Virginia, and undertake the defense of one Jodie Bailey, who stood indicted for the murder of one Luther P. Rockwell, when you had not been employed or retained for such purpose by the said Jodie Bailey or any person connected with or a party to the said case." He did the same thing in November 1950 in a rape case, it was further alleged, and again in 1952, when he offered to defend Tabb Watts, though he had not been retained to do so. All three cases involved interracial conflict. Bailey was a sharecropper accused of murdering his white landlord, the rape case involved a white man accused of raping a black sixteen-year-old girl, and Tabb Watts, also black, had been involved in a fight with a white man. Again, those accusing Tucker were stalemated, this time by the court ruling that the bill of particulars against him was improperly drawn up and thus could not be proceeded upon.[41]

The Bar Association had another try in 1961, having refiled their bill of particulars. This time members were represented by commonwealth attorney Harold L. Townsend, indicative of how serious was the campaign against Tucker. Once again they failed. A three-judge court dismissed the case against him, ruling that the plaintiff be "non-suited without prejudice." Angry and defiant, Townsend vowed to "have new charges brought in the case" once he had consulted with the state bar committee, but that body decided to give up the fight. Though NAACP lawyers continued to suffer routine harassment during the civil rights struggle, never again would a concerted attempt be made to secure their disbarment in retaliation for their activities. In Tucker's case, the law had worked for him, perhaps an indication that the climate of southern justice was at last beginning to change.[42]

When textile workers fought for economic and social justice, they often found themselves facing armed troops across the barricades. In strike situations state governors frequently used guardsmen, ostensibly to restore order, or to prevent violence and lawlessness. It took Tennessee's governor less than a week to order 800 guardsmen to Elizabethton in March 1929, despite protests from AFL president William Green. Governor O. Max Gardner of North Carolina acted with similar dispatch a month later. Within two days of the strike call at the Loray Mill, five units of the North Carolina National Guard had arrived in Gastonia, where they remained for some weeks. Similarly, guardsmen were sent to Marion at the height of the disturbances there, again for a prolonged period. In the general textile strike of 1934, southern governors were equally quick to mobilize the guard at the first signs of trouble, none more so than South Carolina's Ibra Blackwood. He had them out within two days, with orders to "shoot to kill," ostensibly to combat the threat to order and property posed by the strikers' motorized "flying squadrons." Governor Ehringhaus of North Carolina was more circumspect, waiting nearly a week before sending troops to his state's trouble spots. Again, the "increasing number of strike-bent motorcades" on the move was the excuse. In Georgia, Governor Eugene Talmadge, deeply involved in a primary campaign for which he needed labor's support, at first refused to follow his fellow governors' example, despite the entreaties of the mill owners. Once safely elected, however, he changed his tune, and soldiers quickly blanketed the state. In 1929 and 1934, when mill management demanded the guard be mobilized, state authorities were quick to comply. With the arrival of the troops, strike momentum slowed. Soldiers patrolling the streets or on duty outside the mills were an intimidatory presence as far as strikers were concerned. They placed restrictions on picketing and on strike rallies, at no time more obviously than in 1934, when they effectively halted the strikers' most potent weapon, the motorized pickets. Above all, troops protected those who wanted to return to work or had remained at their posts, neutralizing the effect of picketing. Effectively, the guardsmen served as strikebreakers, and union leaders frequently described them as such.[43]

For these reasons, striking workers bitterly opposed the troops' presence, and took every opportunity to tell them so, and none more so than the young women. In Elizabethton, women constantly taunted the troops, marching down the highway "draped in the American flag and carrying the colors," thus forcing the soldiers to present arms every time they passed, shouting obscenities at them, embarrassing the young men with constant sexual innuendo. It was a similar scene in Gastonia a month later, as young women followed the soldiers about with cries of "Boy Scouts" and "nasty guardsmen," sometimes grappling with their weapons. Occasionally they did more than grab. Bertha Tompkinson, a striker, once broke through the lines and commenced "pummeling one of the guardsmen with a stout stick." "A little thing like a bayonet would not stop her," she asserted. A bayonet did stop Gracie Pickard in Burlington, North Carolina, in 1934, during the height of strike tension there. There a guardsman lost his cool and stabbed her during a scuffle on the picket line. Some thought Pickard had had it coming, for she had followed the troops around town for days, abusing them constantly—and obscenely. Given the anger the troops' presence engendered—anger partly arising from the frank recognition that whatever the ostensible reason for their dispatching, the reality was that they were the servants of management—it is surprising that there were not more serious incidents of violence.[44]

Guardsmen killed no strikers in 1929, and only one in 1934. This occurred in Belmont, North Carolina, as the strike sputtered to a stop. On the night of September 17, an angry crowd of strikers attacked Belmont's sheriff, Clyde Robinson, guardsmen came to his aid, and in the fierce struggle that followed, two men were severely bayoneted, one of whom, Ernest K. Riley, died soon afterward. There were allegations that the guardsmen had been drinking that evening, though this was vigorously denied by their young commanding officer, Capt. Sam Ervin. At the inquiry into Riley's death, the future United States senator was cleared of any blame. Indeed, Riley's death was found to be the result of "a lawful act," given the circumstances. No one was ever even identified as his killer. For his family and his strike comrades, however, it remained the ultimate act of strikebreaking, for which Ervin and his men were culpable. Riley's widow remained immensely proud of her dead husband, for in her mind he had died for a noble cause, "he died for organized labor."[45]

Unlike textile workers, civil rights activists rarely had to deal with the national guard, and when they did, they were much more likely to view them as protectors or deliverers than as adversaries. When Alabama's Governor John Patterson reluctantly sent the Alabama guard into Montgomery in 1961 at the height of the freedom rides crisis, it was to protect Martin Luther King and his supporters from being burned alive in First Baptist Church by an angry mob, local police having manifestly failed to do so. Though furious with King and the Kennedys, Patterson used the guard to protect those in the church, to disperse the white mobs baying for blood, to protect black neighborhoods from bomb throwers, and to protect the freedom riders themselves as they continued their journey. Two years later, the Alabama guard had a vital role to play in the integration crisis at the University of Alabama, when, acting under federal control, they symbolically forced Governor George Wallace to vacate the schoolhouse door and then protected the two African American students who passed beneath it. In 1965, Alabama's guardsmen stood guard along the highway as King led his triumphant foot soldiers on their victory march between Selma and Montgomery. Then, as in other instances, though they may not have approved of the cause, Alabama's guardsmen acted to protect those fighting for social change and economic justice, not, as in the textile mill struggles, opposing them as agents of reprisal.[46]

A further means of reprisal, one common to all the southern struggles, remains to be discussed. This was the widespread use of espionage by those most resistant to change. The La Follette Committee hearings, for example, revealed that mill owners routinely used spies and informers as a means of combating union activity. Profoundly shaken by the violence which occurred during the textile strike of 1934, Spencer Love of Burlington Mills and other mill managers hired private detectives from Pennsylvania's violent coal mines and iron foundries, well versed in the techniques of strikebreaking and industrial espionage, to try to catch the perpetrators. Love also engaged the Railway Audit and Inspection Company to provide spies for his mills henceforth, specifically to report any attempts to rebuild UTW locals. Throughout 1935, undercover operatives were active in all Love's North Carolina mills, in Burlington itself, in Mooresville, and in Fayetteville. They provided regular reports, not only on union activity but also on the cleanliness of the mill villages, the extent of gambling and drinking among his employees, even the efficiency of his superintendents. Though Love's spy network was much more extensive than most, mill managers had long relied on informants to help check union activism, and on professional strikebreakers to combat outbreaks of militancy. Earlier, in the prolonged strike in Atlanta's Fulton Bag and Cotton Mill in 1914–15, management relied on a network of spies in its efforts to break the strike, while Gastonia's management were similarly well served by informers in 1929. From the start they had a spy at the center of the strike network. Ed Spenser, ostensibly one of Fred Beal's most loyal deputies, was actually working for the Loray Mill's chief security officer, Bruce Abernethy. Often management knew the details of strike committee demands even before Beal had formally presented them, so assiduously did Spenser perform his duties. Unsurprisingly, he was rewarded with an executive position once the strike was broken. In the post-1945 South, mill managers continued to make use of spies, often anti-union operatives, though less blatantly or obviously. There was less need to do so. Nevertheless, when the chips were down, as at Dan River in 1951, "the less sophisticated strike-breaking methods that had been the stock in trade of southern mill owners in past labor wars" were there to be trotted out: "thugs acting at the employers' instigation, . . . legal harassment from state and local police, prosecutors, and judges disposed to include strikebreaking among their official duties," and company spies. Large-scale espionage, then, infiltration of workers' ranks, was always a key means by which mill managers fought back against those who challenged their authority.[47]

It was a similar story during the civil rights era. Local WCC chapters, State Sovereignty Commissions, and other investigative bodies all had their networks of informers. Some were blacks with personal ties to their white employers or patrons, but most were hired to go underground for specific purposes, usually by the various state commissions formed to combat civil rights activism. Some, like Paul and Sylvia Crouch, had once been Communists and closely identified in the textile workers' struggle. Both had been in Gastonia in 1929, for example, exhorting the workers not to give up their fight. Similarly, they had also both appeared in 1934, once the strike was lost, fiercely denouncing the UTW for their capitulation and urging the strikers to continue the struggle under the Communist Party's banner. Now they worked as informers for hire, ready to testify against those with whom they had once identified. One of the most celebrated displays of infiltration occurred in 1957, on the occasion of the Highlander Folk School's twenty-fifth anniversary celebrations. Among those present were Rosa Parks, Martin Luther King, Ralph Abernathy, leftist folk singer Pete Seeger, Aubrey Williams, and two uninvited guests, Abner Berry, a black reporter for the *Daily Worker*, and an employee of the Georgia's State Sovereignty Commission, sent there by Governor Marvin Griffin and posing as an employee of the state government's water pollution prevention agency. Berry took many photographs of the various activities, including interracial dancing, most of which subsequently appeared in the *Daily Worker*, and he inserted himself into one—alongside King, Myles Horton, and Aubrey Williams —taken by Griffin's spy. This picture, labeled the "four horsemen of racial agitation," was distributed widely throughout the South; it was reproduced in numerous segregationist publications, and the extreme right-wing John Birch Society eventually turned it into a postcard. It was also used on billboards which were displayed prominently on the region's freeways. Griffin's venture into espionage certainly had had the desired result, effectively tying the civil rights cause with that of the Communist Party. Mississippi's State Sovereignty Commission modeled itself on the FBI, even employing a former FBI agent, Zack Van Landingham, as its head. The commission systematically spied on civil rights organizations, compiling dossiers on scores of suspected agitators. It penetrated many local NAACP chapters, always working closely with the WCC. Alabama, too, created an espionage apparatus, aimed at selecting blacks considered targets for economic reprisal, often arranging for the publication of their names in the local press. Those who signed petitions calling for school integration were particularly vulnerable to this brand of exposure. From time to time blacks and their supporters attempted counterespionage, on one occasion even infiltrating a Citizens Council meeting in Shades Valley, Alabama, where they gained valuable information on their policies and tactics, especially the purging of local "voting lists of niggers," but in general such attempts were unsuccessful. Espionage during the civil rights struggle, as it had been during the unionization battles, was generally a one-way street.[48]

Thus, throughout the twentieth century, those white and black southerners determined to bring change to their region faced common and equally determined resistance. They were killed, jailed, beaten, deprived of their livelihood and their civil rights. The full strength of the law was used against them, yet they could rarely find legal redress. They were spied upon, and they were denied the space to expand their lives and to enlarge their own and their children's horizons. And yet they endured, until finally the federal government acted on at least some of the injustices that had long been part of the very fabric of their lives.

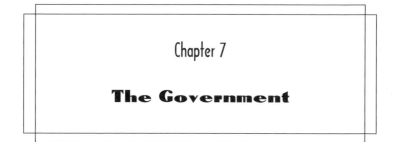

Chapter 7

The Government

On June 16, 1933, when southern textile workers danced and sang in the unpaved streets of their villages, they did so because they thought their southern struggle was over. The national government had a last joined the battle and tipped the scales decisively in their favor. The passage of the National Industrial Recovery Act, especially section 7(a), which gave to all workers the right to join unions of their choice, and the subsequent approval of the cotton textile code seemed to signal their comprehensive victory. Similarly, in 1965, as Martin Luther King sat with his SCLC lieutenants listening to President Johnson's speech to Congress and the nation in which he called for the speedy enactment of a comprehensive voting rights act, a speech in which the president consciously used the refrain of the civil rights anthem, "We Shall Overcome," he too believed the moment of victory had arrived. His friend Andrew Young movingly described the scene in the documentary series, *Eyes on the Prize*. King was focused intently in the television screen, he reported, and after Johnson had used their words, tears ran down his cheeks. His struggle too was over now that the national government had at last joined the fight. King soon found his elation was premature, as did the textile workers more than thirty years before. Yet the importance textile unionists and civil rights activists alike placed on federal intervention is indicative of the growing realization that only through national action could their causes be won. Their victories proved to be partial at best, and long in coming, yet in the end it was the federal government that made the difference.[1]

As has been noted, it did not take long for southern workers to comprehend that the NRA was not going to work in their favor, indeed, that the conditions of their lives were getting worse, not better, as employers took control of the Textile Code's machinery and used it to their advantage. Their anger spilled over in September 1934, in the brief, violent national textile strike. Again they were defeated, but it took a little time for its dimensions of their loss to become apparent. They marched back to work wearing the banner of victory, under a settlement negotiated by the national government in their favor, or so they believed. This was far from the case. In the bitter months ahead, most of its provisions were ignored, as employers took their revenge. Moreover, as historians Janet Irons and George Waldrep both document, the one provision of the strike settlement which seemed unequivocally to favor labor, the creation of a new Textile Labor Relations Board, which would be completely independent of the Cotton Textile Code Authority and seemingly had the power to end the stretch-out once and for all, turned out to be an empty vessel. Hailed by the *Textile Worker* as "the quiet but resistless power of the nation" that would "surround these mill towns with a sense of power hitherto unknown to them," it was seriously understaffed from the beginning, so dependent on the Code Authority for its expertise, and even its field staff, that its independence was hopelessly compromised. It went out of existence, with the NRA in 1935, judged unconstitutional by the United States Supreme Court. Textile workers mourned its passing, seeing it still as a symbol of the government's concern for their cause. It was far from that.[2]

To replace the labor provision of the NIRA, the New Dealers quickly shepherded the National Labor Relations Act, better known as the Wagner Act, through Congress. Signed into law in July 1935, the Wagner Act provided the foundation stone of industrial law for the rest of the century. Its purposes were multifarious, but central to the concern of those who fought for it was a determination to provide a framework through which workers could exercise their right to join unions, untrammeled by employer opposition, and to settle industrial disputes in an impartial manner. Again, textile workers believed that their hour had come, even more so once the Supreme Court had declared the act constitutional, and that it was the national government which had made the difference. Once again, they would soon be brought back to reality.[3]

The Wagner Act worked through a permanent administrative body, the National Labor Relations Board, with powers sufficiently broad to intervene in almost every aspect of the industrial milieu. While it took time to develop its own modes of operation, and it was not until after the Supreme Court's 1937 ruling that employers faced the unpalatable truth that the NLRB was here to stay and that they would have to deal with it thereafter, there can be no doubt as to its profound effect on the fabric of American society. The Wagner Act, in Waldrep's apt comment, "laid the groundwork for all future mediation in American industrial life." Its effect in the nation's great industrial centers was especially profound and altered the balance between capital and labor for the rest of the century. It was under its aegis that the CIO was able to move so swiftly to organize the nation's great industries. By 1941 the CIO's Steel Workers Organizing Committee had largely completed the task, begun only five years earlier, of organizing the nation's steelworkers into the United Steelworkers of America. Here the National Labor Relations Board was vital in challenging management's opposition, and in conducting the elections through which workers voted for the union, most often by margins of around 80 percent. Similarly, the United Automobile Workers of America had won their battle by 1941, when Ford at last capitulated, and again the NLRB had been vital to the struggle. Moreover, these new and lusty industrial unions were soon a vital component of the New Deal coalition, giving the Democratic Party a huge bloc of support in the nation's industrial cities. More than industrial balances had been altered by the NLRB, the political map had also been redrawn.[4]

Yet in the South, the effect of the NLRB was muted, the victories much less clear cut. In 1937, the Textile Workers Organizing Committee was formed, based on the SWOC model, aimed at bringing industrial democracy to that chaotic industry. The committee was in trouble right from the start. There were textile plants in twenty-nine states, a bewildering kaleidoscope of silk workers, rayon workers, hosiery workers, woollen workers, finishers, dyers, jacquard weavers—as well as those in the South's cotton mills. The industry was highly decentralized, with its components holding very different problems and perspectives. Yet the key region was the South. The TWOC workers understood this well, it was just that it was much easier to work with the industry's nonsouthern components, located as they were in New England, New Jersey, or Pennsylvania, where labor unions had existed for decades and management was much less ferocious.[5]

The TWOC did send organizers South, however, around 500, in fact, at the same time hiring prominent southern liberals as its publicists and spokespersons. Of these, Lucy Randolph Mason was the most significant. In 1937, this middle-aged Virginia blueblood, descended on both sides from Founding Fathers and connected to Robert E. Lee, was enticed from her position as general secretary of the National Consumers League to become the CIO's southern public relations representative and, in particular, to work with TWOC's southern campaign—in short, to bring the new national industrial relations framework to southern mills. It was inordinately difficult. Northern managers may have taken their time to recognize the reality of the Wagner Act and its implications, but even their bitter resistance eventually ended. Southern mill people were a different breed; most resisted the new dispensation with a ferocity that even she, a daughter of the region, found quite disheartening. "When I came South I had no idea of the frequency of attacks on people peacefully pursuing legitimate purposes," she wrote FDR soon after her arrival. "I am appalled at the disregard of the most common civil rights and the dangers of bodily harm to which organizers are exposed." The white South was "Fascist," she told Molly Dewson. The long domination of black southerners had made it easy "to repeat the pattern for organized labor." The federal government needed to do more, much more, if the region was to change. The NLRB, on its own, could not do the job. Mason was right, of course. The enduring power of Jim Crow was in convincing white southerners that black southerners had no rights. One result of this collusion with illegality was that their own rights, including the right to join labor unions, were compromised.[6]

Gradually, however, Mason's sense of despair was replaced by a dogged determination to bring change, no matter what the cost or how long it took. In this, she reflected the position of most southern organizers. And the going was painfully slow. In October 1938, at the end of nearly two years of hard work, TWOC had only 2 percent of cotton textile workers under contract, with no dramatic breakthrough to provide even mild optimism for the future. Indeed, organizers in other southern industries, like tobacco in North Carolina or iron and steel in Alabama, had enjoyed far greater success, and this despite the handicap of working across the color line. Moreover, the most respected southern organizer and director of the TWOC's regional drive, Steve Nance, had died suddenly in April, worn out by the impossibly difficult conditions, as managers continued to defy the NLRB. In 1939, the 302 new locals resulting from the TWOC drive merged with 126 former UTW locals to form the new Textile Workers Union of America–CIO, under the leadership of President Emil Rieve and Vice President George Baldanzi. Baldanzi, formerly of the dyers federation, with proven strength as an organizer, was given the South as his bailiwick, and he certainly went to work with a will. Between May 1939 and May 1941, for example, the new union won fifty-one NLRB elections in southern mills, only to find that even then employers could legally delay the signing of contracts. Of those fifty-one victories, only twenty-nine contracts were secured. The New Deal labor legislation, the "national solution," had again proved insufficient to overcome the resistance of southern mill management.[7]

There was a shift in these balances during World War II, in large part due to the stronger provisions against employer defiance mandated by the federal government during the exigencies of wartime. The National War Labor Board (NWLB) had the power to compel employers to accept contracts properly arrived at, and did so. Between 1943 and 1946 the TWUA won 436 contracts in the South, breaking some of region's largest and most resistant chains, including Cone Mills in Greensboro, North Carolina, Dan River in Danville, and a Cannon Mills plant in North Carolina, the only one to be penetrated until 1998. In April 1946, more than 20 percent of southern cotton workers were under contract, the highest percentage in the industry's history. Without doubt, this was in large part due to the NWLB, which for a time had tipped the struggle in labor's favor, a fact union leaders should have paid more attention to as they prepared for the final battle to organize the textile South, Operation Dixie. In particular, they should have understood that southern mill owners and managers had not forsaken the ferocity of their anti-unionism, they had simply been forced to accede to extraordinary pressure in an extraordinary situation.[8]

With peace came a return to the prewar industrial relations framework. The NWLB ceased operating in 1946. Operation Dixie, therefore, took place within the old NLRB framework, which again proved inadequate in the face of open employer defiance. Moreover, the Wagner Act, the centerpiece of the New Deal's industrial relations policy, was itself soon under attack. The Taft-Hartley Act of June 1947 reduced significantly the government's capacity to protect unions from employer defiance, in particular it reshaped the functions of the NLRB, greatly increasing the rights of employers and the public viz a viz those of the workers. The stronger industrial unions of the North and Midwest, the UAW, the Steelworkers, and the United Mine Workers, though undoubtedly slowed up, were able to survive Taft-Hartley. Its effect was most pronounced on the nation's weakest unions, among which was the TWUA. Operation Dixie, therefore, took place in an industrial climate where the balances had swung back decisively in the employers' favor. Their ability to use the provisions of national legislation originally designed to protect workers' rights against the unions was increased, as was their capacity simply to defy the law with impunity, much as they had done with the 1934 textile code. In such a climate, Operation Dixie, and the TWUA's continued drive to capture the textile South, was bound to fail, and fail it did, its end starkly symbolized by the disastrous textile strike of 1951. The national mechanisms set in place by the New Deal, which southern workers had hailed as signifiers of victory in their struggle, had proved woefully inadequate to the task.[9]

The decade following the 1951 defeat was a bleak one for the TWUA. Wracked by bitter internal disputes and with its treasury nearly empty due to declining membership, the union was in no position to wage further war on behalf of its remaining members. In 1960, its dues-paying members numbered no more than 150,000, less than 40 percent of the list a decade earlier. Moreover, with mill management in full control in the South, where the industry was now concentrated, there was little chance of reversing this trend, no matter how hard local organizers plugged away. As Julian Cloutier, president of Local 462 in Lewiston, Maine, warned despairingly in 1964, "I shudder at the thought of our future when the employers discover how divided we have become." The New Deal's attempt to create a national framework for the future conduct of industrial relations had borne bitter fruit for white southern textile workers.[10]

The first branch of the national government to have a decisive impact on the struggle of black southerners to win their civil rights was the federal judiciary. From the late 1930s a team of skilled young lawyers, most trained at Howard University's law school under its dynamic dean, Charles H. Houston, once described as a man who linked "the passion of Frederick Douglass demanding black freedom and of W. E. B. Du Bois demanding black equality to the undelivered promises of the Constitution of the United States," had been challenging the outer walls of segregation under the aegis of the NAACP. Initially they concentrated on inequalities in public education. Their first victory came in 1937, when in *Gaines v. Canada*, a case which Houston himself argued, the U.S. Supreme Court agreed that Lloyd Gaines, an African American, was entitled to enter the University of Missouri's law school, given that the state provided no state-supported legal training for its black citizens. It was a judgment on which precedents were built.[11]

Other victories followed, often argued by Houston's most able disciple, Thurgood Marshall, from 1938 the NAACP's national counsel. In 1950, in *Sweatt v. Painter*, the Supreme Court ruled that Herman Sweatt be admitted to the University of Texas law school, even though there was an alternative law school for blacks in the state, specifically created in 1946 after Sweatt's initial application. Marshall argued that given its inadequacies, Sweatt had no chance of an equal education there. The Court agreed. On the same day, the Court also ruled in favor of George McLaurin, a black school teacher, sixty-eight years old, and a doctoral candidate at the University of Oklahoma. He had been admitted, under pressure, in 1949 but kept separate from the white students thereafter, taking classes in an anteroom, made to sit at a special desk in the library, permitted to use the cafeteria only when white students were absent. Such discrimination denied McLaurin the chance of an equal educational experience, Marshall argued, and again the Court agreed, thus laying the groundwork for a challenge to segregation in public education itself.[12]

That challenge came with the NAACP's decision in 1951 to join together five cases involving desegregation in public schools then making their way through the lower court system under the name of one of them, *Brown v. Board of Education of Topeka*. The other cases were from Delaware, South Carolina, Virginia, and the District of Columbia, but the argument in all of them was the same. Challenging the Court's 1896 decision in *Plessy v. Ferguson*, that the maintenance of separate but equal public facilities did not contravene the fourteenth amendment, Marshall and the NAACP went far beyond their arguments of the earlier victories. Drawing on the expertise of psychologists and historians as well as legal precedent, they contended that segregation was inherently unequal, and thus unconstitutional, despite the maintenance of equal facilities, which in Topeka at least was clearly the case. It was a risky strategy, and Marshall knew it, but it was successful. On May 17, 1954, in his first judicial opinion, Chief Justice Earl Warren announced to a hushed courtroom the nine justices' unanimous decision that in the field of public education the doctrine of "separate but equal has no place. Separate educational facilities are inherently unequal." It was the Supreme Court's most important judgment in the civil rights struggle, its implications reaching far beyond the realm of public education. The judicial branch of the national government had spoken with rare decision.[13]

Because of this, those who had fought for civil rights cheered. The national government had tipped the balances. All over the country, black people rejoiced and prepared for a new dawn. Julius Chambers recalled that "we assumed that *Brown* was self-executing. The law had been announced and people would have to obey it. Wasn't that how things worked in America, even in white America." Sara Lightfoot, ten years old at the time, believed she saw "the veil of oppression lift from my parents' shoulders. It seemed they were standing taller." Even Marshall permitted himself a rare moment of elation. "I was so happy, I was numb," he wrote later. Yet he also recognized that hard work lay ahead, if as he firmly believed, school segregation could be eliminated throughout the country in "up to five years."[14]

Marshall, like most people in the civil rights movement, had underestimated the strength and the ferocity of white resistance to the decision. Moreover, like the textile workers of the 1930s, the NAACP, and all black southerners, would learn that national solutions, seemingly clear cut, could easily be evaded by regional and local resistance, through legal obfuscation and delay, through economic reprisals, and through violence and defiance of the law. Though the national government had indeed defined the law through its judicial arm, the executive and legislative branches for a long time lacked the will to enforce it. Into the vacuum thus created moved the forces of southern resistance. Far from ending school segregation within five years, as Marshall had so confidently predicted, in the fall of 1963, nearly ten years after *Brown*, just over 1 percent of southern black school children attended school with whites. So much for the aspirations of Julius Chambers, Sara Lightfoot, and all who, like them, believed that the national government had ended their struggle.[15]

The national government's executive branch had from time to time confronted southern resistance—but only as a last resort. In Little Rock, Arkansas, in 1957, when Governor Orval Faubus intervened to prevent the admission of nine black students to Central High School, he so blatantly defied federal court orders, as well as creating such a potentiality for widespread violence, that President Eisenhower was forced to send in the 101st Airborne to restore order, reassert federal authority—and ensure Central High was integrated. Similarly, in 1962, President Kennedy sent in troops to ensure James Meredith's enrolment at the University of Mississippi, again after a night of violence. The lesson was not lost on Alabama's Governor George Wallace. A mob had prevented the integration of the University of Alabama in 1956, without federal intervention. In 1963, after the Mississippi example, he stood aside at the last minute, and Vivian Malone and James Hood walked in the door. Yet in many similar situations there was no call for troops, there was no executive response, and the schools or colleges remained segregated.[16]

It was not until 1964, in the omnibus Civil Rights Act of that year, that the third branch of the national government, the Congress, joined the battle to impose the national solution mandated by the *Brown* decision ten years earlier. Title VI of the act empowered federal officials to cut off aid from all school districts that still practiced de jure segregation, at the same time insisting that the provision could not be used to impose racial quotas in schools. Though the act was primarily aimed at racial segregation in public accommodations and employment, this provision was nevertheless eventually to be used effectively to hasten the collapse of segregated schools; in the South, especially when applied in conjunction with the provisions of the Elementary and Secondary Education Act, part of Lyndon Johnson's vision of a "Great Society," which provided massive federal aid to the nation's schools and colleges, aid the South needed desperately. The three branches of the national government were finally working together to enforce the 1954 decision.[17]

There was still, however, much deliberate delay. When, in the fall of 1965, schools in Crawfordville, in Taliaferro County, Georgia, were scheduled for integration, white parents organized fleets of buses to take their children to all-white schools in neighboring Wilkes, Washington, and Lincoln Counties. The county school superintendent then closed the former white school, and police prevented black students getting on the buses with whites. Thus they were forced to return to their old school, and segregation continued. Black activists in Martin County, North Carolina, organized a boycott of all county schools in 1968 in protest at the continuation of the two systems there, given the quickening pace of desegregation elsewhere. Despite the increased federal pressure, and the carrot of federal funds, many southern school boards remained intransigent.[18]

Yet the climate was changing, as federal officials committed to school desegregation imposed their will, with the encouragement of President Johnson, who constantly urged them to "come down hard" on southern recalcitrants. "Get 'em!" he once reputedly ordered. "Get 'em! Get the last ones!" In March 1968, Department of Health, Education and Welfare (HEW) officials told those southern school districts where segregated systems still prevailed to submit plans for complete racial balance by the fall of 1969 or lose their federal funding. And as James Patterson points out, the enormous increase in federal aid since the Elementary and Secondary Education Act gave such officials the "power to help or to hurt." Reluctantly, angrily, the white South gave way and the national solution took, even in the Deep South. In 1965, only 2.23 percent of its black students attended majority-white schools. By 1968, 14 percent did—with far greater increases planned for 1969. There was still evasion, still subterfuge, still open defiance, but these were on the wane.[19]

Not even the election of a Republican president, Richard M. Nixon, who had openly sought the southern white vote by urging that the pace of social change be slowed and, in particular, that judicial activism be curbed, could do much to halt the pace of school desegregation in the South. The HEW activists stood their ground, while federal southern judges like John Minor Wisdom, impatient with the subterfuges of southern school boards, moved actively to end them. When a series of Mississippi school cases came to his Fifth Circuit Court of Appeals in 1966, he used the opportunity to do this. In *United States v. Jefferson County Board of Education*, he ruled that "the only adequate redress for a previously overt system-wide policy of segregation against Negroes as a collective entity is a system-wide policy of integration" and then issued specific instructions on how this was to be done, bringing the courts directly into the detailed business of operating southern schools. In 1968, the Supreme Court effectively endorsed, in *Green v. County School Board of New Kent County, Va,* Wisdom's interventionist approach. Henceforth courts could strike out all delaying tactics, all freedom of choice plans, all the subterfuges southerners had used to soften *Brown's* impact. Desegregation had to be real. Georgia governor Lester Maddox, when he read the decision, knew the game was up. Angrily, he "ordered all state flags to be flown at half-mast." He was right. In a very short period of time, *Green* ended de jure segregation in the public schools of the South.[20]

Green was the last civil rights decision in which Chief Justice Warren took part. He retired in 1968, to be followed within three years by three of his associates on what had become the most activist court of the twentieth century. President Nixon, who had promised to curb such activism, now had the chance to make good on his word. His choice for chief justice, Warren Burger, was a conservative Republican, but two of his other three nominees were more moderate. The third, William Rehnquist, a supporter of Senator Barry Goldwater's presidential bid in 1964, was clearly from the Right. Thus, the political complexion of the court, to the dismay of liberals, had been altered decisively, and they feared for the future of the school desegregation drive. They need not have done so. In two key decisions, the Burger Court soon showed that it had no interest in reversing the activist trend of the past decade. *Alexander v. Holmes County Board of Education* overturned an administration attempt to delay the desegregation timetable in Mississippi—causing George Wallace to observe that the Burger Court and the Warren Court were indistinguishable—while *Swann v. Charlotte-Mecklenburg County Board of Education* upheld the use of court-ordered busing of students to achieve racial balance in cities where residential segregation remained the norm. The impact of this decision was enormous. "After years of defying *Brown*," writes Dean Kotlowski, "southern whites chose to retreat with dignity rather than continue fighting." Added to *Green* and *Alexander*, it resulted in southern schools being more desegregated than those of the rest of the nation. Indeed, the focus of desegregation turned northward, where court-ordered busing to achieve racial balance caused violence and civic anger in cities like Boston and Denver that rivaled, if not exceeded, that formerly confined to the segregated South. Southern schools were as effectively desegregated as they could become. Problems remained, debate continued to rage, but henceforth it was over its effect rather than its prospect. The national response to this aspect of black southerners' struggles finally had its victory.[21]

The same could be said of the struggle for equal use of public accommodation and facilities. The Montgomery bus boycott had been about this issue, as had the sit-in campaign of 1960. Throughout the quickening civil rights drive, the exclusion from equal access had been the most visible symbol of inferiority, certainly the one most readily understood by white America. Martin Luther King repeatedly referred to it in his speeches, throughout the summer of 1963 it was the main emphasis in the South-wide mass demonstrations, and, as such, it was a key component of the Civil Rights Act of 1964. Title II outlawed discrimination in "such places of public accommodation as restaurants, motels, theaters and gas stations," heretofore the most obvious face of segregation.[22]

It was also the arena in which the South was most ready to concede defeat, indeed, scores of southern cities had already done so before the act's passage, while blacks and whites had been sharing aspects of each other's culture, especially music, for decades. After the act passed, most public facilities quickly moved to comply. Andrew Young recalled returning to a motel in St. Augustine, Florida, just five days after its enactment. The previous week a waitress had poured hot coffee over him, while the motel's manager had thrown hydrochloric acid in the pool to prevent Young and his group from using it. After the act, though, everything had changed. "We went back to the same restaurant," Young recalled, "and those people were just wonderful. They were apologetic. They said 'we were afraid of losing out on business. We didn't want to be the only ones to be integrated. But if everybody's got to do it, we've been ready for it for a long time. We're so glad the president signed this law and now we can be through these troubles.'" Throughout the urban South the response was similar, even in the small motels attached to owner-operated gas stations, historically the preserve of lower-class whites. A 1965 survey showed that only in Savannah and Jackson did significant pockets of discrimination remain.[23]

Change came more slowly to the rural South, where tradition often kept blacks at the back window of places where the law now permitted them through the door. In southwestern Louisiana, for example, Jacques Thibeaux, owner of a grocery-liquor store continued to refuse blacks permission to drink on the premises despite the law, while in all sorts of public facilities, especially the county courtrooms, blacks usually continued to sit on one side, whites on the other. Moreover, in town and country alike there were those determined to resist the hated law, violently if necessary. Two black servicemen, both in uniform, were arrested in Macon, Georgia, in 1964 as they attempted to wash their clothes in a previously segregated suburban laundromat. In Atlanta, Lester Maddox, owner of the Pick-Rick restaurant, issued his customers with pickax handles for use in beating any blacks seeking service there. When federal authorities moved to force him to comply with the law, he closed his doors rather than accommodate blacks. Other southern restaurateurs did the same, then reopened as "private clubs," usually short-lived. Maddox did not. Instead, he rode on the publicity his defiance gained him to the

Georgia statehouse. In the 1966 Democratic primaries, this outspoken but unknown segregationist defeated a galaxy of impressive opponents, including former governor Ellis Arnall and future president Jimmy Carter, before tackling Republican Howard H. Callaway in the election. A write-in campaign for Arnall resulted in an inconclusive result, and Maddox became governor on the vote of the Democratic legislature—the last overt segregationist to become so—and all because of his resistance to Title II. In Batesville, Mississippi, in February 1965, twenty-two high school students were "thrown out bodily" from a café they had attempted to integrate, while another closed rather than serve them. The next month, in Marks, all the restaurants closed once black students had tried to enter. In Indianola, the public library finally integrated, under pressure, but with all its tables and chairs removed. Throughout Mississippi, in fact, SNCC field workers found widespread defiance of the law, despite pleas from the governor down for compliance. Even Earle Johnston Jr., head of the State Sovereignty Commission, warned that the state could not afford the loss of federal aid that continued disobedience put at risk.[24]

Then, it should be remembered it was the refusal of the owner of the All Star Bowling Alley to open his doors to black patrons, again in defiance of the 1964 act, that was the precipitating event in the killings in Orangeburg. Resistance to it continued for a while, traditional patterns of segregation may have moderated its impact, yet historian Allan Matusow is surely right when he stresses that what is remarkable about Title II was the speed of its general acceptance, "the ease," he says, "with which white waitresses learned to be polite to black patrons, the routine mixing of the races at lunch counters and theaters." Again, the branches of the national government, working together, had ended a century of public discrimination, of the public humiliation of one group of southerners by another. That aspect of the struggle, too, was over.

The national solution to voter discrimination based on race had rather more mixed results. From 1957, the legislative and executive branches had moved against this—initially with great caution. Two civil rights acts were passed during the Eisenhower administration, in 1957 and 1960, the first since Reconstruction. Attorney General Herbert Brownell, who at least understood the need for some federal response to the quickening forces for change, hoped to get cabinet to support a strong four-part measure aimed at creating a civil rights commission to investigate southern violence, to establish a civil rights division within the Department of Justice, to strengthen existing measures protecting the right to vote, and, most important, to authorize the Justice Department to intervene in school desegregation suits. The president, under pressure from southern senators, at first supported only the voting rights section, and though the whole package was eventually passed, its provisions had been so watered down, especially its enforcement mechanisms, that Georgia's segregationist senator Richard Russell described it as "the sweetest victory in my twenty-five years as a senator." By 1959 not one voter had been added to the rolls as a result of its provisions. Acknowledging its failure, Congress passed another act in 1960 supposedly safeguarding the right to vote. It, too, had most of its substance removed along the way to the extent that one of its sponsors described it as "a crushing defeat." President Eisenhower had promised to remove the barriers to equal voting rights for America's black citizens. He had manifestly failed to do so. Nevertheless, as J. Morgan Kousser points out, the very passage of the 1957 act was a milestone, as for the first time since 1890 a Senate filibuster on a civil rights matter had been broken. In a changing political and social climate, this gave liberals some grounds for optimism.[25]

The omnibus civil rights bill of 1964, though its primary targets were discrimination in public accommodation, and then, after a liberal revolt on the house floor, job discrimination, also contained provisions aimed at guaranteeing the right to vote. In particular, it greatly reduced the power of local registrars to use literacy tests in a discriminatory way, as henceforth a sixth-grade education would be the national literacy standard. Moreover, minor errors in filling out registration forms could no longer be the excuse for disqualifying applicants, as southern registrars had been doing for decades. Indeed, both President Johnson and the civil rights leadership expected that the act should take care of the issue once and for all—no further national action would be needed.[26]

They were wrong, as an analysis of the 1964 election returns clearly showed. Despite the new provisions, in Mississippi, only 6 percent of voting age blacks were registered, 19 percent in Alabama, 32 percent in Louisiana—all states, incidentally, won by President Johnson's Republican opponent. Moreover, there was ample evidence that southern registrars were both ignoring or evading the provisions of the new act, often through such tested devices as opening their offices at irregular hours, or at times inconvenient to black southerners. Accordingly, the president decided on a final attempt to end the injustice through national action, even promising, in his 1965 State of the Union address, to eliminate "every remaining obstacle to the right and opportunity to vote." Yet he was vague as to timing, knowing that the Congress was in no mood to deal with further civil rights legislation, and that a comprehensive voting rights bill would be hard to pass.[27]

Again, Martin Luther King changed the national agenda when he decided to support a local campaign for voting rights in Selma, Alabama. Selma typified southern recalcitrance. Out of a voting age black population of 15,000 in 1965, only 383 were registered. With his swagger stick and his tin helmet, the sheriff, Jim Clark, was a caricature of the repressive white law enforcement officer, a man, said historian Allan Matusow, who "habitually lost his self-control at the sight of a marching Negro" and thus could be guaranteed to provide splendid images for the national television networks. The script went to plan, and the escalating violence, with Clark at the center, helped create a sympathetic national climate for new legislation. After the confrontation on the Edmund Pettus Bridge, which shocked the country, the president knew the time was right. Accordingly, on March 15 he addressed the nation, appropriated the words of the movement's anthem, and proposed legislation so comprehensive as to make further southern resistance futile. Again targeting literacy tests, its main provision was to make it automatic for federal registrars to take over in all states still using them where less than 50 percent of its citizens had been registered in 1964. As Matusow said, "In Mississippi, where less than half the state's voting age population was registered, either local officials would enroll blacks—literate or not—or the Johnson administration would do it for them." The same held true for Louisiana, Alabama, Georgia, South Carolina, Virginia, thirty-nine counties in North Carolina, and Alaska, one of a handful of nonsouthern states and counties caught by the bill. But its intention was to enfranchise southern blacks, and it succeeded in doing so. Johnson signed it into law on August 5, 1965, and in so doing took the biggest single step in imposing a national solution on the southern struggles.[28]

Of course, like all national actions, it took time to bite at the local level. Voter registration efforts by the SCLC were greatly expanded after the act's passage under the acronym SCOPE, for Southern Community Organization and Education Program. Initially, field workers' reports were depressingly familiar. John Worcester, director of a SCOPE project in

Wilcox County, Alabama, for example, told of routine police harassment, the disruption of rallies, even the shotgun shooting of eight local youths who were inside the Antioch Baptist Church. In Clayton, Alabama, SCOPE workers were arrested for "operating in Alabama too long without a permit," while in Albany, Georgia, blacks, discouraged by years of failure and repression, were slow to respond to calls to register. Four weeks after Johnson signed the Voting Rights Act, only eleven new voters had been added to the rolls. Moreover, there had been a noticeable increase of "police harassment" of SCOPE volunteers, mainly for driving offences. It was still hard going.[29]

Yet by the end of the year, the Voting Rights Act was clearly beginning to bite. The minutes of the Georgia Voters League in 1966 recorded a "slow but steady climb" in new black registrants after the act's passage. R. B. Cottonreader, director of the Butler County, Alabama, Scope Project, reported that of the county's 603 new registrants, 422 were black. Even in rural Mississippi, resistance was crumbling. Alice Blackwood reported in late 1965 from Sidon that the police no longer harassed voter registration workers there, partly because a group of local white women had come to their support. "The white women of Sidon told them [the local police] what would happen if they bothered them," she told Annell Ponder, and as a consequence voter registration was now proceeding relatively freely. By 1968, national statistics confirmed these local trends. In the six fully covered states of the Deep South, black registration had increased by 740,000 in three years, from 31 to 57 percent of the eligible population. Most impressive was Mississippi, from 6 to 44 percent, but Alabama, from 19 to 53 percent, and Louisiana, 32 to 60 percent, were not far behind. In Selma, Alabama, there were now 6,789 black voters poised to consign Jim Clark to oblivion. Scores of those like him, mayors, police chiefs, and sheriffs, were to be similarly dispatched in the years ahead. Others, including Alabama's George Wallace, found it expedient to renounce the old ways, and embrace their new constituency as the price of retaining power. "The act, then," Matusow aptly commented, "did nothing less than cleanse the poisoned atmosphere of southern politics."[30]

National action to end discrimination in voting was overwhelmingly successful, much more so than that directed at enabling textile workers to join labor unions without discrimination. Its most obvious effect was at the local and state levels. Since 1970 black voters have been essential to winning political coalitions. In the cities, the towns, and the villages of the

South, blacks were elected to the local positions of power historically denied them. Before long, the region's major cities—Richmond, Raleigh, Birmingham, Atlanta, Houston, Charlotte, and even Jackson, Mississippi —had each elected a black mayor, men who achieved power by combining black votes with those of liberal whites, just like Carl Stokes, the first African American to be elected mayor of a major American city, had done in Cleveland, Ohio. Once in office, working with biracial councils and boards of management, they transformed local administration, successfully building coalitions of local elites, including the predominantly white business leadership. In many small towns and hamlets of the South, where the brutal face of segregation went for so long unchecked, the franchise eventually had a transforming effect. Men like Jim Clark and "Bull" Connor were swept away, replaced often by African Americans such as Charleston's Reuben Greenberg or by whites who needed black votes to achieve office—and spoke and acted accordingly. Nowhere was the transformation more dramatic than in Mississippi, where by 1984, 75 percent of its eligible black citizens were registered. By 1992, there were more black elected officials there than in any other state, including twenty-eight black mayors. One was Unita Blackwell, who was "choppin cotton" at three dollars a day in 1964 when SNCC workers first came to Mayersville in Issaquena County. Politicized by the movement, she became a Freedom Democrat Party delegate to Atlantic City. Eventually, she was elected Mayersville's first black mayor, and in 1984 she addressed the Democrat National Convention as a leader of her state's delegation, a dramatic symbol of victory in the struggle. There were many like her throughout the region, including in Philadelphia, Mississippi, where Schwerner, Goodman, and Chaney had been murdered in 1964, and in symbolic Hancock County in eastern Georgia, which in 1968 became the first United States county since Reconstruction to come under black political control.[31]

In 1993, there were forty-two blacks in the Mississippi state legislature, again more than in any other state. Alabama was close, though; indeed, all southern state legislatures by the 1990s had a substantial African American membership. Some African Americans, like Jesse Oliver from Dallas, who steered a far-reaching health-care measure through the Texas legislature in 1986, or North Carolina's powerful House speaker, Dan Blue, or Ernest Finney, later South Carolina's first black Supreme Court judge since Reconstruction, became men of influence and power, able to build coalitions with powerful white political interests. Douglas

Wilder of Virginia was so skilled a political consensus builder that he was elected governor of Virginia in 1989, the only black to achieve the office. A longtime state senator, he was "not a threat" to the state's Democratic establishment, "he was a colleague." No other state has followed Virginia's example, yet the enfranchisement of blacks surely changed southern statehouses nonetheless. It paved the way to power for men like Georgia's Jimmy Carter or Arkansas's Bill Clinton, postsegregationists with powerful appeal to blacks and whites. It brought about the public repentance of George Wallace, who, having confessed his sins, was henceforth kept in power by the support of black voters whose enfranchisement he formerly had violently opposed. Such was the transforming effect of the national solution.[32]

Black southerners now sit in the U.S. House of Representatives. Some, like Georgia's John Lewis, are veterans of the 1960s and have achieved power and influence within the Democratic Party. Others, like Cynthia McKinney, again of Georgia, or North Carolina's Mel Watt, have largely grown up in the postsegregationist southern political world. Lewis represents an Atlanta constituency which is overwhelmingly black, and thus his experience parallels that of the first African Americans to represent nonsouthern districts in Washington. They came from the black districts of the nation's largest cities. Both McKinney and Watt, however, have had to build coalitions which cross racial lines, as electoral redistricting, upheld by the Supreme Court, have steadily reduced the number of winnable seats available to blacks in federal and southern state legislatures. Creative redistricting was, and is, the main mechanism by which the white political structure fought back against the Voting Rights Act, usually by redrawing boundaries in order to confine black voters to a few seats with overwhelmingly black majorities, while diluting their influence elsewhere. This, together with the post-1964 dominance of the Republican Party in the white South makes it harder for blacks to get elected on black votes alone. They will win fewer elections, as historian David Goldfield rightly observes, "by the strength of numbers." Thus the achievements of McKinney and Watt are not only impressive in themselves but also provide models for the future. All politically successful black southerners, however, be they from black majority districts or from mixed constituencies, owe their achievements to the 1965 Voting Rights Act. Without it, their "southern struggle" would have been far harder.[33]

John F. Kennedy decided not to include a ban on job discrimination in the civil rights bill he sent to Congress in June 1963. He thought it might jeopardize the whole package. What became Title VII of the 1964 act was added once the bill had left the White House, as civil rights activists allied with Congressional liberals to strengthen the bill's provisions. When finally passed, Title VII outlawed all discrimination in employment, making it unlawful practice "to fail or refuse to hire or to discharge any individual, or otherwise to discriminate against any individual with respect to his compensation, terms, conditions of privileges of employment, because of such individual's race, color, religion, sex or national origin" and created the Equal Employment Opportunity Commission (EEOC) to monitor the act and enforce compliance. The EEOC, hopefully, would deal with most complaints through "conference, conciliation and persuasion," but if these failed, Title VII gave it the power to bring civil action. After the act's passage, incidentally, Title VII, not even part of the original legislation, became, in Vice President Humphrey's words, "the heart of the Act. Nothing," he told a White House Conference in 1965, was "more important to the Negro in his struggle to free himself from the circle of frustration than the ability to have and to hold a good job." President Johnson made the same point a year later when he agreed that African Americans could not be full participants in "the American promise . . . until the job question is settled and settled rightly." Title VII was the national government's attempt to do this. Moreover, in its application to the South's flagship industry, cotton textiles, the two southern struggles, those of textile workers for the right to form unions and those of black southerners against the caste system which had constricted them for so long, came together.[34]

George C. Waldrep Jr., an executive with Burlington Industries, had no doubt as to the 1964 Civil Rights Act's importance in integrating the textile industry. It was, he said, "the driving force behind the integration of the plants." Before its passage, the industry had been almost entirely white, with those few blacks who worked in it confined to nonproduction jobs, restricted to service or janitorial positions, sweeping the areas where white workers operated the machinery or hauling the heavy bales of finished product. Calvin Quarles recalled that when he started sweeping at the Eagle and Phoenix Mill in Columbus, Georgia, in 1952, "you wasn't even supposed to go down an alley where a white person was. You had to get out that alley when they come in, and then when they got out of the way, then go and sweep the alley." In South Carolina, state law reinforced southern custom to keep textile production white. South Carolina's Segregation Act of 1915, which was still on the books in 1960, made it illegal for anyone "engaged in the business of cotton textile manufacturing . . . to allow operatives of different races to labor and work together within the same room." Those few mills like Cone Mills in Greensboro, North Carolina, which had used blacks on production work before 1964 had confined them to the lowest-paying and most unpleasant work, leaving the prestigious spinning and weaving jobs still completely white. For civil rights activists, the industry was in 1964 what it always had been, "a symbol of the racist South."[35]

Yet those same activists saw its potential as a source of employment opportunity for blacks. Most jobs, even the most prestigious ones, could easily be learned, and had been so for decades by white southerners forced to leave their farm or their mountains. There was no need for prior industrial experience, an excuse employers in other industries had frequently used to deny jobs to blacks. Title VII, civil rights lawyers believed, would provide the means to force the industry open, and they quickly moved to do so once the act had been passed. As Julius Chambers, the attorney responsible for bringing most lawsuits against the mills, recalled, it was the low skill base required that made it such an easy target—that and its strategic importance to the industrial South. "One could sort of apply general assumptions that most people would be able to operate a machine," he told historian Tim Minchin. "You could make some general assumptions that just about everybody would be able to do it."[36]

Of course, as did Thurgood Marshall and his team after the *Brown* decision, or even the CIO's leaders following the passage of the Wagner Act, Chambers and his colleagues greatly underestimated the tenacity with which whites resisted Title VII and the subterfuges they would resort to in order to avoid full compliance. For a start, the 1964 act did not become effective until July 1965. Most mills postponed placing blacks in traditionally white jobs until that date, and at first hired only a trickle, deliberately, as their records showed, to avoid charges of discrimination, not unlike the token school desegregation plans which followed *Brown*. But the charges and the lawsuits came anyway, and as they did blacks came into the mills in ever increasing numbers. Often the filing of EEOC charges against textile companies was sufficient to change their hiring policies. Management, realizing it they would have to prove in federal court that they did not discriminate, decided that further resistance was useless. An EEOC study in South Carolina in 1967, for example, reported a surge in the hiring of blacks in June and July, four times as great as any previous two-month period. By the end of the year, of the 6,000 new operatives hired since January, 4,000 were African American. Moreover, as the managers of J. P. Stevens told their employees, equal employment opportunity was federal law; to resist was not only fruitless, it could result in them losing their jobs. Textile mills all over the South needed government business to survive. They had no hope of getting it if they ignored Title VII. Thus white employers and employees alike were in a common situation. They may not have agreed with integration, but they had no choice but to accept it. Recalled Fletcher Beck of Rock Hill, South Carolina, "My feeling was the reason they were changing the hiring practices and hiring blacks was that they were complying with the law." He was right. National action had begun to work.[37]

Much more was changed by Title VII than the hiring policies of southern mill management. In *Ellison v. Rock Hill Printing and Finishing Company*, federal law nullified the 1915 South Carolina statute requiring segregation in the state's textile mills. Henceforth, every facility in the mill was to be integrated, the toilets, the water fountains, the showers, the changing rooms, the lunch facilities, the time clocks—everything. As Minchin writes, "These were major changes in workers' lives," especially as the workplace was where blacks and whites were most in contact. The significance of the change was described poignantly by Oscar Gill, one of the plaintiffs in *Ellison*. Before the Civil Rights Act, Rock Hill Printing was completely segregated, its few black employees not even allowed in the main building. Now, he said, the mill had been transformed. He was able to mix with the whites there. "We sat down and ate together," he said. "I'd sit down with my white brothers . . . and nobody said nothing. They all seemed to like me, and I liked them." Not everyone had such positive experiences. At the Celanese Fibers Plant in Rome, Georgia, some white workers simply refused to use the cafeteria once it was integrated. They might have to work beside "niggers" henceforth, they said, but they "wouldn't go eat with them." Similarly, some whites refused to use the newly upgraded locker rooms and showers once integration came. "I'm not going to take no bath with no nigger," shouted one worker at a meeting called by management to explain the changes, before angrily walking out of the hall. Some black workers had their clothes and personal property damaged in protest at integration, yet in a world where rigid social separation had persisted for so long, Title VII transformed the working lives and social interaction of thousands of southerners, black and white.[38]

Then, there was the matter of promotion, of progress up the ladder of success. African American workers who thought that getting into the production rooms was hard enough, found that getting promoted to more skilled or even white collar jobs was infinitely more difficult, and it was in this area that discrimination persisted longer. Management may have been forced to integrate by the federal government, and their white workers had accepted it. Promoting blacks over whites was another matter altogether, and here, for a time, the line was drawn, until it became the main concern for black textile workers in the 1970s. As white workers with less seniority were promoted above them, as pay differentials became more obvious, they often experienced "alienation, anger, and disillusionment," and so they returned to the courts. In February 1971, a group of black male employees from Fieldcrest Mills in Eden, North Carolina, initiated a major class-action suit, the first of its kind. In *Galloway v. Fieldcrest Mills*, they alleged that blacks were restricted to lower-paying jobs and were systematically refused promotion opportunities. The data they produced to support their case was most impressive, and they eventually won. More important, they inspired other African American workers to do likewise. The largest and most significant of these cases was *Sledge v. J. P. Stevens*, involving more than 3,000 petitioners, against the nation's second largest textile company. Eventually, it too was won, after years of testimony and argument. Other victories followed, some African Americans were promoted or reclassified as a result, yet progress remained painfully slow. Moreover, even as the cases were making their way through the various tribunals and courts, the southern textile industry as a whole was declining. Blacks won the right to advance up the ladder precisely as the ladder was losing its rungs. In that sense, victory was bittersweet.[39]

Sledge v. J. P. Stevens was not only brought as a result of the company's discriminatory promotion policies but also aimed at ending the pattern of discrimination against the hiring of black women. There is little doubt that once the 1964 act had integrated the mills, it was much easier for males to get through the doorways. In an industry which traditionally had hired white women in large numbers, black women initially "found it very difficult to secure textile jobs and faced far more discrimination in hiring than their male counterparts." Moreover, those who were taken on too often found themselves in the most unpleasant, lowest-paying positions, at times doing heavy work previously reserved for white males. And, much more than black men, they were likely to face hostility and abuse from their white co-workers. Gladys Trawick of Andalusia, Alabama, one of the first black women to work in production, recalled that the white workers called her all sorts of names, "but we were told that when they hired us, that we would be called names." She had not bargained for threats to her family, however, nor to her home if she continued to work there. She believed "race relations in the mill were worse than those in the town as a whole." White workers "just didn't want you in because they felt they were superior to you, and you could have the same jobs as they did." Hundreds of black women felt as Trawick did, yet despite this they enjoyed the work. Getting into the mills was still the main priority, and that remained hard. Company records produced at court and EEOC hearings showed that as late as 1974 white women were hired at four times the rate of black females.[40]

In time the situation improved, partly due to lawsuits or the threat of such action. Faced with its likelihood, several of the larger companies began to hire black women in much greater numbers, even for the better-paying production jobs that white women had held exclusively. Management also started to promote them; indeed, by the late 1970s the data showed that they were moving into the better jobs at a greater rate than black men. Another reason was their increasing activism; more than the men they engaged in union activity, as Laura Ann Pope's story amply shows. She organized the Oneita Knitting Mills in Andrews, South Carolina, then led her fellow workers out in January 1973, under the banner of the TWUA, until the company capitulated, conceding most union demands, including an end to discriminatory hiring and promotion practices because of race or gender. As mentioned earlier, the TWUA leadership, frankly amazed at the comprehensive victory, attributed it to "the overwhelming support and militancy of the black women strikers." To the extent that the employment of blacks in the South's textile mills did lead to some increase in union activism and a renewed determination to organize, it brought together these two components of the southern struggles. Historian Michelle Haberland, incidentally, found the same connections in the southern apparel industry. Her study of the Vanity Fair factory in Jackson, Alabama, showed that after the 1964 act had forced the company, reluctantly, to hire black women, the International Ladies Garment Workers Union had a new and fertile field with which to work. Yet the downside also remained; employers could still use the race issue as they had always done, to divide their workers and blunt union solidarity. Union organizers knew this well. Though the presence of blacks in the mills introduced a new and militant group to work with, and though some whites were also radicalized as a result, the racial divide was always there, and had to be bridged, sometimes painfully, often slowly, mill by mill—and made even more difficult by the industry's post-1970s decline. It is still there, slowing the progress of all southern workers, black and white.[41]

Moreover, the resurgence of local activity in southern mills has to be set against the steady decline of textile unionism as a whole, and indeed of the industry itself. The TWUA's decline in membership and influence could not be reversed, despite the eventual settling of the internal disputes which had paralyzed it for so long. In 1972, Sol Stetin, who had first joined the UTW in 1933, took over as head, determined to hold the organization together, and to provide what help he could to those southern locals embroiled in battles with management. The task was too great, yet southern director Scott Hoyman was in no doubt that had Stetin not supported them, local unionists would have lost both the Oneita strike and the Elkin, North Carolina, strike against the Chatham Manufacturing Company in 1972. They were to be among the TWUA's last southern victories. Its treasury empty, its membership falling away, the TWUA voted itself out of existence in 1976 when members agreed to a merger with Murray Finley's Amalgamated Clothing Workers to form the Amalgamated Clothing and Textile Workers Union (ACTWU). Southern textile struggles in the future would be fought under a new banner.[42]

The 1964 Civil Rights Act affected all southern industries, not just textiles, and in each there was delay and evasion at first, as employers attempted to preserve as much of past practice as they possibly could. Tim Minchin's recent study of the integration of the paper industry chronicles a depressing story of resistance by employers and the white-dominated union. Indeed, they worked together to limit the effect of Title VII in what had been a thoroughly segregated industry, with every job racially designated black or white. Again it took constant recourse to the EEOC and the civil courts, action defined by the 1964 act, before the situation changed. Yet finally, national action worked to ameliorate these inequalities, as it had done in textiles. The story was the same across the face of southern industry—initial joy at the passage of the act quickly tempered by the realization that there was still hard work to be done to make its provisions work. Even after court and commission challenges had succeeded, too often blacks found that the industries to which they at last had equal access, as with steel in Alabama or textiles in general, were in decline. Always their victories were bittersweet.[43]

A final result of Title VII remains to be discussed. When Leander Perez, segregationist boss of Plaquemine Parish, Louisiana, needed labor, it was his practice simply to round up local blacks and put them to work. In September 1965, a hurricane hit the parish, damaging it extensively and forcing nearly 500 people, almost all black, from their homes and into a Red Cross center opened at Scottsville School in La Grange. When Perez decided it was time to clean up the storm damage, he simply went to the school, rounded up these refugees at gunpoint, and forced them to start the clean-up. He also commandeered the school bus and its driver and violently threatened those Red Cross officials and teachers who protested this. When Andrea Lawrence, the school principal, tried to intervene, Perez reportedly called her a "nigger," then said to the staff, "Damn what you have to do, get your asses on that bus." In Placquemine Parish, where his word was still law, Perez was used to obedience from the black citizens.[44]

The arch-segregationist's world was changing, however. These particular citizens found it expedient to obey him at the time and get on the bus, but after the incident was over they complained to the FBI, the NAACP, and, later, President Johnson himself. In time, Perez found himself in court, charged with several violations of the 1964 Civil Rights Act, including Title VII's provisions against unfair employment practices. The reach of the national solution had finally caught up with him, and with Plaquemine Parish.[45]

Eventually, then, these southern struggles, white textile workers for economic justice, black southerners for their civil rights, became the subject of national concern and action. The three branches of the federal government became actively involved, and if their solutions were not always totally successful, and often the result of political expedience or compromise, they nevertheless transformed the boundaries within which black southerners had formerly lived. As a result, they profoundly altered the white South as well.

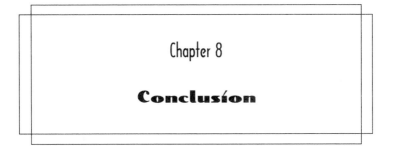

Chapter 8

Conclusion

This book has been highly selective. Its concern has not been to examine the broad sweep of racial and class conflict in the twentieth-century South but to focus in a comparative way on two key areas of struggle, that of white textile workers to achieve economic justice through union power and that of black southerners to cleanse their region of the evils of segregation through both legal action and mass protest. This gives it its originality, its point of emphasis, but consequently, much of importance has been left out. Throughout the twentieth century, as has been noted, black southerners also fought for economic justice and civil rights through union activism—though often in segregated locals, with their white co-unionists bitterly opposed. Tim Minchin has recently described in detail the attempts of black paper workers, in an industry with "more segregated locals than any other industry in the South," to achieve a measure of economic and racial justice through union activity. For decades progress was painfully slow, as white executives and white workers alike fought them every step of the way. But after the 1964 Civil Rights Act, when Title VII provided access to the courts in discrimination disputes, together with the end of racially segregated locals, the balance was altered. White union officials and black civil rights leaders now joined to help African American unionists in their court battles, to the extent that by 1990 the traditional practices of discrimination in the industry were finally of the past. But it had been a long struggle.[1]

Similarly, Michael Honey has shown that an earlier generation of black workers had used their unions as a means of fighting the battle for civil rights. From the 1930s, African Americans in Memphis had fought against discrimination through militant union action—again either through segregated locals or unions they controlled. Eventually, through the efforts of the CIO's national leadership, some biracial unions were created in the city. Their formation "did not abolish racism, but could and did lead to important changes in the thinking of many whites." Yet coming together in unions "was only one step toward breaking down white prejudices." The abandonment of "deep-seated racial attitudes" took much longer to occur, if indeed it ever did. In some southern industries, of course, black workers predominated, and there much more militant action was possible. The black steel workers of Birmingham, Alabama, had showed this dramatically in the early days of CIO activity there. So did tobacco workers—mainly black, mainly women—at the Reynolds Tobacco Company plant in Winston-Salem, then the largest in the world, when they staged their successful strike in June 1943. There were 10,000 workers in the Reynolds plant, including "the largest concentration of black workers in the South," working in a strictly segregated environment, doing the dirtiest and most dangerous of jobs. Shunned as union material by the conservative Tobacco Workers International Union (TWIU AFL), they had been organized instead by the leftist United Cannery Agricultural Packinghouse and Allied Workers of America–CIO (UCAPAWA), soon to change its name to the Food, Tobacco, Agricultural and Allied Workers of America (FTA). In June 1943, black women in one of the departments stopped work to protest specified grievances, including a recent speedup. Quickly this broadened into a plant-wide strike, forcing Reynolds to agree to an NLRB election, which the CIO union won. As a result, Local 22 of the FTA was formed. The victory was significant, not only because both black and white workers gained some improvement in their working conditions but also because the continued presence and strength of the union gave them, for a time, a new visibility and strength in the Winston-Salem community, until cold war politics destroyed the FTA and its locals. Still, the point is made. African Americans, working within segregated locals, or in CIO locals where they formed a majority of members, had a tradition of fighting for their civil rights which predated the wider struggle of the 1960s.[2]

The story of Winston-Salem's Local 22 has a particular poignancy, for it showed, briefly, what might have been in the South. For a time, white and black tobacco workers transcended the barriers of race. They worked together in the union, bringing some improvement to their workplace and to their community. Both black and white votes were necessary to secure the election of an African American minister to the Winston-Salem Board of Aldermen in 1947, the first to defeat a white candidate anywhere in the South since Reconstruction. Black and white unionists, too, had provided a year earlier the crucial votes in Rep. John Folger's victory in North Carolina's Fifth Congressional District. Folger, a New Dealer and CIO supporter, had faced a fierce challenge from an avowedly antilabor opponent. But the strength of black and white workers, together, won the victory. Yet the forces arrayed against Local 22, and those few similar examples of interracial action, were too strong. Race won out against class. Local 22 had lost its charter by 1950, and the southern labor force remained divided along racial lines, despite such brief glimpses of hope. Both white and black workers suffered as a result; segregation hurt them all.[3]

In the textile mills, not even such fragile exceptions as Local 22 were possible, given the racial exclusivity of the work force, and here lies even deeper sadness. This book has compared the struggles of southern mill workers for economic justice to that of blacks fighting for an end to the caste system, of which economic injustice was a part. They displayed the same strength of leadership, especially at the local level, they used the same symbols—the message of the Scriptures and of the wellsprings of their culture—to sustain them. In so many ways, they fought a common fight. Moreover, they were opposed by the same enemies using the same weapons: terror, state power, police repression, economic reprisal, the destruction of livelihood. And yet they remained enemies to each other, until the great civil rights legislation of the 1960s changed forever the parameters of the American South. This has been the purpose of this book, to show how much these two groups of southerners shared as they fought their class battles. Yet they could not fight them together. The power of racial division, stemming from the depths of southern history, was far too strong. That is the greatest tragedy of all.

Black southerners, in general, found the organized labor movement rather lukewarm to their concerns, for organizers were always much more sensitive to the fears and prejudices of white workers. Race kept the white and black female tobacco workers of Durham, North Carolina, divided, despite the efforts of labor activists to stress the commonalties of class and gender. They remained divided until the post–civil rights era. One of the reasons commonly advanced for the failure of Operation Dixie in the immediate postwar years was the CIO's policy on interracial unions. Employers could and did raise the specter of race mixing as the inevitable consequence of unionization—the CIO would "force their daughters to work with Negro girls and would subject them to fines if they refused to work under Negro overseers and second hands," they warned—while local CIO organizers themselves did little to mobilize black workers, fearful of antagonizing the white textile workers whose support would determine the campaign's success. As the black struggle for equality quickened, African Americans became increasingly impatient with the labor movement, believing it insensitive to their demands. They had considerable justice on their side, yet as historian Alan Draper has brilliantly shown, labor leaders were classic victims of Gunnar Myrdal's American dilemma. Belatedly aware that a black-white working-class coalition would not "emerge spontaneously in the South" despite the heady enthusiasm of the liberal optimists of the SCHW in 1945, they eventually realized that their white members enjoyed racial privileges under segregation that integration, whether of the local or the larger society, profoundly threatened. The AFL-CIO did aid the black struggle, but in a measured manner, and usually from well behind the front lines. Only after Title VII had profoundly altered the composition of the southern work force was a frontal approach possible, and then often with black leadership of formerly all-white locals. By then, it was too late, and once more we are left wondering what might have been had, like Myles Horton, more CIO activists recognized the futility of treating one group of southern workers differently from the other. But his was a forlorn voice, and as a result, all southern workers were the losers. They still are.[4]

The southern struggles discussed in this book are about social and economic justice. That is their common denominator. In their determination to end the conditions of discrimination under which they lived, the white southerners of Marion and Honea Path and the black southerners of Birmingham and Orangeburg and Fayette County, Tennessee, were at one. They themselves did not see it that way, as the dividers of race and history remained too strong. Yet as we have reflected on their struggles, on their leadership, their local strength, the sustaining power of their women leaders, and on their Christian faith, even the mechanisms by which those who opposed them so vehemently sought to maintain their control, commonalties have nonetheless emerged. And in the end, blacks and whites alike sought the aid of the national government to bring them some measure of victory. Charles Joyner writes movingly and truly of the "shared traditions" of southern folk culture, traditions which have always had the potential to bridge the racial divide. In their struggles, black and white southerners alike have helped confirm this wisdom.[5]

Notes

Chapter 1. Introduction

1. Dittmer, *Local People*, passim.

2. For Marion, see Tippett, *Southern Labor*, 109–55. For Honea Path, see Simon, *Fabric of Defeat*, 115–18; Irons, *Testing the New Deal*, 147–50; and my own *General Textile Strike of 1934*.

3. Reggie Robinson, field reports, January 6–12, 13–19, 21–26, March 31–April 6, 1963, all in Student Non-violent Coordinating Committee Papers, 1959–1972, Series XV State Project Files, 1960–1968 (hereafter cited as SNCC Papers XV), Reel 40, File 237.

4. Bulletin from SNCC National Headquarters, February 9, 1968. Jack Nelson, "Orangeburg: A Tragedy of Police Panic and Official Defensiveness," reprint from *Los Angeles Times*, in SNCC Papers XV, Reel 40, File 239. *New York Times*, February 9, 1968. For the background to the shooting, see Carson, *In Struggle*, 249–50. Sellers with Terrell, *River of No Return*, 206–28. Nelson and Bass, *Orangeburg Massacre*, passim.

5. Nelson and Bass, *Orangeburg Massacre*, passim.

6. Ibid.

7. Nelson, "Orangeburg."

8. Dunbar, *Against the Grain*, 1–14. Honey, *Southern Labor and Black Civil Rights*, 1–10. Minchin, *Color of Work*, passim. Kelley, *Hammer and Hoe*, 138–52.

9. Korstad, "Daybreak of Freedom," passim. Korstad's revised dissertation was published in June 2003, titled *Civil Rights Unionism*.

Chapter 2. The Story of the Struggles

1. Hall et al., *Like a Family*, 215–17. Tippett, *Southern Labor*, 135–39. Mary Heaton Vorse, "Eye Witnesses Describe the Marion Massacre," newsletter found in American Civil Liberties Union Papers (microfilm), Reel 65, New York Public Library (hereafter cited as ACLU Papers).

2. *Asheville Citizen*, October 3, 1929. *Marion Progress*, October 3, 1929. Tippett,

Southern Labor, 64–66, 135–41. Hall et al., *Like a Family,* 213–15; Salmond, *Gastonia,* passim.

3. Hall, Korstad, and Leloudis, "Cotton Mill People," 245. See also Waldrep, *Southern Workers,* 11–18; Hall et al., *Like a Family,* passim; Hodges, *New Deal Labor Policy,* passim; and Irons, *Testing the New Deal,* 13–15.

4. Salmond, *Gastonia,* 2–3. Herman Newton Truitt, interview with Allen Tullos, December 5, 1978, January 19, 30, 1979, Southern Oral History Collection (hereafter cited as SOHC), Southern Historical Collection, Wilson Library, University of North Carolina at Chapel Hill (hereafter cited as SHC). Wright, *Old South, New South,* 124–32.

5. Hodges, *New Deal Labor Policy,* 26–27. Waldrep, *Southern Workers,* 19–20. Hall, Korstad, and Leloudis, "Cotton Mill People," 247–54. Hall et al., *Like a Family,* 106–80.

6. Salmond, *Gastonia,* 5–6. Wright, *Old South, New South,* 139–46; Flamming, *Creating the Modern South,* 58–59, 97–104.

7. Wright, *Old South, New South,* 150. Flamming, *Creating the Modern South,* 112.

8. Wright, *Old South, New South,* 147–48. Irons, *Testing the New Deal,* 21–23.

9. Salmond, *Gastonia,* 7. Hall, Korstad, and Leloudis, "Cotton Mill People," 266.

10. Brooks, "United Textile Workers," 223–37. McCartin, *Labor's Great War,* 166–67. Irons, *Testing the New Deal,* 20–22.

11. Salmond, *Gastonia,* 7–8. Irons, *Testing the New Deal,* 19–22. Hall et al., *Like a Family,* 187–95.

12. Tippett, *Southern Labor,* 54. Hall et al., *Like a Family,* 240–48. Salmond, *Gastonia,* 8. Irons, *Testing the New Deal,* 22. Waldrep, *Southern Workers,* 32–33.

13. Salmond, *Gastonia,* 9. Irons, *Testing the New Deal,* 22–23.

14. Salmond, *Gastonia,* 9. Flamming, *Creating the Modern South,* 184–85. Irons, *Testing the New Deal,* 22–25.

15. Irons, *Testing the New Deal,* 32–34. Tippett, *Southern Labor,* passim.

16. Salmond, *Gastonia,* passim. Hall et al., *Like a Family,* 213–15. Tippett, *Southern Labor,* passim.

17. Hall et al., *Like a Family,* 217–19. Tippett, *Southern Labor,* 235–40, 262–65.

18. Bellush, *Failure of the NRA,* 6–11. Hodges, *New Deal Labor Policy,* 45–53. Simon, *Fabric of Defeat,* 87–89.

19. Brooks, "United Textile Workers," 349–51. Irons, *Testing the New Deal,* 101. Hodges, *New Deal Labor Policy,* 60–70. Hall et al., *Like a Family,* 307–8. Kennedy, "General Strike," 10–11. See also my own *General Textile Strike of 1934.*

20. Carl Welch to President Roosevelt, December 11, 1933, Records of the National Recovery Administration, RG 9, National Archives, Washington D.C., Records Relating to Employee complaints in the Textile Industry, File 398, Employee Complaints.

21. Simon, *Fabric of Defeat,* 96–101.

22. *New York Times,* August 28, 29, 30, 31, September 1, 1934. *Birmingham Age-*

Herald, July 17, 18, 19, 1934. Hoffman, "United Textile Workers," 190–97. Hodges, *New Deal Labor Policy,* 90–104. Irons, *Testing the New Deal,* 113–19.

23. Transcripts of interviews made for the documentary film *The Uprising of 1934* (hereafter cited as Film Transcripts), Box 23, Honea Path, South Carolina, Southern Labor Archives, Georgia State University. Mack Fretwell Duncan, interview by Allen Tullos, June 7, August 30, 1979, SOHC. Duplessis, "Massacre at Honea Path," 60–63. *Anderson Independent,* September 6, 7, 1934. *State,* Columbia, South Carolina, September 6, 7, 1934. Simon, *Fabric of Defeat,* 116–19. Irons, *Testing the New Deal,* 147–50. For a survey of the strike as both a national and a local event, see Salmond, *General Textile Strike of 1934.*

24. Irons, *Testing the New Deal,* 150. Hall et al., *Like a Family,* 347–54.

25. Waldrep, *Southern Workers,* 86–112. Irons, *Testing the New Deal,* 154–69.

26. Zieger, *CIO,* 75–78. Hodges, *New Deal Labor Policy,* 116–18. Irons, *Testing the New Deal,* 169–73. Paul Christopher to Gorman, March 3, December 31, 1936, February 22, 1937, Box 1867, UTW Records, AFL-CIO Region 8 Records, 1933–1969, Southern Labor Archives, Georgia State University.

27. Minchin, *What Do We Need,* 27–31. See also Griffith, *Crisis of American Labor,* passim.

28. Minchin, *What Do We Need,* 37–43.

29. Ibid., 44–47. Salmond, *Miss Lucy of the CIO,* 124–45.

30. Minchin, *What Do We Need,* 48–68.

31. Ibid., 154–76. Daniel, *Culture of Misfortune,* 184–205.

32. Lewis, *Cheap and Contented Labor,* 26. Tippett, *Southern Labor,* 110–11.

33. Lewis, *Cheap and Contented Labor,* 5. Tippett, *Southern Labor,* 110–12.

34. Tippett, *Southern Labor,* 117–55. Hall et al., *Like a Family,* 218. *Justice—North Carolina Style,* ACLU pamphlet in North Carolina Collection, Wilson Library, University of North Carolina at Chapel Hill, 11–13.

35. Tippett, *Southern Labor,* 125. Jack Herling to N.T. and P.P., July 31, 1929, ACLU Papers, Reel 69.

36. Irons, *Testing the New Deal,* 135. Hall et al., *Like a Family,* 233–35. Vesta Finley and Sam Finley, interview with Mary Frederickson and Marion Roydhouse, July 22, 1975, SOHC (hereafter cited as Finley interview).

37. Salmond, *My Mind Set on Freedom,* 132–33. There are many good short histories of the civil rights movement. Among the best are Sitkoff, *Struggle for Black Equality;* Marable, *Race, Reform and Rebellion;* and Powledge, *Free at Last.*

38. Eagles, "Towards New Histories," 815–48. Salmond, *My Mind Set on Freedom,* 55.

39. Salmond, *My Mind Set on Freedom,* 72–77, 123–25.

40. Ibid., 79–80.

41. Ibid., 126–48.

42. Nelson and Bass, *Orangeburg Massacre,* 3–11, 24–25, 174. Salmond, *My Mind Set on Freedom,* 64–67. Grant, *Ella Baker,* 105–46. Ransby, *Ella Baker,* 273–74.

43. Salmond, *My Mind Set on Freedom,* 87–93.

44. Ibid., 4–9, 23–25.

45. Ibid., 27–50.

46. Ibid., 81–86. SNCC Papers XV, Reel 38, File 119, and Reel 40, Files 241, 242.

47. Nelson and Bass, *Orangeburg Massacre*, 73–74, 90, 95–96. Branch, *Pillar of Fire*, 280–81, 324, 326.

48. Salmond, *My Mind Set on Freedom*, 10–14. Kelley, *Hammer and Hoe*, 36–56.

49. Feldman, *Politics*, 54, 221–25, 249. Egerton, *Speak Now Against the Day*, 53–56. Sullivan, *Days of Hope*, 141–43.

50. Sullivan, *Days of Hope*, 194, 202–7. Salmond, "Fellowship of Southern Churchmen," 179–99.

51. Tyson, *Radio Free Dixie*, passim, but especially 1–3, 86–89. For Columbia, see the excellent recent study by O'Brien, *The Color of the Law*.

52.   See Minchin, *Hiring the Black Worker*, passim.

53. Kelley, *Hammer and Hoe*, passim. Honey, *Southern Labor and Black Civil Rights*. Michael Honey, "Martin Luther King Jr., the Crisis of the Black Working Class, and the Memphis Sanitation Strike," in Zieger, *Southern Labor in Transition*, 146–69. Michael Honey, "Industrial Unionism and Racial Justice," in Zieger, *Organized Labor*, 135–57. Minchin, *Color of Work*.

54. Daniel, *Lost Revolutions*, passim.

55. O'Brien, *Color of the Law*, passim.

Chapter 3. Local Men, Local Women

1. Salmond, *Gastonia*, 126–27.

2. *Charlotte Observer*, September 15, 1929, November 25, 1977; *Daily Worker*, September 16, 1929. Salmond, *Gastonia*, 127–28, 187–88.

3. Salmond, *Gastonia*, 50–51. Haessly, "Mill Mother's Lament," 1–4.

4. Haessly, "Mill Mother's Lament," 4–19.

5. Salmond, *Gastonia*, 61–62. Beal, *Proletarian Journey*, 153–59. *Charlotte Observer*, May 16, 19, 1929. *News and Observer*, September 18, 1929.

6. *Baltimore Evening Sun*, September 19, 1929.

7. Lee, *For Freedom's Sake*, 10, 14.

8. Ibid., 44–46.

9. Ibid., 47–48.

10. Fannie Lou Hamer, Open Letter from Fannie Lou Hamer, September 30, 1963, and interview with Hamer, March 19, 1964, SNCC Papers XV, Reel 38, File 122. Lee, *For Freedom's Sake*, 48–51.

11. Interview with Hamer, March 17, 1964, SNCC Papers XV, Reel 38, File 122.

12. Lee, *For Freedom's Sake*, 87–89.

13. Ibid., 25–33.

14. Ibid., 166–67, 177–78.

15. Finley interview. Tippett, *Southern Labor*, 159, 164–65. Hall et al., *Like a Family*, 215, 225, 233.

16. Irons, *Testing the New Deal*, 100. *Atlanta Constitution*, September 17, 18, 19, 1934. *Newnan Herald*, September 21, 1934. Film Transcripts, Boxes 7 and 9, East Newnan, Georgia. *New York Times*, November 15, 1936.

17. Minchin, *What Do We Need*, 91–98, 101.

18. Minchin, *Hiring the Black Worker*, 248–51.

19. Dittmer, *Local People*, 49, 101–3, 121–24, 166–67.

20. For what follows, I am entirely indebted to an excellent article by David C. Carter. See Carter, "Williamston Freedom Movement," 1–42.

21. Ibid., 13, 16–17, 20–22, 35–36, 41–42.

22. SNCC Papers XV, Reel 40, Files 241, 242.

23. Statement of John McFerren, May 13, 1960; of O. D. Maclin, May 13, 1960; of Harpman Jameson, May 13, 1960, all in Papers of the National Association for the Advancement of Colored People, Part 20 White Resistance and Reprisals, 1956–1965 (hereafter cited as 20 White Resistance), Reel 11, File 0424.

24. Report on a visit to Fayette and Haywood Counties, Tennessee, January 3, 4, 5, 1961, by Ross Anderson, Wallace Nelson, and Maurice McCrackin of Peacemakers, 20 White Resistance, Reel 11, File 0888.

25. Ibid.

26. Ibid. Salmond, *Gastonia*, 60–61, 74–75. Dunbar, *Against the Grain*, 178–80.

27. Gloster B. Current to Roy Wilkins, December 29, 1960, 20 White Resistance, Reel 11, File 0642.

28. Ibid. See also NAACP Press Releases, Fayette County; Gloster Current to H. T. Lockard, January 24, 1961; memo of telephone conversation, January 30, 1961, all in 20 White Resistance, Reel 11, File 0888.

29. NAACP Press Release, January 3, 1961; John A. Morsell, Assistant to the Executive Secretary, NAACP to Barry Gray, January 31, 1961, both in 20 White Resistance, Reel 11, File 0888.

30. J. Francis Polhaus, Counsel, Washington Bureau, NAACP to Gloster Current, November 24, 1961; L. C. Bates to Current, December 11, 1961; Morsell to Prof. A.J.C. Priest, Law School, University of Virginia, April 26, 1961; Current to Robert L. Carter, February 2, 1962, all in 20 White Resistance, Reel 11, File 0888. *New York Times*, June 15, 1961.

31. *Charlotte Observer*, November 26, 27, 1929. *Asheville Citizen*, November 26, 27, 1929.

32. Hall, "Disorderly Women," 372–74. See also Hall et al., *Like a Family*, 213, 229.

33. *Charlotte Observer*, April 5, 1929. *Gastonia Daily Gazette*, April 18, 25, 1929. Salmond, *Gastonia*, 47–56, 69.

34. *Burlington Daily Times-News*, September 14, 1934. *Greensboro Daily News*, September 15, 16, 1934. *News and Observer*, September 15, 1934. Salmond, "Burlington Dynamite Plot," 398–434.

35. Film Transcripts, Box 7, East Newnan, Georgia. *Atlanta Constitution*, September 17, 18, 22, 1934. *Newnan Herald*, September 21, 1934.

36. Minchin, *What Do We Need,* 56–58, 66–68.

37. Ibid., 79–80, 131–32. Griffith, *Crisis of American Labor,* XIV, 82–83.

38. James A. Hodges, "The Real Norma Rae," in Zieger, *Southern Labor in Transition,* 251–72.

39. Minchin, *Hiring the Black Worker,* 196–203.

40. Hall et al., *Like a Family,* 222–23. Hall, "Disorderly Women," 356, 370–72.

41. *Charlotte Observer,* April 5, 1929. Salmond, *Gastonia,* 33, 46, 60–62. Minchin, *Hiring the Black Worker,* 199.

42. Garrow, *Montgomery Bus Boycott,* passim.

43. Fleming, *Soon We Will Not Cry,* passim. The quotation is on page 97.

44. Evans, *Personal Politics,* 74–75. Carter, "Williamston Freedom Movement," 16. Nelson and Bass, *Orangeburg Massacre,* 90–91, 95–96.

45. Powledge, *Free at Last,* 74–76.

46. Daniel, *Lost Revolutions,* 257–58, 264–66. Rabby, *Pain,* 230–43. Knowles continued to fight for school integration in Tallahassee long after her son had graduated from Leon High.

47. Rabby, *Pain,* 9–16, 40–41. Robnett, *How Long?* passim.

48. Daniel, *Lost Revolutions,* 230–31, 286–88. Sullivan, *Days of Hope,* 142, 145–46. Dittmer, *Local People,* 433–34. Grant, *Ella Baker,* passim.

49. Payne, *I've Got the Light of Freedom,* 265–83.

50. *New York World,* January 20, 1926, clipping in Papers of the National Association for the Advancement of Colored People, Part 12, Southern Branch File, 1912–1939 (hereafter cited as NAACP Papers 12, Southern Branch), Reel 1, Box G-1. Statement of Mary White, Gadsden, Alabama, May 20, 1922, Mary White to James W. Johnson, June 21, 1922, NAACP Papers 12, Southern Branch, Reel 1, Box G-1. Daisy Lampkin to Jonnie Blount, March 13, 1935, Reel 3, Box G-4; to Frank Turner, February 27, 1934, Reel 2, Box G-2. Mary White Ovington to Charles A. J. McPherson, March 3, 1933, Reel 1, Box G-2. Althea Hart to W. E. B. Du Bois, February 11, 1930; G. W. Lucas, President, New Orleans Branch, NAACP to Walter White, February 21, 1930; NAACP Press Release, April 7, 1930, all in NAACP Papers 12, Southern Branch, Reel 14, Group 1, Box G-82. Tuck, *Beyond Atlanta,* 58–59. A fine book on the civil rights struggle in rural Louisiana, unfortunately published after this study had been completed, is de Jong, *A Different Day.*

51. Evans, *Personal Politics,* 74–76. Theresa Del Pozzo, "The Feel of a Blue Note," in Curry et al., *Deep in our Hearts,* 194.

52. Salmond, *Gastonia,* 55–60, 98–99. *Charlotte Observer,* June 28, 29, 30, 1929.

Chapter 4. The Way of the Lord

1. Tippett, *Southern Labor,* 143.

2. Ibid., 141–44. *Asheville Citizen,* October 5, 1929. *Charlotte Observer,* October 5, 1929.

3. *Greensboro Daily News,* September 14, 18, 1929. *News and Observer,* September 18, 1929. Salmond, *Gastonia,* 132–33.

4. *State,* Columbia, South Carolina, September 9, 1934. *New York Times,* September 9, 1934. *Anderson Independent,* September 9, 1934.

5. Dittmer, *Local People,* 284.

6. Manis, *Fire You Can't Put Out,* 404–7.

7. Ibid. See also Branch, *Parting the Waters,* 891–92.

8. Dittmer, *Local People,* 284–85. Stanton, *From Selma to Sorrow,* 176–78. Eagles, *Outside Agitator,* 179–84, 191–93.

9. Chafe, *Unfinished Journey,* 367. Fairclough, *To Redeem the Soul of America,* 380–82. King's funeral service is available on videotape and is brilliantly and movingly presented in the second series of the acclaimed documentary on the civil rights years, *Eyes on the Prize.*

10. The Atlanta Branch of the NAACP to the Ministry of Fulton County, February 12, 1919, NAACP Papers 12, Southern Branch, Reel 9, Group 1, Atlanta, Georgia.

11. NAACP Branch News, Mobile, Alabama, March 4, 1934, clipping from the *Mobile Press-Register,* March 10, 1935, both in NAACP Papers 12, Southern Branch, Reel 3, Group 1, Mobile, Alabama. Broadsheet from Little Rock, NAACP Branch, undated, Reel 2, Group 1, Camden, Arkansas. C. H. Myers, President, Monroe Branch NAACP to all co-workers in Civil Improvement, December 10, 1931, Reel 13, Group 1, Monroe, Louisiana. Clipping from *Atlanta World,* May 16, 1933, Reel 10, Group 1, Atlanta, Georgia.

12. Salmond, *My Mind Set on Freedom,* 54–55.

13. Branch, *Parting the Waters,* 265–68. Fairclough, *To Redeem the Soul of America,* passim. The quotation is from page 49.

14. Egerton, *Speak Now Against the Day,* 589–95. Patterson, *Brown v Board of Education,* 23–27, 35–36. Rev. J. A. DeLaine to Roy Wilkins, November 28, 1961, 20 White Resistance, Reel 10, South Carolina.

15. Manis, *Fire You Can't Put Out,* passim, but especially 14–17, 280–82, 343–92, 441. Eskew, *But for Birmingham,* 121–24, 130, 135–38, 140–42. See also J. Mills Thornton's magisterial new book, *Dividing Lines.*

16. Gadsden County, Florida, Free Press, Gadsden County Citizen Project, Newsletter No. 2, August 9, 1964, Papers of the Congress of Racial Equality (hereafter cited as CORE Papers), Reel 3, Florida Field Reports, April to October 1964. Tuck, *Beyond Atlanta,* 2, 46–54, 71–73.

17. Dittmer, *Local People,* 182–84, 247, 303–9. Carter, "Williamston Freedom Movement," 12–21. List of churches and pastors homes bombed or otherwise destroyed, dated 1965, found in 20 White Resistance, Reel 8, File 0429.

18. Suggested outline for a report on Voter Education Programs; Rev. Elton B. Cox to Dear Ministers of Northern Florida, October 27, 1964; Field Report, North Florida Citizen Education Project, January 15, 1965, all in CORE Papers, Reel 2, Voter Registration in Florida.

19. Salmond, *Gastonia,* 28–29. Waldrep, *Southern Workers,* 122. Hall et al., *Like a Family,* 221–22. Tippett, *Southern Labor,* 143. Honey, in *Southern Labor and Black Civil Rights,* 122–23, tells the story of Red Davis, a Memphis CIO organizer and a

devout Baptist, who left the church because of the hostility of most white clergy to the labor movement.

20. Lewis, *Cheap and Contented Labor*, 5. *Asheville Citizen*, November 9, 10, 11, 12, 1929. Salmond, *Gastonia*, 39. Salmond, *Miss Lucy of the CIO*, 132–37. Minchin, *Hiring the Black Worker*, 229. Hodges, "Real Norma Rae," 258.

21. *Charlotte Observer*, April 8, 1929; *News and Observer*, April 7, 1929. Pope, *Millhands and Preachers*, 273–77.

22. Film Transcripts, box 7, East Newnan, Georgia. *New York Times*, September 2, 3, 4, 1934. *Macon Evening News*, September 17, 20, 1934. Irons, *Testing the New Deal*, 34, 47, 81–84.

23. Salmond, *Miss Lucy of the CIO*, 132–35. Korstad, "Daybreak of Freedom," 9, 282–92.

24. *New York Times*, September 2, 3, 4, 1934. Irons, *Testing the New Deal*, 82, 121–22. *Augusta Chronicle*, September 6, 10, 1934.

25. Branch, *Parting the Waters*, 880–83. Martin L. King Jr., "Letter from a Birmingham Jail," in Chafe and Sitkoff, *History of Our Time*, 184–97.

26. See "Voices of the Civil Rights Movement," passim.

27. Ibid. See also Salmond, *Gastonia*, 61–63.

28. "Voices of the Civil Rights Movement," passim.

29. Waldrep, *Southern Workers*, 119–22.

30. Ibid. Irons, *Testing the New Deal*, 82.

31. Salmond, *My Mind Set on Freedom*, 79–80. Evans, *Personal Politics*, 28–38.

32. King, "Letter from a Birmingham Jail," 189–93. Simon, *Fabric of Defeat*, 83, 88, 129, 136.

33. *New York Times*, September 5, 6, 9, 23, 24, 26, 1934. *Charlotte Observer*, September 5, 1934. *Spartanburg Journal*, September 21, 23, 27, 28, 1934. *Gastonia Daily Gazette*, September 6, 1934. *Greenville News*, September 6, 1934. *State*, South Carolina, September 9, 1934. Hall, "Disorderly Women," 372–74. Salmond, *Gastonia*, 183.

34. Dittmer, *Local People*, 49, 166–67. Branch, *Parting the Waters*, 527–61, 825–30. For dramatic shots of flags being removed from demonstrator's hands, see the acclaimed television documentary series *Eyes on the Prize*, first series, episodes 3 and 5.

Chapter 5. Agitators

1. Report on violence in Natchez, 1964–5, in SNCC Papers XV, Reel 40, File 201, Natchez. Hodges, "Real Norma Rae," 257–58, 263–64. Irons, *Testing the New Deal*, 100, 114. Irons incorrectly identifies Dean as having been born in North Carolina.

2. Salmond, *Gastonia*, 16–18.

3. Ibid., 19–22. Beal, *Proletarian Journey*, 109–32.

4. *Gastonia Daily Gazette*, April 3, 1929.

5. Ibid., April 11, 1929. Salmond, *Gastonia*, 33–36, 60. Weisbord, *Radical Life*, 103–5, 207–17.

6. Kelley, *Hammer and Hoe*, 15, 40–43.

7. Rosengarten, *All Gods Dangers*, passim. Kelley, *Hammer and Hoe*, 43–53.

8. Kelley, *Hammer and Hoe*, 53–56, 158–71.

9. Ibid., 139–43, 185–88.

10. Carter, *Scottsboro*, 53–55, 97–108, 119–31, 181–82.

11. Hall et al., *Like a Family*, 218–19, 340–41. Tippett, *Southern Labor*, 60–66.

12. Hall et al., *Like a Family*, 233. Tippett, *Southern Labor*, 118–25, 146–47, 215.

13. *Charlotte Observer*, September 11, 19, 20, 24, 1929. Salmond, *Gastonia*, 123–24, 133–35.

14. *Birmingham Age-Herald*, August 6–7, 1934. Salmond, *Miss Lucy of the CIO*, 82–83. Kelley, *Hammer and Hoe*, 129–31. David Kennedy, *Freedom from Fear*, 309–10.

15. Minchin, *What Do We Need*, 37.

16. Salmond, *Miss Lucy of the CIO*, 135–36. Minchin, *What Do We Need*, 37.

17. Minchin, *What Do We Need*, 44–47. Brattain, *Politics of Whiteness*, 128–29.

18. Branch, *Parting the Waters*, 168–73, 516–17, 573–74, 675–79, 835–59.

19. Tyson, *Radio Free Dixie*, passim, but especially 47, 62–66, 141, 281–93, 307–8.

20. The persistent HUAC and SISS pursuit of SCEF during the 1950s has been well documented by a number of historians. I have discussed it extensively from the perspective of individuals so accused in *Southern Rebel* and *Conscience of a Lawyer*. See also Brown, *Standing Against Dragons*, passim, and Reed, *Simple Decency and Common Sense*.

21. Sullivan, *Days of Hope*, 5, 97–100, 242–43, 274. Salmond, *Miss Lucy of the CIO*, 159–65. Salmond, *Southern Rebel*, 219–46.

22. Salmond, *Southern Rebel*, 219–46. Brown, *Standing Against Dragons*, 141–77.

23. Ibid. Salmond and Brown.

24. Branch, *Parting the Waters*, 291–93, 446–49.

25. Ibid., 325–31. See also Dittmer, *Local People*, 101–3, 326.

26. Dittmer, *Local People*, 138, 145, 149–51, 157–58. Branch, *Parting the Waters*, 533–34. Daniel, *Lost Revolutions*, 288–89.

27. Dittmer, *Local People*, 208–11.

28. Ibid., 246–48.

29. Ibid. Eagles, *Outside Agitator*, passim.

30. Salmond, *My Mind Set on Freedom*, 81–85.

31. Branch, *Parting the Waters*, 171, 261–64, 390–91. See also Lewis with D'Orso, *Walking with the Wind*, passim. Chappell, *Inside Agitators*.

32. Robnett, *How Long?* 95, 99, 101–10. Branch, *Parting the Waters*, 295, 392–93, 428–31.

33. Fairclough, *To Redeem the Soul of America*, 69–70. Robnett, *How Long?* 88–96.

34. Nan Watson to Dorothy Cotton, July 2, 1963, Records of the Southern Christian Leadership Conference, microfilm in Perkins Library, Duke University (hereafter cited as SCLC Records), Part 4, Records of the Program Department (hereafter cited as 4), Reel 14. Clara N. Riggs to Cotton, May 17, 1962, SCLC Records, 4, Reel 16.

35. Sally Tuggle to Dorothy Cotton, May 13, 1965; Magdalene Jackson to Hosea Williams, April 7, 1963; and Daisy Jones to Williams, March 4, 1963, all in SCLC Records, 4, Reel 16. Susie Green, report for March 1962, SCLC Records, 4, Reel 17.

36. *Charlotte Observer,* November 25, 1977. *Let's Stand Together.*

37. *Charlotte Observer,* June 28, 29, 30, 31, 1929. *Birmingham Age-Herald,* August 6, 7, 1934. Salmond, *Gastonia,* 98–99. Matusow, *Unraveling of America,* 78.

38. Branch, *Parting the Waters,* 144. Timothy B. Tyson, "Dynamite and the Silent South," in Dailey, Gilmore, and Simon, *Jumpin' Jim Crow,* 275–97.

39. Chappell, *Inside Agitators,* 177, 257, 275. Salmond, *Southern Rebel,* passim. Salmond, *Conscience of a Lawyer,* passim.

40. Sarah Cunningham, "Woman Beyond Her Times," *Churchwoman: An Interdenominational Magazine* 32 (December 1966): 5–13. Helena Huntington Smith, "Mrs. Tilly's Crusade," *Colliers,* December 1950, 29, 66–67. Florence B. Robin, "Honeychile at the Barricades," *Harpers Magazine,* October 1962, 173–77. All offprints in Dorothy Rogers Tilly Papers, Special Collections, Robert H. Woodruff Library, Emory University (hereafter cited as Tilly Papers), Box 2. "Workbook of the Fellowship of the Concerned," October 23, 1968, Tilly Papers, Box 4.

41. Smith, "Mrs. Tilly's Crusade," 66–67.

42. Ibid. See also Report of Mrs. Tilly on Fellowship of Concerned Activities, First Quarter, 1956, Tilly Papers, Box 1. Jessie Ash Arndt, "Women's Crusade Spurs Fairer Treatment of Negroes in the United States," *Christian Science Monitor,* January 9, 1953, clipping in Tilly Papers, Box 2.

43. Martin "Critique of Southern Society and Vision of a New Order," 66–67. Salmond, "Fellowship of Southern Churchmen," 179–99.

44. Morton to William Jernagin, January 31, 1947. Don West, "The Case for Work Camps," n.d., typescript; "Have You Heard About this Work Camp?" n.d., FSC flyer, all in Fellowship of Southern Churchmen Papers, SHC (hereafter cited as FSC Papers). Dallas Blanchard, interview with Nelle Morton, June 25, 1983, SOHC, SHC.

45. Salmond, "Fellowship of Southern Churchmen," 185–92. Morton, *Journey Is Home,* 188–89. *News and Observer,* August 19, 1947. *Greensboro Daily News,* August 21, 1947. *Atlanta Journal,* July 17, 1948. Cornelia Lively to Maynard Catchings, April 30, 1947; George Hauser to Morton, May 14, 1947; Morton to Rev. R. W. Underwood, January 7, 1947; FSC newsletter, February, 1947, all in FSC Papers.

46. K'Meyer, *Interracialism and Christian Community,* 5, 46–47, 81, and passim.

47. Ibid., 109. Sullivan, *Days of Hope,* 150–51. For Highlander, see Glen, *Highlander,* passim.

48. Sullivan, *Days of Hope,* 209, 235. Glen, *Highlander,* 129–72.

49. Glen, *Highlander,* 195–223. Horton, *Highlander Folk School,* 253, 271.

Chapter 6. Reprisals

1. *News and Observer,* April 23, 24, 1929. *Charlotte Observer,* April 24, 1929.

2. Julia Small to Dorothy Cotton, July 11, 1965; Julia Small to Septima Clark, July 30, 1965, both in SCLC Records, 4, Reel 17.

3. Statement by Maggie Gordon, Holmes County, Mississippi, in SNCC Records, Reel 40, File A:XVI:12. Statement of Lt. Emanuel D. Schreiber, March 26, 1964, in SNCC Records, Reel 42, A:XVII:61, Case Studies of Intimidation, Mississippi, February–April 1964.

4. Report of demonstration in Somerville, Tennessee, July 23, 1963, SNCC Records, Reel 40, File 247, Fayette County, Tennessee.

5. Salmond, *My Mind Set on Freedom*, 75–76, 130–32.

6. Gloster Current to Roy Wilkins, September 23, 1963, 20 White Resistance, Reel 9. Margaret Price, "Joint Interagency Fact Finding Project on Violence and Intimidation," Reel 11, File 0335.

7. NAACP Press Release, Florence, South Carolina, April 24, 1956, 20 White Resistance, Reel 10.

8. La Follette Committee—Hearings, Part 5, Labor Espionage, Pinkerton's National Detective Agency Inc., February 8, 9, 10, 11 and 12, 1937, 2488–93.

9. Ibid. Part 2, Labor Espionage and Strikebreaking, 727–29.

10. Gilbert R. Mason deposition, May 3, 1960, 20 White Resistance, Reel 1. "Tot Survives Mississippi Atrocity," NAACP Press Release, Reel 3. Lee, *For Freedom's Sake*, passim. Dittmer, *Local People*, passim.

11. Eddie Mayberry, Affidavit, July 21, 1957, 20 White Resistance, Reel 6, Reprisals, Arkansas.

12. Salmond, *Gastonia*, passim. Tippett, *Southern Labor*, passim. Salmond, *General Textile Strike of 1934*, passim. Nelson and Bass, *Orangeburg Massacre*, 185–221. Dittmer, *Local People*, passim. SNCC Papers XV, Reel 41, A:XVI:36, Biographical Sketches. A:XVI:52, report on the death of Freddie Lee Thomas, August 20, 1965.

13. *News and Observer*, April 19, 1929. *Charlotte Observer*, April 19, 1929. *Gastonia Daily Gazette*, April 18, 1929.

14. Branch, *Parting the Waters*, 888–91. Manis, *Fire You Can't Put Out*, 107–11. Report on violence in Natchez, 1964–5, in SNCC Papers XV, Reel 40, File 201, Natchez.

15. Koinonia Farms, newsletter no. 10, January 18, 1957, no. 11, February 10, 1957, 20 White Resistance, Reel 9, Georgia, Koinonia Farm, 1957. K'Meyer, *Interracialism and Christian Community*, passim.

16. Pope, *Millhands and Preachers*, 255. Tippett, *Southern Labor*, 89. *News and Observer*, November 7, 1929. *Gastonia Daily Gazette*, May 22, 1929. Salmond, *Gastonia*, 42–45, 122–27.

17. *Gastonia Daily Gazette*, April 9, 1929. *News and Observer*, November 7, 8, 9, 1928, April 11, 1929. Salmond, *Gastonia*, 37–38.

18. *Anderson Independent*, September 5, 6, 7, 14, 1934. Minchin, *What Do We Need*, 112–14, 186–87.

19. Minchin, *What Do We Need*, 40–42. Daniel, *Culture of Misfortune*, 179. Finley interview.

20. Feldman, *Politics*, 273–80.

21. "Pro-Segregation Groups in the South," a special report from the Southern

Regional Council, November 19, 1956, 20 White Resistance, Reel 8. Brown, *Standing Against Dragons*, 119. Harry T. Moore bombing file, in Stetson Kennedy Papers, held privately by Stetson Kennedy. Author's interview with Stetson Kennedy, July 5, 1991. Raymond A. Mohl, "South of the South," 5–6.

22. Dittmer, *Local People*, 215–19, 266–68. Daniel, *Lost Revolutions*, 213–15.

23. "Pro-Segregation Groups." Daniel, *Lost Revolutions*, 212–13.

24. "Pro-Segregation Groups" and "The Assault upon the National Association for the Advancement of Colored People," March 1957, both in 20 White Resistance, Reel 8. Daniel, *Lost Revolutions*, 210–12. Dittmer, *Local People*, 45–52.

25. R. S. Fisher to Wesley W. Law, July 11, 1961; Clarence Mitchell to Hon. J. Edward Day, Postmaster General, July 20, 1961, both in 20 White Resistance, Reel 9.

26. W. D. Burgess to Roy Wilkins, May 26, 1960; L. E. Jarma, New Bern, N.C., December 4, 1957, both in 20 White Resistance, Reel 10. Daniels, *Lost Revolutions*, 211.

27. C. O. Pearson, Chair Legal Redress Committee, North Carolina State Conference of the NAACP to Roy Wilkins, November 20, 1959, February 8, 1960, January 6, 1961; Dora M. Farmer to Wilkins, January 26, 1960, all in 20 White Resistance, Reel 10, North Carolina.

28. I. DeQuincey Newman to John A. Morsell, December 4, 1959. Statement of Billie S. Fleming before the Senate Subcommittee on Constitutional Rights, April 16, 1959. Margaret Price, "Joint Interagency Fact Finding Project on Violence and Intimidation," undated, all in 20 White Resistance, Reel 11, South Carolina, Government Actions. Salmond, *Southern Rebel*, 243–46.

29. Salmond, *Gastonia*, 55–58. Mary Heaton Vorse, "Gastonia Strike Diary," in Mary Heaton Vorse Papers, Walter P. Reuther Archive for Labor History and Urban Affairs, Wayne State University, Detroit, Michigan, Box 122.

30. Daniel, *Lost Revolutions*, 257–59.

31. Salmond, *Gastonia*, 146–48, 161–64. *Charlotte Observer*, October 18, 19, 1929. *News and Observer*, October 19, 1929.

32. Dittmer, *Local People*, 55–58.

33. Ibid., 418. Daniels, *Lost Revolutions*, 214.

34. Nelson and Bass, *Orangeburg Massacre*, 138–46, 218–21.

35. Leonard H. Carter, field secretary, NAACP, to Aaron Henry, president, Mississippi state conference, March 11, 1964, 20 White Resistance, Reel 1, Group 3, Box A 90, Mississippi, Crime.

36. Medgar Evers to Roy Wilkins, February 11, 1958; Hazel Brannon Smith to Hyman Bookbender, Director, Eleanor Roosevelt Memorial Foundation, August 24, September 7, 1963; clipping from *Lexington Advertiser*, September 5, 1963, all in 20 White Resistance, Reel 5, Mississippi, Relief Funds, 1956–1963. Dittmer, *Local People*, 323.

37. "Supreme Court Orders Bail for 3 La. Women," press release in 20 White Resistance, Reel 9, Reprisals La. General, 1956–59. C. C. Battle to Roy Wilkins, September 25, 1956, Reel 1, Group III, Box A-90.

38. Salmond, *Southern Rebel*, 218–46, 261–65. Clipping from *Macon News*, April 5, 1957; Statement by Koinonia Farm, April 15, 1957, both in 20 White Resistance, Reel 9, Koinonia Farm, 1957. K'Meyer, *Interracialism and Christian Community*, 90–92.

39. Branch, *Parting the Waters*, 160–62, 239–42, 276–77, 351–71, 550–56, 601–7, 621–30, 734–45, 784–87.

40. SCLC Records, Part 2, Records of the Executive Director and Treasurer, Reel 1, Series II, Ella J. Baker, Field Report, Louisiana, March 1960, Files 32–41.

41. "The Assault upon the National Association for the Advancement of Colored People," March 1957, paper in 20 White Resistance, Reel 8, File 0077. Clipping from *Washington Post*, December 22, 1959, S. W. Tucker defense file, Reel 13, Group 3, Virginia.

42. S. W. Tucker defense file.

43. Tippett, *Southern Labor*, 64–69, 126–27. Salmond, *Gastonia*, 28, 38, 44. Salmond, *General Textile Strike of 1934*, passim.

44. Hall et al., *Like a Family*, 229–31. Salmond, *Gastonia*, 24–25. Salmond, "Burlington Dynamite Plot," 410–11.

45. *Gastonia Daily Gazette*, September 19, 20, 1934. *New York Times*, September 19, 1934. *Charlotte Observer*, September 20, 21, 23, 1934. Transcript, Court of Inquiry into Death of Ernest K. Riley, Papers of Governor J. C. B. Ehringhaus, North Carolina State Department of Archives and History, Box 139 (Adjutant General).

46. Branch, *Parting the Waters*, 460–71, 821–23. Patterson, *Grand Expectations*, 579–83.

47. Wright, "Aftermath," 100–102. See also Salmond, "Burlington Dynamite Plot," passim. Salmond, *Gastonia*, 24. Fink, *Fulton Bag and Cotton Mills Strike*, passim. Daniel, *Culture of Misfortune*, 215.

48. Salmond, *Southern Rebel*, 233–39, 257–60. Salmond, *Gastonia*, 28, 35, 185. Daniel, *Lost Revolutions*, 211–12. Minutes of Shades Valley Citizens Council Meeting, February 28, 1957, 20 White Resistance, Reel 4.

Chapter 7. The Government

1. Simon, *Fabric of Defeat*, 87–89. Salmond, *General Textile Strike of 1934*, passim. *Eyes on the Prize*, second series, Part 3.

2. Irons, *Testing the New Deal*, 155–60. Waldrep, *Southern Workers*, 86–89.

3. Zieger, *CIO*, 35, 40, 61–64. Minchin, *What Do We Need*, 33. Waldrep, *Southern Workers*, 89.

4. Minchin, *What Do We Need*, 32–33. Waldrep, *Southern Workers*, 89. Zieger, *CIO*, 34–38, 124–25.

5. Zieger, *CIO*, 74–75. Daniel, *Culture of Misfortune*, 57–92.

6. Daniel, *Culture of Misfortune*, 92–93. Lucy Mason to FDR, August 12, 1937; to Molly Dewson, September 6, 1937, both in Lucy Randolph Mason Papers, Perkins Library, Duke University, Box 1, Folder 2.

7. Zieger, *CIO*, 76–78. Daniel, *Culture of Misfortune*, 94–96, 100. Salmond, *Miss Lucy of the CIO*, 80. Minchin, *What Do We Need*, 15–17.

8. Minchin, *What Do We Need*, 16. Daniel, *Culture of Misfortune*, 141–42.

9. Minchin, *What Do We Need*, 32–37, 99–118.

10. Daniel, *Culture of Misfortune*, 254–57. For a poignant discussion of the effect of this decline at the local level, see Clark, *Like Night and Day.*

11. Salmond, *My Mind Set on Freedom*, 4–6. Patterson, *Brown v Board of Education*, 12.

12. Patterson, *Brown v Board of Education*, 16–20.

13. Salmond, *My Mind Set on Freedom*, 24–26. Patterson, *Brown v Board of Education*, 65–69.

14. Patterson, *Brown v Board of Education*, xiii–xiv, 70–71.

15. Salmond, *My Mind Set on Freedom*, 50.

16. Ibid., 34–50. Daniel, *Lost Revolutions*, 251–84.

17. Patterson, *Brown v Board of Education*, 137.

18. SCLC Records, 4, Reel 19, Field Reports, Georgia, June-December, 1965. SCLC Records, 4, Reel 20, Field Reports, North Carolina, 1965–1968. Tuck, *Beyond Atlanta*, 204–5.

19. Patterson, *Brown v Board of Education*, 138–39.

20. Ibid., 142–46.

21. Ibid., 147–59. For a balanced recent discussion of the Nixon administration's policies, or lack of them, on school desegregation, see Kotlowski, *Nixon's Civil Rights*, 15–37. The quotation is from page 37.

22. Matusow, *Unraveling of America*, 187.

23. Ibid. See also Goldfield, *Black, White and Southern*, 144–48.

24. Goldfield, *Black, White and Southern*, 207. Matusow, *Unraveling of America*, 187. Nelson and Bass, *Orangeburg Massacre*, 22–25. Salmond, *My Mind Set on Freedom*, 120. Bartley, *New South*, 390–91. "Chronology of Terrorism in Mississippi," SNCC, special report, March 1965, in CORE Papers, Reel 14. Tuck, *Beyond Atlanta*, 194–97.

25. Salmond, *My Mind Set on Freedom*, 107–8. Matusow, *Unraveling of America*, 187. Goldfield, *Black, White and Southern*, 150–51. Kousser, *Colorblind Injustice*, 54.

26. Matusow, *Unraveling of America*, 90. Kousser, *Colorblind Injustice*, 202.

27. Matusow, *Unraveling of America*, 181.

28. Ibid., 181–87. Salmond, *My Mind Set on Freedom*, 127–33.

29. "A SCOPE Evaluation of Four Weeks in Albany, Georgia, September 1965; John Worcester to Junius Griffin, July 1965; Barbour County, Alabama, field report, July 29, 1965, all in SCLC Records, 4, Reel 21, SCOPE Field Reports. Tuck, *Beyond Atlanta*, 197–201.

30. Alice Blackwell to Annell Ponder, December 15, 1965, SCLC Records, 4, Reel 17. Minutes of Georgia Voters League, 1963–1966, Reel 20. R. B. Cottonreader, Field

Report, undated, Reel 21. Matusow, *Unraveling of America*, 187–88. Salmond, *My Mind Set on Freedom*, 149–50. Tuck, *Beyond Atlanta*, 214–15.

31. Dittmer, *Local People*, 253, 300, 484. Goldfield, *Black, White and Southern*, 227–31. Salmond, *My Mind Set on Freedom*, 151–53. Tuck, *Beyond Atlanta*, 220–25.

32. Goldfield, *Black, White and Southern*, 231–37.

33. Ibid., 238–41. See also Kousser, *Colorblind Injustice*, passim, but especially, 223–24, 403.

34. Matusow, *Unraveling of America*, 90–91. Minchin, *Hiring the Black Worker*, 1–2. Minchin, *Color of Work*, 3–4.

35. Minchin, *Hiring the Black Worker*, 12–16, 47.

36. Ibid., 28–29.

37. Ibid., 46–47, 50–54.

38. Ibid., 55. Brattain, *Politics of Whiteness*, 238–42.

39. Minchin, *Hiring the Black Worker*, 137–60.

40. Ibid., 36–37, 166, 178–79.

41. Ibid., 174, 196–203, 254–63. Haberland "After the Wives Went to Work." Brattain, *Politics of Whiteness*, 279–81.

42. Daniel, *Culture of Misfortune*, 271–81.

43. Minchin, *Color of Work*, passim. Goldfield, *Black, White and Southern*, 204.

44. Arthur J. Chapital, Sr. Executive Secretary, New Orleans Branch NAACP, September 27, 1965; affidavit of Clarence L. Marchand Jr., undated, and of Fred Patterson Jr., September 22, 1965, all in 20 White Resistance, Reel 9, Louisiana.

45. Ibid.

Chapter 8. Conclusion

1. Minchin, *Color of Work*, 74–90, 207–15.

2. Kelley, *Hammer and Hoe*, 142–43. Honey, *Southern Labor and Black Civil Rights*, passim; quotation from 219. See also Honey, *Black Workers Remember*. Robert Korstad, "Those Who Were Not Afraid, Winston-Salem, 1943," in Miller, *Working Lives*, 184–99. Korstad and Lichtenstein, "Opportunities Found and Lost," 786–811. See too the essays by Lichtenstein and Zieger in Eskew, *Labor in the Modern South*. For steel, see Nelson, *Divided We Stand*, chapter 4.

3. Korstad, "Daybreak of Freedom," 250–60, 282–92.

4. Janiewski, *Sisterhood Denied*, 152–78. Draper, *Conflict of Interests*, 161–71. Brattain, *Politics of Whiteness*, 143.

5. Joyner, *Shared Traditions*, 3–6.

Bibliography

Primary Sources

MANUSCRIPT COLLECTIONS

Microfilmed Collections

American Civil Liberties Union Papers, 1929–30. In author's possession.

Papers of the Congress of Racial Equality, 1947–1980. Baillieu Library, University of Melbourne.

Papers of the National Association for the Advancement of Colored People, 1920–1980. Borchardt Library, La Trobe University.

Papers of the Southern Christian Leadership Conference, 1957–1970. Perkins Library, Duke University.

Papers of the Student Non-violent Coordinating Committee, 1961–1970. Davis Library, University of North Carolina at Chapel Hill.

University of North Carolina at Chapel Hill

Fellowship of Southern Churchmen Papers, 1935–1956.

Southern Oral History Collection.

Southern Labor Archives, Georgia State University

Transcripts of interviews made for the documentary film *The Uprising of 1934*.

United Textile Workers Records, 1934–1937.

Walter P. Reuther Archive for Labor History and Urban Affairs, Wayne State University

Mary Heaton Vorse Papers, 1929.

Robert H. Woodruff Library, Emory University

Dorothy Rogers Tilly Papers, 1948–1963.

National Archives, Washington D.C.
National Recovery Administration Records, 1933–1934.

North Carolina State Department of Archives and History
Papers of Governor J. C. B. Ehringhaus, 1934.

Perkins Library, Duke University
Lucy Randolph Mason Papers, 1937–1959.

Private Collections
Stetson Kennedy Papers.

NEWSPAPERS

Anderson Independent, 1934.
Asheville Citizen, 1929.
Atlanta Constitution, 1934, 1961–67.
Atlanta Journal, 1934.
Atlanta World, 1934.
Augusta Chronicle, 1934.
Baltimore Evening Sun, 1929.
Birmingham Age-Herald, 1934, 1961–1965.
Burlington Daily Times News, 1934, 1947.
Charlotte Observer, 1929–1934, 1963–1970.
Daily Worker, 1929, 1934.
Gastonia Daily Gazette, 1929, 1934.
Greensboro Daily News, 1929, 1934, 1947–1949.
Greenville News, 1934.
Macon Evening News, 1934.
Marion Progress, 1929.
Newnan Herald, 1934.
News and Observer (Raleigh, N.C.), 1929–1970.
New York Times, 1929–1980.
New York World, 1934.
Spartanburg Journal, 1934.
State (Columbia, S.C.), 1934, 1968.

GOVERNMENT DOCUMENTS, PAMPHLETS, INTERVIEWS

Author's interview with Stetson Kennedy, Jacksonville, Florida, July 5, 1991.
Let's Stand Together: The Story of Ella Mae [sic] *Wiggins.* Charlotte: Metrolina
    Chapter, National Organization for Women, 1979. In North Carolina Collection,
    University of North Carolina at Chapel Hill.

Lewis, Sinclair. *Cheap and Contented Labor.* New York: United Textile Workers of America, 1929. In North Carolina Collection, University of North Carolina at Chapel Hill.

Violation of Free Speech and Rights of Labor. Hearings Before a Subcommittee of the Committee of Education and Labor, United States Senate, 75th Congress, First Session pursuant to S. Res. 266 74th Congress Resolution to Investigate Violations of the Right of Free Speech and Assembly and Interference With the Right of Labor to Organize and Bargain Collectively. Washington, D.C.: United States Government Printing Office, 1937.

Secondary Sources

Bartley, Numan. *The New South: The Story of the South's Modernization, 1945–1980.* Baton Rouge: Louisiana State University Press, 1995.

Beal, Fred E. *Proletarian Journey: New England, Gastonia, Moscow.* New York: Hillman Curl, 1937.

Bellush, Bernard. *The Failure of the NRA.* New York: Norton, 1975.

Branch, Taylor. *Parting the Waters: America in the King Years, 1954–63.* New York: Simon and Schuster, 1988.

———. *Pillar of Fire: America in the King Years, 1963–65.* New York: Simon and Schuster, 1998.

Brattain, Michelle. *The Politics of Whiteness: Race, Workers and Culture in the Modern South.* Princeton: Princeton University Press, 2001.

Brooks, Robin R. "The United Textile Workers of America." Ph.D. diss., Yale University, 1935.

Brown, Sarah Hart. *Standing Against Dragons: Three Southern Lawyers in an Era of Fear.* Baton Rouge: Louisiana State University Press, 1998.

Carson, Clayborne. *In Struggle: SNCC and the Black Awakening of the 1960's.* Cambridge: Harvard University Press, 1981.

Carter, Dan T. *Scottsboro: A Tragedy of the American South.* Baton Rouge: Louisiana State University Press, 1969.

Carter, David C. "The Williamston Freedom Movement: Civil Rights at the Grass Roots in Eastern North Carolina, 1957–1964." *North Carolina Historical Review* 76, no. 1 (January 1999): 1–42.

Chafe, William H. *The Unfinished Journey: America Since World War II.* New York: Oxford University Press, 1995.

Chafe, William H., and Harvard Sitkoff. *A History of Our Time: Readings on Postwar America.* New York: Oxford University Press, 1991.

Chappell, David L. *Inside Agitators: White Southerners in the Civil Rights Movement.* Baltimore: Johns Hopkins University Press, 1994.

Clark, Daniel J. *Like Night and Day: Unionization in a Southern Mill Town.* Chapel Hill: University of North Carolina Press, 1997.

Curry, Constance, et al. *Deep in Our Hearts: Nine White Women in the Freedom Movement*. Athens: University of Georgia Press, 2000.

de Jong, Greta. *A Different Day: African American Struggles for Justice in Rural Louisiana, 1900–1970*. Chapel Hill: University of North Carolina Press, 2002.

Dailey, Jane, Glenda Elizabeth Gilmore, and Bryant Simon, eds. *Jumpin' Jim Crow: Southern Politics from Civil War to Civil Rights*. Princeton: Princeton University Press, 2000.

Daniel, Clete. *Culture of Misfortune: An Interpretive History of Textile Unionism in the United States*. Ithaca: ILR Press, 2001.

Daniel, Pete. *Lost Revolutions: The South in the 1950s*. Chapel Hill: University of North Carolina Press, 2000.

Dittmer, John. *Local People: The Struggle for Civil Rights in Mississippi*. Urbana: University of Illinois Press, 1994.

Draper, Alan. *Conflict of Interests: Organized Labor and the Civil Rights Movement in the South, 1954–1968*. Ithaca: ILR Press, 1994.

Dunbar, Anthony P. *Against the Grain: Southern Radicals and Prophets, 1929–1959*. Charlottesville: University Press of Virginia, 1981.

Duplessis, Jim. "Massacre at Honea Path." *Southern Exposure* 17 (Fall 1989): 60–63.

Eagles, Charles W. *Outside Agitator: Jon Daniels and the Civil Rights Movement in Alabama*. Chapel Hill: University of North Carolina Press, 1993.

———. "Towards New Histories of the Civil Rights Era." *Journal of Southern History* 66, no. 4 (November 2000): 815–48.

Egerton, John. *Speak Now Against the Day: The Generation Before the Civil Rights Movement in the South*. New York: Knopf, 1994.

Eskew, Glenn. *But for Birmingham: The Local and National Movements in the Civil rights Struggle*. Chapel Hill: University of North Carolina Press, 1997.

———, ed. *Labor in the Modern South*. Athens: University of Georgia Press, 2001.

Evans, Sara. *Personal Politics: The Roots of Women's Liberation in the Civil Rights Movement and the New Left*. New York: Random House, 1979.

Eyes on the Prize. Television documentary series. Blackside Productions, 1986, 1990.

Fairclough, Adam. *To Redeem the Soul of America: The Southern Christian Leadership Conference and Martin Luther King Jr.* Athens: University of Georgia Press, 1987.

Feldman, Glenn. *Politics, Society and the Klan in Alabama, 1915–1949*. Tuscaloosa: University of Alabama Press, 1999.

Fink, Gary M. *The Fulton Bag and Cotton Mills Strike of 1914–1915: Espionage, Labor Conflict and New South Industrial Relations*. Ithaca: ILR Press, 1993.

Flamming, Douglas. *Creating the Modern South: Millhands and Managers in Dalton, Georgia, 1884–1984*. Chapel Hill: University of North Carolina Press, 1992.

Fleming, Cynthia Griggs. *Soon We Will Not Cry: The Liberation of Ruby Doris Smith*. Lanham, Md.: Rowman and Littlefield, 1998.

Garrow, David, ed. *The Montgomery Bus Boycott and the Women Who Started It:*

The Memoir of Jo Ann Gibson Robinson. Knoxville: University of Tennessee Press, 1987.

Glen, John M. *Highlander: No Ordinary School, 1932–1962.* Lexington: University Press of Kentucky, 1985.

Goldfield, David R. *Black, White and Southern: Race Relations and Southern Culture, 1940 to the Present.* Baton Rouge: Louisiana State University Press, 1990.

Grant, Joanne. *Ella Baker: Freedom Bound.* New York: John Wiley, 1998.

Griffith, Barbara S. *The Crisis of American Labor and the Defeat of the CIO.* Philadelphia: Temple University Press, 1988.

Haberland, Michelle. "After the Wives Went to Work? Organizing Women in the Southern Apparel Industry." Unpublished paper in author's possession.

Haessly, Jo Lynn. "Mill Mother's Lament: Ella May, Working Women's Militancy and the 1929 Gaston County Strikes." Master's thesis, University of North Carolina at Chapel Hill, 1987.

Hall, Jacquelyn Dowd. "Disorderly Women: Gender and Labor Militancy in the Appalachian South." *Journal of American History* 73, no. 2 (September 1986): 354–82.

Hall, Jacquelyn Dowd, with Robert Korstad and James Leloudis. "Cotton Mill People: Work, Community and Protest in the Textile South, 1880–1940." *American Historical Review* 91, no. 2 (April 1986): 245–86.

Hall, Jacquelyn Dowd, James Leloudis, Robert Korstad, Mary Murphy, Lu Ann Jones, and Christopher B. Daly. *Like a Family: The Making of a Southern Cotton Mill World.* Chapel Hill: University of North Carolina Press, 1987.

Hodges, James A. *New Deal Labor Policy and the Southern Textile Industry, 1933–1941.* Knoxville: University of Tennessee Press, 1986.

Hoffman, James L. "A Study of the United Textile Workers of America in a Cotton Mill in a Medium-sized Industrial City: Labor Revolt in Alabama, 1934." Ed.D. thesis, University of Alabama, 1986.

Honey, Michael. *Black Workers Remember: An Oral History of Segregation, Unionism and the Freedom Struggle.* Berkeley: University of California Press, 1999.

———. *Southern Labor and Black Civil Rights: Organizing Memphis Workers.* Urbana: University of Illinois Press, 1993.

Horton, Aimee Isgrig. *The Highlander Folk School: A History of Its Major Programs, 1932–1961.* New York: Carlson Publishing, 1989.

Irons, Janet. *Testing the New Deal: The General Textile Strike of 1934 in the American South.* Urbana: University of Illinois Press, 2000.

Janiewski, Dolores. *Sisterhood Denied: Race, Gender and Class in a New South Community.* Philadelphia: Temple University Press, 1985.

Joyner, Charles. *Shared Traditions: Southern History and Folk Culture.* Urbana: University of Illinois Press, 1999.

Kelley, Robin D. G. *Hammer and Hoe: Alabama's Communists During the Great Depression.* Chapel Hill: University of North Carolina Press, 1990.

Kennedy, David M. *Freedom from Fear: The American People in Depression and War, 1929–1945.* New York: Oxford University Press, 1999.

Kennedy, John W. "The General Strike in the Textile Industry, September, 1934." Master's thesis, Duke University, 1947.

K'Meyer, Tracy E. *Interracialism and Christian Community in the Post War South: The Story of Koinonia Farm.* Charlottesville: University Press of Virginia, 1997.

Korstad, Robert R. *Civil Rights Unionism: Tobacco Workers and the Struggle for Democracy in the Mid-Twentieth Century South.* Chapel Hill: University of North Carolina Press, 2003.

———. "Daybreak of Freedom: Tobacco Workers and the CIO, Winston Salem, North Carolina, 1943–1950." Ph.D. diss., University of North Carolina, 1987.

Korstad, Robert, and Nelson Lichtenstein. "Opportunities Found and Lost: Labor Radicals and the Early Civil Rights Movement." *Journal of American History* 75, no. 3 (December 1988): 786–811.

Kotlowski, Dean J. *Nixon's Civil Rights: Politics, Principle and Policy.* Cambridge: Harvard University Press, 2001.

Kousser, J. Morgan. *Colorblind Injustice: Minority Voting Rights and the Undoing of the Second Reconstruction.* Chapel Hill: University of North Carolina Press, 1999.

Lee, Chana Kai. *For Freedom's Sake: The Life of Fanny Lou Hamer.* Urbana: University of Illinois Press, 1999.

Lewis, John, with Michael D'Orso. *Walking with the Wind: A Memoir of the Movement.* New York: Simon and Schuster, 1998.

Manis, Andrew M. *A Fire You Can't Put Out: The Civil Rights Life of Birmingham's Reverend Fred Shuttlesworth.* Tuscaloosa: University of Alabama Press, 1999.

Marable, Manning. *Race, Reform and Rebellion: The Second Reconstruction in Black America, 1945–2000.* Jackson: University Press of Mississippi, 2000.

Martin, Robert. "Critique of Southern Society and Vision of a New Order: The Fellowship of Southern Churchmen, 1934–1957." *Church History* 52 (March 1983): 66–80.

Matusow, Allen. *The Unraveling of America: A History of Liberalism in the 1960's.* New York: Harpers, 1984.

McCartin, Joseph A. *Labor's Great War: The Struggle for Industrial Democracy and the Origins of Modern American Labor Relations, 1912–1921.* Chapel Hill: University of North Carolina Press, 1997.

Miller, Marc S., ed. *Working Lives: The Southern Exposure History of Labor in the South.* New York: Pantheon, 1980.

Minchin, Timothy J. *The Color of Work: The Struggle for Civil Rights in the Southern Paper Industry, 1945–1980.* Chapel Hill: University of North Carolina Press, 2001.

———. *Hiring the Black Worker: The Racial Integration of the Southern Textile Industry, 1960–1980.* Chapel Hill: University of North Carolina Press, 1999.

———. *What Do We Need a Union for? The TWUA in the South, 1945–1955.* Chapel Hill: University of North Carolina Press, 1997.

Mohl, Raymond. "'South of the South?' Jews, Blacks, and the Civil Rights Movement in Miami, 1945–1960." *Journal of American Ethnic History* 18, no. 2 (Winter 1999): 3–36.

Morton, Nelle. *The Journey Is Home*. Boston: Beacon Press, 1985.

Nelson, Bruce. *Divided We Stand: American Workers and the Struggle for Black Equality*. Princeton: Princeton University Press, 2001.

Nelson, Jack E., and Jack Bass. *The Orangeburg Massacre*. New York: World Publishing, 1970.

O'Brien, Gail Williams. *The Color of the Law: Race Violence and Justice in the Post–World War II South*. Chapel Hill: University of North Carolina Press, 1999.

Patterson, James T. *Brown v Board of Education: A Civil Rights Milestone and Its Troubled Legacy*. New York: Oxford University Press, 2001.

———. *Grand Expectations: The United States, 1945–1974*. New York: Oxford University Press, 1996.

Payne, Charles M. *I've Got the Light of Freedom: The Organizing Tradition and the Mississippi Freedom Struggle*. Berkeley and Los Angeles: University of California Press, 1995.

Pope, Liston. *Millhands and Preachers: A Study of Gastonia*. New Haven: Yale University Press, 1942.

Powledge, Fred. *Free at Last: The Civil Rights Movement and the People Who Made It*. Boston: Little Brown, 1991.

Rabby, Glenda Alice. *The Pain and the Promise: The Struggle for Civil Rights in Tallahassee, Florida*. Athens: University of Georgia Press, 1999.

Ransby, Barbara. *Ella Baker and the Black Freedom Movement: A Radical Democratic Vision*. Chapel Hill: University of North Carolina Press, 2003.

Reed, Linda. *Simple Decency and Common Sense: The Southern Conference Movement, 1938–1963*. Bloomington: Indiana University Press, 1991.

Robnett, Belinda. *How Long? How Long? African-American Women in the Struggle for Civil Rights*. New York: Oxford University Press, 1997.

Rosengarten, Theodore. *All Gods Dangers: The Life of Nate Shaw*. New York: Knopf, 1974.

Salmond, John A. "'The Burlington Dynamite Plot': The 1934 Textile Strike and Its Aftermath in Burlington, North Carolina." *North Carolina Historical Review* 75, no. 4 (October 1998): 398–434.

———. *The Conscience of a Lawyer: Clifford J. Durr and American Civil Liberties, 1899–1975*. Tuscaloosa: University of Alabama Press, 1990.

———. "The Fellowship of Southern Churchmen and Interracial Change in the South." *North Carolina Historical Review* 69, no. 2 (April 1992): 179–99.

———. *Gastonia 1929: The Story of the Loray Mill Strike*. Chapel Hill: University of North Carolina Press, 1995.

———. *The General Textile Strike of 1934: From Maine to Alabama*. Columbia: University of Missouri Press, 2002.

———. *Miss Lucy of the CIO: The Life and Times of Lucy Randolph Mason, 1882–1959*. Athens: University of Georgia Press, 1959.

————. "My Mind Set on Freedom": A History of the Civil Rights Movement, 1954–1968. Chicago: Ivan Dee, 1997.

————. A Southern Rebel: The Life and Times of Aubrey Willis Williams, 1890–1965. Chapel Hill: University of North Carolina Press, 1983.

Sellers, Cleveland, with Robert Terrell. The River of No Return: The Autobiography of a Black Militant and the Life and Death of SNCC. Jackson: University Press of Mississippi, 1973.

Simon, Bryant. A Fabric of Defeat: The Politics of South Carolina Millhands, 1910–1948. Chapel Hill: University of North Carolina Press, 1998.

Sitkoff, Harvard. The Struggle for Black Equality, 1954–1980. New York: Oxford University Press, 1980.

Stanton, Mary. From Selma to Sorrow: The Life and Death of Viola Liuzzo. Athens: University of Georgia Press, 1998.

Sullivan, Patricia. Days of Hope: Race and Democracy in the New Deal Era. Chapel Hill: University of North Carolina Press, 1996.

Thornton, J. Mills III. Dividing Lines: Municipal Politics and the Struggle for Civil Rights in Montgomery, Birmingham and Selma. Tuscaloosa: University of Alabama Press, 2002.

Tippett, Tom. When Southern Labor Stirs. New York: Jonathan Cape, 1931.

Tuck, Stephen G. N. Beyond Atlanta: The Struggle for Racial Equality in Georgia, 1940–1980. Athens: University of Georgia Press, 2001.

Tyson, Timothy B. Radio Free Dixie: Robert F. Williams and the Roots of Black Power. Chapel Hill: University of North Carolina Press, 1999.

————. The Uprising of 1934. Documentary film. Produced by George Stoney and Judith Helfand. PBS, 1994.

————. Voices of the Civil Rights Movement: Black American Freedom Songs, 1960–1980. Washington D.C.: Smithsonian Institution Press, 1980.

Waldrep, G. C. Southern Workers and the Search for Community: Spartanburg County, South Carolina. Urbana: University of Illinois Press, 2000.

Weisbord, Vera Buch. A Radical Life. Bloomington: University of Indiana Press, 1997.

Wright, Annette C. "The Aftermath of the General Textile Strike: Managers and Workplace at Burlington Mills." Journal of Southern History 55, no. 1 (February 1994): 81–112.

Wright, Gavin. Old South, New South: Revolutions in the Southern Economy Since the Civil War. New York: Basic Books, 1986.

Zieger, Robert H. The CIO: 1935–1955. Chapel Hill: University of North Carolina Press, 1995.

————, ed. Organized Labor in the Twentieth-Century South. Knoxville: University of Tennessee Press, 1991.

————, ed. Southern Labor in Transition. Knoxville: University of Tennessee Press, 1997.

Index

John A. Salmond recently retired as professor of American history and pro-vice chancellor at La Trobe University, Australia. He is the author of *Gastonia 1929: The Story of the Loray Mill Strike* (1995) and *"My Mind Set on Freedom": A History of the Civil Rights Movement, 1954–1968* (1998).